The Making of the 20th Century

This series of specially commissioned titles focuses attention on significant and of often controversial events and themes of world history in the present century. each book provides sufficient narrative and explanation for the newcomer to the subject while offering, for more advanced study, detailed source-references and bibliographies, together with interpretation and reassessment in the light of recent scholarship.

In the choice of subjects there is a balance between breadth in some spheres and detail in others; between the essentially political and matters economic or social. The series cannot be a comprehensive account of everything that has happened in the twentieth century, but it provides a guide to recent research and explains something of the times of extraordinary change and complexity in which we live. It is directed in the main to students of contemporary history and international relations, but includes titles which are of direct relevance to courses in economics, sociology, politics and geography.

The Making of the 20th Century

In search of Detente

The Politics of East-West
Relations since 1945

S. R. Ashton

St. Martin's Press
New York

First published in the United States of America in 1989

Printed in China

ISBN 0-312-02465-7

LIBRARY OF CONGRESS

Library of Congress Cataloguing-in-Publication Data

Ashton, S. R.
In search of détente : the politics of East-West relations since
1945 / S.R. Ashton
p.   cm. — (The Making of the 20th century)
Bibliography: p.
Includes index.
ISBN 0-312-02465-7 : $35.00 (ast.)
1. World politics—1945–   I. Title. II Series.
D843.A743 1988   88–21135
909.82—dc19   CIP

Contents

Preface

LARGELY through the combined efforts of political leaders, their permanent officials, academics and journalists, international relations have a habit of producing new concepts or terminologies at regular intervals. Such concepts are usually thrust upon an unsuspecting public in an attempt to illuminate in basic and simple terms what essentially are highly complex and intricate issues. All too often, however, this objective is never realised. Frequently the concepts produced serve only to confuse or to mislead. Such considerations would seem to apply with particular relevance to the concept of détente.

It is nonetheless undeniable that at the beginning of the 70s détente was an extremely fashionable concept. Those who used it did so in anticipation of a new era of peace, harmony and cooperation in international affairs. At the outset, such optimism seemed justified. Richard Nixon, during a visit to Moscow in the spring of 1972 described by Henry Kissinger as 'the greatest diplomatic coup of all time', appeared on Soviet television to proclaim, with reference to the early SALT negotiations, that the leaders of the two superpowers had taken a first decisive step in the limitation of strategic nuclear weapons. A year later Leonid Brezhnev, returning the compliment by visiting the United States, signed with Nixon an agreement calling for the prevention of nuclear war and declared that the Cold War was over. After over two decades of crises and tensions the world suddenly seemed a safer place in which to live. Or did it? Within the space of three years, which had been tarnished in American eyes by the traumas of Watergate, the communist conquest of South Vietnam and the Soviet-Cuban intervention in Angola, many observers in the United States began to question the entire 'détente' process. Confronted by an increasingly critical Congress and public opinion, an uncertain Gerald Ford, believing that détente had virtually become synonymous with appeasement, even went so far as to banish the word from the presidential entourage and substituted instead the more subtle euphemism 'peace through strength'. The idealistic Jimmy Carter, who began his presidency by attempting to convince Americans that it was time they rid themselves of their complex about Soviet power and communist influence, went down to an ignominious defeat in 1980 lamenting that his perceptions of the Soviet Union had been completely changed by the invasion of Afghanistan. At the beginning of the new decade Ronald Reagan, capitalising upon the disillusion-ment of the Carter years, captured the prevailing mood in the United States by proclaiming at his first major press conference as president that détente had been a 'one-way street' and that it had been used by the Soviet Union to promote world revolution. Never afraid to express his deepest convictions, Reagan accused the Russians of reserving unto themselves the right to commit any crime, to lie and to cheat in order to achieve their objectives. Clearly, in American eyes at least, détente had failed to live up to expectations.

In attempting to explain what had gone wrong, the problem of definition immediately arises. What exactly does détente mean? The word is French and its literal translation is 'the release of tension when a crossbow is fired'. Hence, within the context of international relations, détente has been taken to mean the relaxation or reduction of international tensions. But it is important to recognise that this does not imply that détente represents a given policy or strategy. Rather it reflects a particular mood or sense of expectation and, like all moods and expectations, it is subject to change and fluctuation. The purpose of this study is to explain how this mood or sense of expectation emerged within the overall context of East-West relations since the end of the Second World War. What were the tensions and how did they originate (Chapters 1 and 2)? How and why were attempts to alleviate these tensions plagued by failure and recurring crises for so long (Chapter 3)? Why, in the mid-60s and early 70s, did the United States and the Soviet Union and their respective allies in Europe seek to establish a meaningful dialogue and what did they achieve (Chapter 4)? Under what circumstances and to what extent did détente collapse at the end of the 70s (Chapter 5) and what, if anything, has survived of détente in the 80s (chapter 6)? The narrative focuses not only on relations between the United States and the Soviet Union: consider-ation is also given to the European perspective (both East and West), to the problems created by the emergence of a communist state in China and to the regional problems in the conflict areas of the Middle East, Indo-China, Africa, South West Asia and Central America.

The events under discussion are part of an ongoing process which makes the drawing of any significant conclusions a hazardous business. But two general observations may be made. First, one of the problems in defining détente is that it means different things to different people. This is particularly relevant in the context of relations between the United States and the Soviet Union. The equivalent of the word détente in the Russian vocabulary is *razryadka*. Détente in the Western sense and *razryadka* in the Russian are not synonymous. It was at first a more painful experience for the United States to realise this than it was for the Soviet Union. Under Ronald Reagan, the United States rejected détente, declared a new Cold War and then shifted to a position in between described in 1985 by George Shultz, the Secretary of State, as one of 'constructive confrontation'. The constructive elements of the Soviet-American relationship entered a new phase when Mikhail Gorbachev came to power in the Soviet Union in 1985. Where previously the United States and the Soviet Union had been concerned to impose limits beyond which their nuclear arsenals should not grow, they now entered into negotiations to reduce them and, in some cases, to eliminate them altogether. But the constructive elements of the relationship remained precariously balanced against the elements of confrontation in the form of political, economic and military rivalry in other areas of the world. Ideological differences, rival geopolitical interests and domestic economic and political pressures have always combined to give the relationship between Washington and Moscow a fiercely competitive edge and also to make it inherently unstable. Under these conditions it would perhaps be unwise to expect too much of any agreements that the United States and the Soviet Union might reach beyond the INF Treaty of 1987.

The second observation is that there has always been much wider agreement amongst Europeans about what they mean by détente. For this reason détente in Europe has become fairly stable and durable. Here also the process has become institutionalised through the successive Conferences on Security and Cooperation. The United States and the Soviet Union were both party to the original Helsinki agreement in 1975 and to the agreements which have been reached since. But the Europeans themselves have played increasingly significant roles in reducing the tensions inherent in the post-war division of their continent. As a result of patient and painstaking negotiations, long-term benefits in terms of personal contacts and economic exchange have accrued on both sides. The Europeans have not allowed their differing political and social structures, as well as their membership of rival military alliances, to undermine the bridges which have been built between East and West. Largely as a result of the relative decline in the economic power of the United States and the Soviet Union, the Europeans have also become increasingly independent. It is now a primary European responsibility to ensure that the achievements of détente in Europe survive.

This book is not intended for the advanced specialist in international relations or politics. It presents neither new theories nor interpretations. Rather, it is designed as an introduction for newcomers to the subject. The idea of writing it developed when I was teaching courses on World Affairs at the South-East Essex Sixth Form College between 1975 and 1981. I have just one acknowledgement to make. Dr Bishwa Nath Pandey, author of two titles in the present series, was for many years both a teacher and a close personal friend at the School of Oriental and African Studies in London. He died in November 1982. An obituary described him as a 'convivial man' with a great gift for friendship who would be sorely missed by the many colleagues and students whom he had helped. I can but echo these sentiments.

S. R. ASHTON
December 1987

Abbreviations

ABM	Anti-ballistic missile
ANC	African National Congress
CDU	Christian Democratic Union (of West Germany)
CEEC	Committee for European Economic Cooperation
Centcom	Central Command
CIA	Central Intelligence Agency
Comecon	Council for Mutual Economic Assistance (also CMEA)
Cominform	Communist Information Bureau
Comintern	Communist International
CSU	Christian Social Union (of West Germany)
DDR	German Democratic Republic (East Germany)
DRV	Democratic Republic of Vietnam
EAM	National Liberation Front of Greece
ECSC	European Coal and Steel Community
EDC	European Defence Community
EEC	European Economic Community
ERW	Enhanced Radiation Weapon (Neutron bomb)
FNLA	National Front for the Liberation of Angola
FRELIMO	National Front for the Liberation of Mozambique
FDP	Free Democratic Party (of West Germany)
FRG	Federal Republic of Germany (West Germany)
GNP	Gross National Product
IC	Intercontinental
ICBM	Intercontinental ballistic missile
INF	Intermediate-range nuclear force
KGB	Committee of State Security (Soviet secret police)
KPD	Communist Party of Germany
LDPD	Liberal Democratic Party of Germany
LR	Long-range
MAD	Mutual Assured Destruction
MBFR	Mutual Balanced Force Reduction

MIRV	Multiple independently-targetable re-entry vehicle
MLF	Multilateral Force
MPLA	Popular Movement for the Liberation of Angola
MX	Missile Experimental
NATO	North Atlantic Treaty Organisation
NFLSV	National Front for the Liberation of South Vietnam
NSC	National Security Council
OEEC	Organisation of European Economic Cooperation
PD	Presidential Directive
PDPA	People's Democratic Party of Afghanistan
PLO	Palestinian Liberation Organisation
PZPR	Polish United Workers Party (Communist Party of Poland)
RENAMO	National Resistance Movement of Mozambique
RDF	Rapid Deployment Force
SADEC	South African Development Coordination Conference
SAM	Surface-to-air missile
SALT	Strategic Arms Limitation Talks/Treaty
SAVAK	Iranian secret police under the Shah
SDI	Strategic Defence Initiative
SEATO	South East Asia Treaty Organisation
SED	Socialist Unity Party of Germany (Communist Party of DDR)
SKP	Communist Party of Finland
SLBM	Submarine-launched ballistic missile
SPD	Social Democratic Party (of West Germany)
START	Strategic Arms Reduction Talks/Treaty
SWAPO	South West Africa People's Party
UNITA	National Union for the Total Independence of Angola
WEU	West European Union

1 In the Shadow of Stalin: The Cold War in Europe 1945–53

YALTA, POLAND AND THE COLD WAR DEBATE

IN February 1945, as the Red Army lay poised to capture Budapest and British and American commanders marshalled their forces for the final assaults on the Rhine bridgeheads, the leaders of the three principal allied powers – Franklin D. Roosevelt, Winston Churchill and Joseph Stalin – met in conference at Yalta in the Crimea. Hitler's thousand-year Reich, its cities already bearing the scars of armageddon as a result of the destruction wrought by allied bombing, lay prostrate and within three months of total collapse. With the approach of an allied victory in Europe but with war still raging fiercely in the Far East, the 'big three' conferred at Yalta in an attempt to resolve some outstanding political and military issues which, it was hoped, would facilitate a swift end to hostilities in all theatres of the war and lay the foundations for a durable peace settlement. The end-product of their week-long labours, the conference meeting between 4 and 11 February, was a number of protocols representing, for the most part, a series of bargains and compromises.

Agreement was reached that Germany should be divided into zones of allied occupation (initially three but extended to four at Yalta with agreement that a French zone should be created out of the British and American zones) and an Allied Control Council established in Berlin. The German armed forces were to be disbanded completely and Nazi ideas and institutions eradicated from public life. German industry capable of military production was to be eliminated and reparations extracted. In response to Stalin's demands, the Western leaders agreed to territorial transfers affecting Poland. In the East, Russian occupation of eastern Poland would become permanent and the Curzon Line re-established as the Russo-Polish frontier; in the West, Poland was to be compensated by extending its frontier at Germany's expense to an extent to be determined ultimately by a peace conference. In return Stalin agreed that the then provisional government of Poland – the

Lublin Committee – a communist body established under Russian auspices in 1944, should be reorganised on a broader basis by the inclusion of non-communist Poles. Once constituted this new Provisional Government of National Unity would be pledged to holding 'free' elections as soon as possible. In deference to Roosevelt's wishes, Stalin agreed to sign a Declaration on Liberated Europe in which the three allies recognised 'the right of all peoples to choose the form of government under which they will live'. Decisions were also reached on voting procedures and Soviet representation at a new United Nations Organisation. Finally, in the context of the Far East, a number of secret bargains were struck. Stalin agreed to declare war on Japan within three months of the German surrender and to negotiate a pact of friendship and alliance with Chiang Kai-shek's Nationalist China. In return, the Soviet Union would gain the Kurile Islands from Japan and a recognition of Outer Mongolia's independence. In addition, the Soviet Union was promised the means to avenge its defeat at the hands of Japan in 1904–5 by the acquisition of southern Sakhalin and the adjacent islands, the lease of Port Arthur as a naval base, the right to use an internationalised port at Dairen and a share in control over the Chinese Eastern and South Manchuria railways.

The Polish settlement was at the time and has remained since the most controversial aspect of the Yalta conference. For Stalin, Poland was a vital security concern. By means of territorial annexation in the east and the imposition of a 'friendly' government, he was determined to ensure that Poland should never again provide a gateway for an invasion of the Soviet Union from the West. Stalin's plans were vehemently opposed by members of the Polish government -in-exile in London whose hostility towards the Soviet Union was based, not simply on Soviet participation in the liquidation of Poland's independence in the autumn of 1939, but also on the Kaytn Forest discovery in 1943 and the events surrounding the Warsaw uprising in 1944.[1] Sympathetic to the plight of the exiled Poles, critics of Yalta in the West accused Roosevelt and Churchill of having betrayed their Polish allies. But at Yalta the hands of the Western leaders had been tied by the concessions they had already made at the Tehran conference in November 1943. Then, in order to placate Stalin, who was becoming increasingly impatient with the Western powers because of their decision to defer for another year the opening of a second front, Roosevelt and Churchill had accepted in principle the territorial transfers affecting Poland which were subsequently confirmed at

Yalta. These frontier changes were hardly likely to be acceptable to a genuinely independent Polish government. Moreover, Polish acquisition of German territory ensured not only future enmity between Poland and Germany but also Poland's dependence on Soviet protection against German irredentism. In short, Tehran as much as Yalta ensured that Poland was destined to become a Soviet sphere of influence.

Soviet advances in Eastern Europe during the latter stages of the war did not of course leave the Western leaders completely unmoved. Churchill's notorious percentage deal with Stalin at Moscow in October 1944 was specifically designed to check a perceived Soviet thrust to the Mediterranean through the Balkans.[2] Moreover, although the Western leaders defended the Yalta settlement on Poland by emphasising the agreement to include non-communists in the government, they were both equally aware that the Soviet conception of what constituted a democratic government differed substantially from their own. Roosevelt, some two months after Yalta, took issue with Stalin over Soviet insistence that the communist members of the existing government in Poland should be given a right of veto over which other Poles should be included in discussions on the composition of a new provisional government. Moreover, when Roosevelt told Churchill in April 1945 that he would 'minimize the general Soviet problem as much as possible' because 'these problems arise every day, and most of them straighten out', he was not, as has often been assumed, expressing an opinion about relations with the Soviet Union in general but replying specifically to an enquiry from the prime minister as to how he should handle questions during a forthcoming parliamentary debate on Poland.[3] Nevertheless, for all his public protestations in favour of self-determination as a means to alleviate the political tensions which had produced two world wars, Roosevelt appreciated that concessions would have to be made to the Russians in Eastern Europe. By so doing and by treating the Soviet Union as a conventional power concerned solely with the pursuit of its own national interests, Roosevelt believed that the Russians could be induced to lend their support to his own 'grand design' which envisaged that the great powers would assume the dominant role in a new system of collective security. Supremely confident in his ability to move Stalin in this direction, Roosevelt accepted that the Russians had the power in Eastern Europe and believed that the only practicable course open to the United States was to use what influence it had to ameliorate the situation.

On 12 April 1945 Roosevelt died. In succeeding months the problems to which he had referred in his advice to Churchill could not be 'minimised', nor could they be 'straightened out'. Instead they became magnified and more protracted. Attitudes on both sides became more inflexible and uncompromising. Roosevelt's 'grand design' began to fade. In its place the Cold War cast its shadow over Europe.

For the most part, historical debate on the origins of the Cold War has centred on two rival interpretations: the orthodox and the revisionist. The orthodox view maintains that responsibility rests with the Soviet Union which attempted to exploit the political and economic uncertainty of the post-war world in order to further its own territorial ambitions and to promote the cause of communist revolution. By way of contrast the revisionists, arguing from one of two points of view, maintain that responsibility rests with the West and primarily with the United States. One view is that Roosevelt's efforts to foster continued cooperation with the Russians were deliberately aborted by the successor Truman administration which resorted to economic blackmail and the brandishing of atomic weapons in order to force a Soviet withdrawal from Eastern Europe and to deny the Russians a presence in the Far East. The other view, which is essentially a critique of the American capitalist system, maintains that American leaders sought economic domination abroad as a means to overcome recurring bouts of depression and overproduction which threatened economic prosperity at home. When the Russians demonstrated their opposition to this approach, and in particular to American plans to maintain the countries of Eastern Europe as suppliers of essential raw materials, American leaders of necessity perceived the Soviet Union as a threat to their own domestic wellbeing against whom a prolonged war of attrition would have to be waged.

Neither orthodox nor revisionist interpretations of the Cold War have commanded universal acceptance. Both are flawed and both overstate their case. The orthodox view tends to overlook the fact that the post-war period was one, not only of opportunity for the Soviet Union, but also, owing to the devastated condition of the Soviet economy, one of considerable danger and uncertainty. The revisionists for their part have either exaggerated the extent to which atomic bombs were used against Japan to influence Soviet behaviour in Eastern Europe or have relied too heavily on assumption, as distinct from actual evidence, in suggesting that the impulse towards economic hegemony was *the* vital factor influencing American foreign policy in the post-war years.

The centrist view, which emphasises fundamental differences in outlook as opposed to individual responsibility, remains therefore the most convincing explanation of the Cold War. In the absence of common bonds and shared values, the wartime alliance disintegrated once the objective upon which it had been based – the defeat of Nazi Germany – had been achieved. Thereafter suspicion and distrust, based for the Western powers on their instinctive fear of communism, and for Stalin on the memory of foreign intervention in the Russian civil war (1918–21) and the appeasement of Hitler in the 30s, were revived as the great powers confronted each other on the question of how to reconstruct the post-war world. The intensity with which the United States and the Soviet Union subsequently waged Cold War, however, can be attributed, not only to the mutual conviction that one constituted a threat to the security of the other, but also to the fact that both considered it necessary to resort to extremes to demonstrate the adversary nature of their relationship.[4]

At the end of the war Stalin considered it of paramount importance to impose a siege mentality upon his country and its people. The full extent of wartime destruction within the Soviet Union had to be concealed from the outside world and the Soviet people had to be isolated lest unfavourable comparisons be made with Western society. Wartime appeals to nationalistic symbols and patriotic pride gave way after 1945 to scrutiny and then repression of anyone – prisoners-of-war (many of whom were sent home against their will by the Western powers) and minority nationalities whose homelands had been occupied by the Germans – who had come into contact with foreigners and foreign influences. Moreover, Soviet society had to be eulogised. In an election address at the Bolshoi Theatre in Moscow in February 1946 Stalin declared: 'Our victory demonstrates first and foremost the victory of our Soviet *social system* . . . secondly, the victory of our Soviet *state*.'[5] Victory in the war had thus been achieved, not simply because of the heroics of the Red Army, but also because of the wise and far-sighted policies of collectivisation and industrialisation which had laid the foundations for survival and success. The nature of the international climate was subsequently used to justify the pace of plans for post-war reconstruction. At the founding conference of the Cominform in September 1947 Andrei Zhdanov, keeper of the ideological keys of the Soviet Union until his death the following year, posited the existence of two rival camps: the imperialist and warmongering led by the United States and the socialist and peace-loving led by the Soviet Union. Although the possibility of coexistence between these two rival systems was acknowledged the Soviet Union had still to be on its guard. American capitalism, in seeking to establish itself on a monopoly basis, had become predatory and aggressive. Zhdanov's remarks must of course be placed in context representing as they did the official Soviet response to shifts in American policy as outlined in the Truman Doctrine and the Marshall Plan. Nevertheless, the implications seemed clear: capitalist encirclement, xenophobia and the enemy within were the essential prerequisites which were needed to sustain the Stalinist system in the Soviet Union during the post-war years.[6]

For the Americans, two vital questions about the Soviet Union confronted policymakers in Washington in the post-war years: the role of ideology in the shaping of Soviet foreign policy and the question whether totalitarian behaviour at home would, of necessity, be duplicated abroad. These questions, pertinent since the revolution of 1917 and dormant during the Second World War, became fundamental after 1945. Roosevelt's belief that Soviet totalitarianism could be mitigated by treating the Soviet Union as a conventional great power interested solely in the pursuit of its own national interests was gradually rejected by the administration which succeeded him. Confronted by the Soviet presence in Eastern Europe, constantly alarmed by the imagined size of the Soviet military establishment,[7] deeply suspicious of Soviet probing in such diverse areas as Iran, Turkey and North Africa, and ever-conscious of the Marxist heritage of the Soviet state, Truman and his advisers eventually concluded that ideology provided *the* key to an understanding of Soviet foreign policy and that communist revolution was the grand design of a Soviet leadership which had become utterly ruthless in its quest for power. Any communist victory in any part of the world was henceforth identified as a corresponding threat to the security of the United States and the free world. Soviet security interests were viewed with the utmost suspicion as the administration began to embrace the domino theory. 'Russian plans for establishing satellite states are a threat to the world and to us', Averell Harriman, American ambassador in Moscow, informed the State Department as early as April 1945: 'The Soviet Union, once it had control of bordering areas, would attempt to penetrate the next adjacent countries.'[8] But Washington's response to the alleged Soviet challenge – a programme of economic and military aid to countries deemed under threat together with an escalating defence budget – encountered domestic opposition in the shape of public indifference and a budget-conscious Congress. To overcome both and to persuade the nation to endorse the administration's own assessment of the gravity of the international situation, Truman and his advisers seized upon isolated and disconnected events to invoke a crisis mentality. To obtain Congressional approval for financial aid to Greece and Turkey, a localised conflict in the former was magnified in the Truman Doctrine of 1947 into a crisis with global implications which required the United States to undertake an open-ended commitment in defence of freedom and democracy. Similarly, the Czech crisis of 1948, which Truman represented as the gravest threat to the United States since Pearl Harbour, was used to secure Congressional majorities for the funds outlined in the Marshall Plan, the reintroduction of selective military service and the Vandenberg Resolution which paved the way for the United States to become a signatory of the North Atlantic Treaty. In short, words as well as deeds were responsible for the intensity of the Cold War and, in the case of the United States, the language employed was designed to intimidate the American people as much as the Soviet leaders.

TRUMAN, POTSDAM AND ATOMIC DIPLOMACY

Although inexperienced in foreign affairs, Harry S. Truman, Roosevelt's successor, made a significant impression during his first six weeks in office. Molotov, the Soviet Foreign Minister, received from the new president a severe rebuke over Russian behaviour in Poland. Land-lease agreements were abruptly terminated and consideration of a post-war loan for the Soviet Union was postponed indefinitely. Revisionists see in the collective impact of these actions, not only a sharp break with Roosevelt's policies, but also a major step towards the Cold War. This, however, is an extreme view. Such evidence as exists suggests that on Poland, the Russians were in breach of both the spirit and the letter of the Yalta agreements. Sixteen leaders of the Polish underground had been arrested and imprisoned having previously received verbal assurances of immunity. The Russians had also transferred large areas of Germany to the administration of the Lublin Poles and, on 21 April 1945, just two days before Truman's meeting with Molotov, they had concluded a defence pact with the same regime in a preemptive move designed to strengthen the claim of the Lublin Poles to be recognised as the legitimate government. Moreover, in considering the implications of Truman's early measures, it should not be forgotten that in May, against the advice of Churchill, the president ordered the withdrawal to the zonal boundaries agreed at Yalta of all American forces which had advanced some 100 miles into the Soviet zone of Germany. Also, at the end of the same month he sent Harry Hopkins, Roosevelt's trusted emissary, to Moscow for talks with Stalin which ended in agreement on the inclusion of non-communists in Poland's provisional government.[9] At this early stage Truman shared Roosevelt's view of the Soviet Union as a conventional great power. The difference between the two presidents lay in Truman's belief that tougher measures were required to induce the Russians to relent in their intimidation of their smaller and more vulnerable neighbours in Eastern Europe.

Truman met Stalin just once – at the Potsdam conference in July and August 1945. Here agreement was reached on the establishment of a Council of Foreign Ministers, charged specifically with the task of making peace treaties with the defeated countries. Sharp disagreements, however, arose over reparations, Poland's frontiers and the composition of the remaining governments in Eastern Europe. To avert a breakdown, compromise solutions, largely the work of James Byrnes, Truman's Secretary of State, were obtained on all three issues. The compromise on Poland was of particular significance. The Western powers agreed, subject to final approval by a peace conference which was expected to follow soon after, that German territory to the east of the Oder and Western Neisse Rivers should be transferred to Poland.

While at Potsdam, Truman received word to the effect that American scientists had successfully tested an atomic bomb at Alamogordo in New Mexico. Revisionists have asserted that bombs were subsequently dropped on Hiroshima and Nagasaki, not so much to bring Japan to her knees, but rather to warn the Soviet Union that the United States now had the means to force compliance with American ideas on the reconstruction of the post-war world. But again the revisionist case has been overstated.[10]

Initially, the Americans approached Potsdam with the aim of reminding Stalin of his pledge at Yalta to enter the war against Japan within three months of Germany's defeat. At the time of Roosevelt's death, Soviet entry into the war was still thought vital to bring hostilities in the Far East to a speedy conclusion with a minimum loss of further American lives. Truman left for Potsdam with the same considerations in mind but the actual timing of his arrival was very much influenced by the approaching Alamogordo test. Moreover, news that the test had been successful significantly altered the military position in the Far East. Soviet entry was no longer deemed vital. There is evidence to suggest that Byrnes, by encouraging procrastination on the part of the Nationalist Chinese in the Sino–Soviet treaty negotiations (Stalin had insisted on a treaty with China incorporating the concessions agreed at Yalta as a precondition of Soviet entry into the war), was attempting to forestall, not only a Soviet invasion of Manchuria, but also a role for the Russians in the Japanese occupation regime. But there is no evidence to suggest that Washington seriously contemplated threatening the Russians with the bomb over Eastern Europe. On the contrary, when the relationship between the bomb and policy towards the Soviet Union had been discussed in June between Truman and his Secretary for War, Henry Stimson, the conversation had turned, not on the idea of using the bomb as a threat, but on using it as a possible bargaining lever. Truman and Stimson suggested an atomic partnership with the Russians in return for an acceptable settlement of, amongst others, the Polish, Romanian, Yugoslav and Manchurian problems. The desire to end the war with the minimum loss of American life remains therefore the principal reason why Truman authorised use of the bomb as a combat weapon against Japan.

Whatever the reason for its actual use, however, the bomb made a decisive impression in Moscow. Averell Harriman reported in November 1945: 'Suddenly the atomic bomb appeared and they [the Russians] recognised that it was an offset to the power of the Red Army. This must have revived their old feeling of insecurity ... the Russian people have been aroused to feel that they must face an antagonistic world. American imperialism is included as a threat to the Soviet Union'.[11] Stimson was one of the first to realise that the bomb, or more specifically Byrnes' post-Potsdam tactic of negotiating with the bomb rather ostentatiously on his hip, was beginning to poison Soviet-American relations. Concerned at the prospect of an arms race, Stimson had already proposed a direct approach to Moscow over the control of atomic energy. But his advice was rejected. When in 1946 the United States produced the Baruch plan for the control of atomic weapons the political climate had changed considerably for the worse. The plan, which suggested that the United States would destroy its stocks of atomic weapons but only after a United Nations Atomic Energy Commission had been established, was clearly designed to preserve America's lead. The Russians countered by proposing an immediate ban on the use and manufacture of all atomic weapons and the destruction of all weapons in existence. The mutual trust required for agreement was entirely absent from the debate. With the Soviet bomb a mere three years away, Stimson's worst fears were soon to be realised.

THE EVOLUTION OF CONTAINMENT

The period between the Potsdam conference and the announcement of the Truman Doctrine in March 1947 was crucial in the evolution of American perceptions about the objectives of Soviet foreign policy. The image of the Soviet Union as a conventional, if somewhat overbearing, great power was abandoned in favour of the theory that the Soviet Union was an expansionist power bent on pursuing a messianic mission to communise the world. Washington's response – the strategy of containment – is significant in that it subsequently dominated American foreign policy for the next 30 years.

Two meetings of the Council of Foreign Ministers were held during the second half of 1945. At London in September, in an attempt to secure non-communist representation in the governments of Eastern Europe, Byrnes offered Molotov a four-power treaty guaranteeing Germany's demilitarisation for 25 years. The offer was not taken up by the Russians but at the second meeting, held at Moscow in December, Molotov agreed to the addition of two non-communists to the governments of Bulgaria and Romania and also promised early elections and the establishment of civil liberties in both countries. Regarding his negotiations with his Soviet counterpart as a painstaking exercise in the art of the possible, Byrnes felt that progress had been made. But this was not a view shared by his Republican critics in Washington. Senators Arthur Vandenberg and John Foster Dulles, who had carefully scrutinised Byrnes every move, argued that there was a point beyond which compromise could not go and lamented what they regarded as the desertion of 'our war pledges to small nations'. Byrnes, it was said, had accepted agreements which fell well short of American ideals and which even smacked of appeasement.

Anxious to maintain the bipartisan nature of American foreign policy and himself irritated by Byrnes' tendency to treat foreign policy as his own personal domain, Truman decided to bring his Secretary of State to heel. In a letter to Byrnes in January 1946, Truman listed what he regarded as Soviet misdemeanours, asserted that America should no longer 'play compromise' and concluded: 'I'm tired of babying the Soviets'.[12] A chastened Byrnes had no option but to fall in line with the anti-Soviet consensus which was rapidly permeating the administration.

This consensus was considerably reinforced by two key events which took place early in 1946. The first, in February, was a telegraphic communication from George Kennan, then Chief of Mission at the American Embassy in Moscow, to the State Department. With experience dating from the 20s, Kennan was one of the State Department's foremost experts on the Soviet Union. In the light of Stalin's election address at the Bolshoi Theatre (see above p. 5), he had been asked to submit an 'interpretive analysis' of Soviet foreign policy. Impatient with the manner in which American leaders were approaching the subject of post-war negotiations with their Soviet counterparts, Kennan responded with the 'Long Telegram' (forerunner of his better known 'Mr X' article which appeared in the July 1947 issue of *Foreign Affairs*), an 8,000-word epistle designed to impress upon its recipients the true character of their adversary.[13]

Kennan's analysis began with the premise that the Soviet Union 'still lives in [a world of] antagonistic "capitalist encirclement" with which in the long run there can be no permanent peaceful coexistence'. This attitude was conditioned, not by an objective analysis of conditions beyond the Soviet Union, but by 'inner-Russian necessities', the most basic of which was the 'instinctive Russian sense of insecurity'. The Soviet leaders felt insecure because they recognised that 'their rule was relatively archaic in form, fragile and artificial in its psychological foundation, [and] unable to stand comparison or contact with political systems of western countries'. This mentality, according to Kennan, explained why Marxism, with its emphasis on the insolubility of economic conflicts by peaceful means, had such a powerful appeal for these same leaders. By claiming that they were the harbingers of a new social order, defying the evil and menacing forces of capitalism, they could disguise their insecurity and justify their domestic repression.

Kennan's analysis led him to draw a chilling conclusion: '[We] have here a political force committed to the belief that with [the] United States there can be no permanent *modus vivendi*, that it is desirable and necessary that the internal harmony of our society be disrupted, our traditional way of life be destroyed, the international authority of our State be broken, if Soviet power is to be secure'. But Kennan also believed that the United States possessed certain advantages which could enable it to withstand the challenge without recourse to war. The Soviets were by far the weaker force, the Soviet system had yet to prove itself and Soviet propaganda, being essentially negative, could easily be counteracted by an 'intelligent and really constructive programme'. Above all, however, Soviet power, unlike that of Hitlerite Germany, was neither schematic nor adventuristic: 'Impervious to [the] logic of reason . . . it is highly sensitive to [the] logic of force. For this reason it can easily withdraw – and usually does – when strong resistance is encountered at any point'. If an adversary maintained sufficient counterforce and made clear its readiness to use it, it would rarely have to do so. Containment was thus the remedy prescribed by Kennan for dealing with the communist contagion.

Kennan's analysis, as he himself later admitted, was clearly flawed.[14] Beyond a fleeting reference to the Soviet system being subject to additional strains by virtue of recent territorial expansion, the Long Telegram made no reference to the problem of maintaining control in Eastern Europe. Nor did it dwell on the implications of the weakness of the Soviet economy. The Stalinist system certainly thrived on the threat of capitalist encirclement but to argue that the Soviet Union would be driven in consequence to seek the destruction of American power was to present an extreme and distorted view of Soviet foreign policy. In short, Kennan had placed too much emphasis on ideology and too little on the role of *Realpolitik* in the shaping of Soviet policy. Nevertheless, the Long Telegram had a dramatic impact on officialdom in Washington. 'A splendid analysis' and 'Magnificent' were just two of the tributes it received. Copies were circulated throughout the administration and also distributed to American diplomatic and military missions abroad. The Long Telegram not only made Kennan a household name in Washington. It also became the bible to which policymakers turned for guidance in their dealings with the Soviet Union.[15]

The second key event was the Iranian crisis of March 1946. In order to prevent Iran gravitating into the German orbit and also to secure the supply lines to Russia, Britain and the Soviet Union had established joint military control in Iran in 1941. The British occupied the south, the Russians the north. The same two powers concluded a further agreement in 1942 for the withdrawal of their troops within six months of the end of the war. During the war, Britain and America used their influence to secure major oil concessions in Iran. As one American official put it: 'We shall soon be in the position of actually "running" Iran through an impressive body of American advisers'. The Russians for their part were determined to strengthen their position in an area long regarded as a traditional Russian sphere of influence and, as in the case of the Western powers, they were anxious to secure an oil concession.

At the end of the war Britain began withdrawing its troops according to the agreed schedule but the Russians did not follow suit. In order to press their claims they sponsored the creation of a separatist regime in the northern province of Azerbaijan. The communist-dominated Tudeh Party, part of the ruling coalition in Tehran, exerted pressure for the opening of negotiations with the Russians who subsequently demanded autonomy, not only for Azerbaijan, but also for the neighbouring province of Kurdistan. The Russians also requested the formation of a Soviet-Iranian oil company. The Western powers reacted sharply to these developments. The continued presence of Soviet troops was an ominous factor in the situation and Truman in particular had no wish to be presented with another *fait accompli* in the shape of a Sovietised Iran. When the deadline for the withdrawal of Soviet troops passed, Washington attempted to undermine the Soviet-Iranian negotiations by encouraging the government in Tehran to raise the issue at the United Nations. Tehran duly obliged, bringing the question of Soviet 'aggression' first before the Security Council in January 1946 and then, simultaneously with the despatch of strong notes of protest from Washington and London to Moscow, before the General Assembly in March. Thereafter the crisis subsided, Andrei Gromyko, the Soviet delegate to the United Nations, pledging at the end of March that Soviet troops would be withdrawn within six months. In April, Tehran and Moscow reached agreement on the formation of a joint-stock oil company and in May Soviet troops were withdrawn. But at the end of the year, to Moscow's chagrin, the Tudeh Party was expelled from the coalition in Tehran and the separatist movements in the north were suppressed. Worse was to follow. In October 1947 the Iranian parliament refused to ratify the agreement for the establishment of a Soviet-Iranian joint-stock oil company.

The Iranian crisis, besides representing a setback for the Soviet Union in an area on its own borders, was also the occasion of the first public breach between the former wartime allies. Winston Churchill, now leader of the opposition in Britain but still an influential voice, added fuel to the fire with his celebrated 'Iron Curtain' speech at Fulton, Missouri, on 5 March 1946 in which he declared that the Russians sought, by means short of war, 'the indefinite expansion of their power and doctrines'.[17] Furthermore, the crisis persuaded policymakers in Washington to take Kennan's analysis a significant step further. It now became the conventional wisdom to assume that the Soviet Union operated on a global basis, each move in its foreign policy being 'carefully planned and integrated with ones on other fronts'.[18] What had been for Moscow an exercise in traditional power politics was identified in Washington as part of a grand expansionist design which also threatened neighbouring Iraq and Turkey. Accordingly the United States had to respond with a global strategy of its own. No longer was it possible to devise policy for separate regions. Nor could foreign policy issues be considered in future on their merits. Instead, American foreign policy was to have a single determinant – the means to resist Soviet expansionism.

By the autumn of 1946, and particularly after the resignation in September of Commerce Secretary Henry Wallace, a lone advocate of the theory that American bellicosity would serve only to induce the same in the Russians, the anti-Soviet consensus reigned supreme in Washington. Beyond the corridors of power, however, lay an apathetic and indifferent public and a Republican-dominated, budget-conscious Congress which defined national security, not in terms of global strategy, but in terms of conventional defence. Aware therefore of the need to educate public opinion, the administration seized upon the next major crisis which arose in the Balkans in the spring of 1947 not so much as a challenge but as an exercise in salesmanship.

In February 1947 Britain informed Washington of its inability to maintain support for the right-wing nationalist forces in Greece in their civil war against the communist-controlled guerrilla forces of the National Liberation Front (EAM). Britain's parlous financial and economic plight was well known in Washington and thus the news did not come as a surprise. Moreover, Washington had already been alerted to the gravity of the situation by reports received from its own observers in Athens which indicated that the Greek government was on the point of collapse and that Moscow, as well as being responsible for the crisis, would also be the chief beneficiary of an EAM victory.

The reality was rather different. The roots of the Greek crisis were local in origin: endemic political instability accompanied by the alienation of both workers and peasants in the face of corruption and oppression on the part of the ruling elite. From the outset, Stalin remained aloof and urged restraint on the Greek communists. At first, EAM appear to have heeded his advice. In July 1944, following the visit of a Soviet military mission to EAM headquarters.led by Colonel Popov, the communists agreed, once the German occupation forces had been removed, to enter the provisional government of Georgios Papandreou which was waiting in exile. With the aid of a small British military force, the Papandreou government was established in Athens in October 1944. In the confusion surrounding the German withdrawal and the British landings, this was arguably EAM's best chance of seizing power. However, the opportunity was missed. The communist leadership appears to have been divided between those who advocated the revolutionary road to power and those who advocated the parliamentary road. Subsequent clashes between the British-backed governments in Athens (Papandreou's government being only the first in a series of liberal experiments which veered increasingly towards the right) and the communists, occurred in December 1944 over the issue of disarming guerrilla forces. Full-scale civil war began in 1946. External aid for the communists was channelled through neighbouring Albania and Yugoslavia but not even moral encouragement was forthcoming from Moscow. Preoccupied with affairs in Eastern Europe, the evidence suggests that Stalin remained committed to the 1944 percentage deal with Churchill which defined Greece as a British sphere of influence. As late as 1948 he is reported to have told Milovan Djilas, one of Tito's lieutenants, that it was 'nonsense' to believe that Britain and America would ever allow their lines of communication in the Mediterranean to be broken.[19]

The realities of the Greek situation, however, were lost on policy-makers in Washington. At the end of February 1947, George Marshall, Byrnes' successor at the State Department, and Dean Acheson, his Under-Secretary, addressed Congressional leaders. With his superior fluffing his lines, Acheson stepped in to warn of dire consequences should the United States fail to respond at once. 'Like apples in a barrel infected by the corruption of one of them', declared Acheson,

'the corruption of Greece would infect Iran and all to the East ...
Africa ... Italy and France'.[20] This was the domino theory in its most
extreme form but Acheson's alarmist tone had the desired effect.
Senator Vandenberg called for a presidential statement in equally
dramatic terms.

The upshot was Truman's speech to Congress – the Truman
Doctrine – on 12 March 1947. Appealing for military and economic
aid to the tune of 300 million dollars for Greece, and 100 million
dollars for neighbouring Turkey, the president declared:

> At the present moment in world history nearly every nation must
> choose between alternative ways of life. The choice is too often not
> a free one. One way of life is based upon the will of the majority,
> and is distinguished by free institutions, representative government,
> free elections, guarantees of individual liberty, freedom of speech
> and religion, and freedom from political oppression. The second
> way of life is based upon the will of the minority forcibly imposed
> upon the majority. It relies upon terror and oppression, a controlled
> press and radio, fixed elections, and the suppression of personal
> freedoms. I believe that it must be the policy of the United States
> to support free people who are resisting attempted subjugation by
> armed minorities or by outside pressures.[21]

The speech, which cast the United States in the role of the world's
policeman, had the desired galvanising effect. Congress dutifully
complied with the president's request for aid, polls indicated an
increase in the numbers of Americans who regarded Soviet behaviour
as aggressive and, by 1949, the communists had been defeated in
Greece.

Nevertheless, like Kennan's Long Telegram, the Truman Doctrine
was open to objection on several counts. It was presented, not as a
policy, but as a crusade and as such it represented an open-ended
commitment which recognised no boundaries in its application. It
implied that the threat of 'subjugation by armed minorities or by
outside pressures' was to be the only criterion dictating the provision
of American military and economic aid. Significant qualifying factors
– whether it would always be within American capabilities to provide
aid, whether the United States would always of necessity benefit
thereby and whether the recipients of such aid would always be
deserving of it – were overlooked. In this latter respect it was singularly

inappropriate to relate the crisis in Greece to the defence of democracy. The beneficiaries of American aid could hardly qualify for it upon the basis of their democratic credentials. Here then in embryo were the two features of post-war American foreign policy which ultimately culminated in the tragedy of Vietnam: an extensive and expensive range of overseas commitments in defence of regimes chosen upon the basis, not of their democratic credentials, but of their strategic location and their anti-Sovietism.

The Truman Doctrine was rapidly followed by a further extension of the containment strategy in the shape of the Marshall Plan. By the early summer of 1947 Washington had become increasingly concerned at the economic plight of Western Europe. The winter of 1946–47, one of the worst in living memory, had aggravated a situation in which there were already serious shortages of food, fuel and raw materials. Rising costs and prices fuelled strike activity which in turn promoted political instability. In this gloomy climate, Marshall returned in April 1947 from a meeting of the Council of Foreign Ministers at Moscow convinced that the Soviet Union was biding its time in anticipation that the worsening economic situation would persuade the voters of Western Europe to turn to the communists as their only means of salvation. In the circumstances it was surely no coincidence that the communist members of the ruling coalitions in France and Rome were forced from office in May 1947.

Whatever its external manifestations, the roots of the European crisis were financial and expressed in terms of the 'dollar shortage'. A trade imbalance between the United States and Europe had developed to the extent that the former was exporting to the latter seven times as much as it received in return in imports. In consequence, Europe had insufficient dollar reserves with which to purchase essential supplies of food and raw materials from the United States. The only means of recovery which suggested itself was that the Americans should finance these purchases by making dollars available.

Accordingly, Marshall appointed a Policy Planning Staff within the State Department under the direction of George Kennan, recently returned from Moscow. The planners were given the task of considering, not so much the details of an American aid programme for Europe, but rather the manner of its presentation. In May 1947 Kennan's staff submitted a report which maintained that an aid programme should be designed to counteract, not communism itself, but rather the economic deprivation which made European society vulnerable to communist exploitation. To convince Congress that the Europeans were willing to help themselves, the report also suggested that the actual details should be worked out by the governments concerned. They would be required to produce a single coordinated plan for the whole region. One further consideration influenced the planners. Fears of a German revival, a recurrent concern of the French in particular, would be mitigated by placing Germany's recovery within the context of overall European cooperation.

Marshall took his cue from the Planning Staff's report when he announced America's willingness to finance a European aid programme in his speech at Harvard on 5 June 1947. He also indicated that the American offer was open to *all* European countries: 'Any Government that is willing to assist in the task of recovery will find full cooperation on the part of the United States Government'. By implication, therefore, the Soviet Union could, if it wished, avail itself of American aid.

The question of Russian participation had been debated at length by State Department officials. Kennan recalled the conclusion reached:

> As for the Russians, we would play it straight. If they responded favourably, we would test their good faith by insisting that they contribute constructively to the program as well as profiting from it. If they were unwilling to do this, we would simply let them exclude themselves. But we would not ourselves draw a line of division through Europe.[22]

Kennan's recollection, however, did not represent the full American position. The State Department was aware that Congress would probably reject Marshall's proposal if the Soviet Union came in.[23] Furthermore, officials felt reasonably confident that the Russians would object to the cooperative nature of the programme as an infringement of their national sovereignty. The constructive contribution to which Kennan referred turned out to be a suggestion that the Russians should be asked to supply raw materials to Western Europe, a remote prospect given their own economic plight. The open invitation was thus deceptive. Unwilling to exclude the Soviet Union and thus incur responsibility for having precipitated an economic division in Europe, the United States chose instead to stipulate conditions known in advance to be unacceptable to the Kremlin.

The Harvard speech produced a flurry of diplomatic activity in

Europe. Bevin and Bidault, the respective British and French Foreign Ministers, arranged a meeting in Paris at the end of June and extended an invitation to the Russians who seemed at first to be taking the matter very seriously. Molotov arrived in Paris at the head of a team of 80 economic specialists. American calculations, however, were soon confirmed when Molotov insisted upon a bilateral approach. Individual countries would be required only to submit a statement of need and would then have the freedom to determine themselves how to spend the money provided by the United States. Bevin and Bidault responded with their own insistence on the collective approach. Individual statements of need would require collective approval and be included in a single consolidated demand. Subsequent spending of the money provided would then be subject to central direction and supervision.

On 2 July 1947, after five fruitless sessions with his British and French counterparts, Molotov stormed out of Paris, unleashing as he departed a bitter attack against American efforts to avoid an economic depression of their own by establishing new markets in Europe. But the Soviet walkout represented a tactical blunder. However unwelcome the conditions, Soviet compliance would have placed Washington in a quandary. Had the administration succeeded in overcoming Congressional reservations, the Russians would have gained access to much needed American dollars. Had it failed, then the deception of the open invitation would have been exposed. Either way the Russians stood to gain. In the event they gained nothing except a bad press in the West.

On 12 July 1947, at British and French bidding, representatives of sixteen West European countries attended a further meeting at which a Committee for European Economic Cooperation (CEEC) was established to determine the collective needs of the participants. In April 1948 Congress passed a European Recovery Programme Bill and in May the CEEC became the Organisation for European Economic Cooperation (OEEC), a permanent body with headquarters in Paris. Over the next five years the OEEC disbursed some 13.5 billion dollars. The results were immediate and effective. Western Europe was hauled back from the precipice of economic collapse and communism in Western Europe, if not halted (the communist parties in France and Italy continued to command considerable electoral followings), had at least been contained. Equally, however, the Soviet response to these events ensured that the Marshall Plan became a major turning point in the evolution of the Cold War.

THE SOVIET RIPOSTE IN EASTERN EUROPE

The Soviet rejection of the Marshall Plan was determined, not simply by an instinctive dislike of foreigners prying into their domestic affairs, but also by their conviction that the plan was in part designed to drive a wedge between the Soviet Union and its neighbours in Eastern Europe. The governments of Czechoslovakia and Poland, both of whom had expressed interest in the plan, were subsequently obliged to withdraw against their will under Soviet pressure. But once the heat generated by Molotov's Paris walkout had subsided, the Russians appear to have elaborated a yet further interpretation of the plan which ascribed more sinister motives to policymakers in Washington. This new interpretation attached more significance to military considerations and maintained that the real purpose of American aid was to facilitate a military build-up in Western Europe which would ultimately enable America's allies to recover, at the expense of Moscow's gains in Eastern Europe, the position lost to the Red Army between 1944 and 1947.[24] The United States in the meantime would remain in the background, shielding Western Europe under the nuclear umbrella provided by Strategic Air Command. This assessment, an early version of the 'liberation' or 'roll-back' theory propagated by American strategists in the mid-50s, suggested answers to hitherto unresolved questions about the long-term objectives of American foreign policy. In particular, it seemed to explain the apparent contradiction whereby the United States was so reluctant either to risk all-out war or to engage in large-scale rearmament and yet, at the same time, so determined to deny to the Russians the fruits of their victory in the war. American strategy was thus identified as a grave, if not as yet imminent, threat to Soviet security and it was this heightened perception of their own vulnerability which prompted the Russians to adopt ruthless measures in tightening their grip on Eastern Europe between 1947 and 1949.

In the summer and autumn of 1947 Moscow negotiated a series of bilateral trade agreements which were designed to harness the economies of Eastern Europe to the economy of the Soviet Union and to forestall any further attempts to seek economic recovery within a Western framework. Joint-stock companies were established. The countries of Eastern Europe were also obliged to sell much of their produce to Russia at prices which were well below those operating on the world market. In return they received Soviet goods at grossly inflated prices. These agreements paved the way for the creation of the Council for Mutual Economic Assistance (Comecon) in January 1949. Ostensibly designed to centralise arrangements for trade, credit and technological assistance, Comecon became an extension of the means whereby the Russians could exploit the economies of Eastern Europe to bolster their own.

A second instrument of control emerged in September 1947 with the establishment of the Cominform (Communist Information Bureau). Besides the Soviet Communist Party, the Cominform included in its organisation the parties of Poland, Czechoslovakia, Yugoslavia, Poland, Hungary, Romania and Bulgaria, as well as the powerful Western parties of France and Italy. The Cominform was more exclusive in membership than the Comintern (Communist International) which had been dissolved in 1943 and its functions taken over by the International Department of the Central Committee of the Soviet Party. Stalin believed then that the communist parties would fare better in the post-war popularity stakes if they were released, in public at least, from the constraints of a centrally controlled international movement. In 1947, however, the eagerness of the governments in Prague and Warsaw to participate in the Marshall Plan, together with the prospect that Western prosperity might have a disintegrating effect on Eastern Europe as a whole, convinced Moscow of the imperative need to re-establish central control. Presented as a somewhat anodyne forum to enable the communist parties to exchange views and information, the Cominform was conceived in reality as an agency through which Moscow could impose ideological uniformity on Eastern Europe, check any 'nationalist' deviations on the road to socialism and dragoon the two largest communist parties in Western Europe into service against the Marshall Plan.

The founding conference of the Cominform, which was held ostensibly at Polish invitation in Silesia some distance from Warsaw, was the occasion of Zhdanov's two-camp analysis of the international situation (see above pp. 5–6). It witnessed vehement attacks against the Marshall Plan, Social Democratic parties in the West and, to the utter bewilderment of their respective delegations, the French and Italian communist parties which were upbraided for having placed excessive reliance on parliamentarism – the very tactic advocated at the seventh and last Congress of the Comintern which had been held at Moscow in 1935. The French and Italian parties were henceforth directed to sabotage by all means short of revolution the implementation of the Marshall Plan and hence Western Europe's economic recovery. The net result was that these two parties were placed in a political straitjacket and Washington provided with retrospective justification for their expulsion from the coalitions in Paris and Rome the previous spring.

The most draconian measures, involving the destruction of non-communist parties, the elimination of non-communist politicians and, following the breach with Tito's Yugoslavia in 1948, the purging of the communist parties themselves, were imposed on individual East European countries. Western observers argued that Stalin intended after the war to instal obedient satellite governments in Eastern Europe, at best as a minimum guarantee of Soviet security, at worst as part of a planned move to advance the cause of communist revolution. As evidence, they pointed to the apparent similarity in political developments throughout Eastern Europe after 1945. Coalitions of all parties except those of the far right gave way in time to 'Popular Fronts' consisting of communists and other parties of the left which in turn were replaced by one-party communist dictatorships or 'People's Democracies' as Moscow euphemistically chose to describe them. Throughout this 'salami' process, communists held the key positions in government – usually the interior (which gave them control over the police and other security forces), broadcasting and information, and education and agriculture. Yet despite outward appearances to the contrary, Eastern Europe still displayed sufficient diversity between 1945 and 1947 to suggest that the Kremlin did not operate from a masterplan for the establishment of Soviet control. Nor does the evidence necessarily suggest that Stalin intended from the outset to establish obedient satellites.

Communist pressure with Soviet backing was most keenly felt in Poland, Bulgaria and Romania. The cosmetic addition of a handful of non-communists to the provisional governments of these countries made little difference to their political outlook and elections in all three, with the Red Army lurking ominously in the background, produced predictable results. In Poland, contrary to opinion in the West both at the time and since, there was never a period when free competition was permitted between the communist and non-communist parties. Power passed directly from the German occupying forces to the Red Army to the Soviet-controlled Provisional Government. Equally, however, there was no need to impose communism by force. With the possible exception of Mikolajczyk, leader of the London Poles and, since 1945, leader of the Polish Peasant Party, the non-communist elements had been eliminated. They were either discredited because of their pre-war failures, deserted by the Western allies or destroyed during the Warsaw uprising. The communists depended on Soviet support during the early post-war years. But given the degree of importance which the Western powers attached to Poland, Stalin was still inclined to tread warily to avoid giving the impression of a direct Soviet takeover. The Polish communists thus possessed some degree of leverage of their own, which explains why friction developed between the communists and Moscow over the questions of the timing of political changes in Poland and the introduction of a socialist programme.[25]

International considerations also had a bearing on developments in Bulgaria and Romania. The Western powers were handicapped, not only by their ignorance of what was actually happening in both countries, but also by their own disinclination to become involved. This was particularly true in Britain's case while Churchill was still prime minister. Churchill believed that Western protests over Bulgaria and Romania would serve only to complicate matters in countries such as Poland and Greece. In 1945 he minuted Eden, his Foreign Secretary: 'I am much concerned lest U[ncle] J[oe] should reproach us for breaking our undertaking with him about Roumania at the same time as the strife about Poland comes to a head. We must keep our word, however painful, if we are to use that agreement to him with effect. I am anxious to go full out over Poland and this requires concentration at the expense of other matters'.[26] Verbally at least, the Labour administration which replaced that of Churchill adopted a tougher attitude over Bulgaria and Romania. But once agreement had been reached with Molotov at Moscow in December 1946 on non-communist representation in the Bulgarian and Romanian governments (see above p. 10), the Americans and the British moved quickly to conclude peace treaties with Bulgaria and Romania, and also with Hungary, in February 1947. These treaties were deemed necessary to get the Russians to sign a peace treaty with Italy which would remove Russian influence and set that country on a firmly pro-Western course.

Elsewhere, not only in Eastern but also in Northern and Central

Europe, the extent and nature of communist influence presented a varied picture. In Northern Europe, the Russians regarded Finland as a defeated enemy. The country was not occupied but a Russian force was established at the naval base of Porkkala, only 30 minutes' driving time from the capital, Helsinki. The Finnish Communist Party (SKP) was not a negligible factor in Finland's domestic politics. By the end of 1945, having transformed itself from an underground movement to a mass party with 20,000 members, the SKP represented a powerful force in the government and led a political front which had the support of a quarter of the electorate. But Stalin preferred to work for what he wanted in Finland through J.K. Paasikivi, a conservative banker and Finland's first post-war prime minister. Stalin wanted, not control of Finland, but formal guarantees to the effect that Helsinki recognised a special relationship with Moscow and renounced all possibility of joining a Western alliance. An agreement to this effect was concluded in the Soviet-Finnish Mutual Assistance Pact which was signed at Moscow in April 1948. By accepting these constraints on their defence and foreign policies, the Finns were able to maintain their internal autonomy.[27]

The Finnish model was applicable in Central Europe. In Austria, which had been placed, like Germany, under four-power control at the end of the war, the Russians again made no attempt to instal a communist regime in their eastern zone of occupation. The questions of communist influence and Soviet policies in Germany merit separate investigation and are discussed below (pp. 30–44). In Czechoslovakia, President Eduard Beneš and other non-communist politicians seemed ready to concede what Stalin wanted. To restore an independent Czechoslovakia to its pre-war borders and to safeguard against another German attack, Beneš, during the war, abandoned the Munich strategy of cooperating with the Western powers and tilted his country towards the Soviet Union. Beneš envisaged a post-war role for Czechoslovakia as a bridge-builder between East and West and between communism and democracy. He believed that the key to Czech security lay in friendly relations with Moscow. A treaty, publicly concluded, was seen by Beneš as a means of committing Stalin to both the protection of Czechoslovakia and to non-interference in Prague's internal affairs. In December 1943 he travelled to Moscow and signed a Russo-Czech Treaty of Friendship, Alliance and Mutual Assistance. During discussions in Moscow with both Stalin and Gottwald, the leader of the Czech communists, Beneš conceded a major role to the communists in a post-war government. This the communists achieved when they secured 38 per cent of the vote in relatively free elections in April 1946. With only 9 of the 27 seats, the communists were in a minority in the new cabinet. But Gottwald was appointed prime minister and the communists also controlled the key ministries of the interior and information.[28] A not dissimilar situation obtained in Hungary after elections in November 1945. Although they had a much smaller share of the vote, the communists shared power with the majority Smallholders or Peasant Party in a coalition which included Ferenc Nagy of the Smallholders as prime minister and Matyas Rakosi, General-Secretary of the Communist Party, as vice-premier.

In the South-East of Europe the picture was different. Stalin regarded Greece as a Western sphere of influence and, as we have seen, he gave no support to the Greek communists. Neighbouring Albania and Yugoslavia were two countries which did not depend upon Red Army assistance to liberate themselves from the axis powers. In both, communist regimes emerged independently of Moscow from the local partisan militias.

Surveying these regional variations it seems quite conceivable that what Stalin wanted in Eastern Europe at the end of the war was not 'Sovietisation' but 'Finlandisation'. But whereas the non-communists of Finland were prepared to accept a 'special relationship' with Moscow which precluded military ties with the West, the non-communists elsewhere were divided. Those in Czechoslovakia were prepared to play the Finnish game but others, particularly those in Poland, were not. The eventual outcome, which produced satellite states in Eastern Europe bound closely to Moscow, was ultimately determined by the climate of East-West relations from the spring of 1947. Stalin's hand was forced by the Truman Doctrine and the Marshall Plan. Given his view of the hostile intent behind both, Stalin could no longer tolerate non-communist politicians in the governments of Eastern Europe. In time-honoured Stalinist fashion, he therefore acted to terminate the regional variations. In May 1947 in Hungary, Nagy was implicated in an espionage case which had already claimed as one of its victims Bela Kovacs, a former General-Secretary of the Smallholders. Nagy chose exile thus enabling the communists to strengthen their grip on the government. Communist-controlled elections in August sent the Smallholders into oblivion. Petkov, the leader of the Bulgarian Peasant Party, was arrested in August on a similar charge of espionage and executed in September. In Romania the

Peasant Party was dissolved in October and its 75-year-old leader, Maniu, sentenced to life imprisonment. In Poland in the same month, Mikolajczyk managed to escape the fate of his Bulgarian and Romanian counterparts by fleeing to Britain.

Parliamentary government lingered on in Czechoslovakia until February 1948. In December 1947 Laurence Steinhardt, the American ambassador in Prague, observed how Moscow's somewhat 'benign' attitude towards Czechoslovakia had hardened as a result of the latter's interest in the Marshall Plan.[29] Certainly Stalin could ill afford to let Czechoslovakia slip. Not only was the Czech state an integral part of the Soviet security zone in Eastern Europe, it was also the Soviet Union's most important source of uranium. Presented in the West as a coup, the communist takeover was in fact precipitated by the resignations of twelve non-communist ministers in protest against the appointment of communists to senior police positions. An ominous factor in the situation was the presence in Prague of Valerian Zorin, the Soviet deputy Foreign Minister. Haunted by the spectre of Munich, President Beneš at first prevaricated and refused to accept the resignations. The communists quickly exploited the crisis, forming Action Committees to take over the vacated ministries and using the police to arrest and intimidate political opponents. At the end of February Beneš succumbed to the pressure and invited Gottwald to form a new communist-dominated government. Jan Masaryk, the Foreign Minister, agreed to remain in office but on 10 March he was found dead on the pavement beneath his office window. Whether his death was suicide or murder remains a mystery.

The events of February and Masaryk's death produced a shock wave of revulsion in the West but no decision to intervene. Washington had shown little appreciation of the precarious geopolitical position in which countries like Czechoslovakia found themselves. Sandwiched between larger and more powerful forces – Germany in the West and the Soviet Union in the East –the countries of Eastern Europe had either gained or regained their independence at the end of the First World War when the influence of their great power neighbours had been temporarily in abeyance. Now, with the eclipse yet again of German power but with Russian power in the ascendant, their ability to preserve a modicum of independence depended, not only on the overall state of East-West tensions, but also on their readiness to acknowledge that they were part of the Soviet sphere and to accept the consequent constraints on the conduct of their foreign policy.

Beneš and Masaryk appreciated this. In describing their strategy, Zenkl, another non-communist Czech politician, formulated an embryonic version of the 1968 Brezhnev Doctrine: 'We know that the freedom of action of every small country is nowadays to a certain extent limited, and we know that this is doubly true about a country in our geographical position. Accepting this limitation, we do so nevertheless in the spirit of Masaryk and Beneš, namely above all in the interest of international understanding which, as is known, demands a certain limitation of sovereignty of every state'.[30] Washington, however, had little respect for the efforts made by Beneš and Masaryk to keep their fences mended with Moscow. The Americans attempted to influence political conditions within Czechoslovakia, and also the orientation of Czech foreign policy, by deliberately withholding credits but they succeeded only in weakening and isolating the non-communist forces and tarnishing still further the reputation of the West. Furthermore, having already decided in November 1947 that Moscow would be forced, in a 'defensive move', to 'clamp down completely on Czechoslovakia',[31] Marshall was rather more concerned about the repercussions should a successful communist coup occur in Western Europe than he was about events in Czechoslovakia. Hence the administration dramatised the crisis to secure Congressional majorities for the funds outlined in the European Recovery Programme Bill and for the Vandenberg Resolution of June 1948 which, in calling for American participation in regional security pacts, paved the way for the North Atlantic Treaty of 1949 (see below p. 41–2).

The communist takeover in Prague was intended to set the seal on the Soviet bloc in Eastern Europe. Beneath the surface, however, a quarrel was simmering between the Soviet Union and Yugoslavia. It became public in June 1948 and thereafter had far-reaching implications for the future of the communist world.[32]

That tension existed between Moscow and Belgrade appeared at first to be somewhat paradoxical. Tito was an orthodox communist who had been relentless in his pursuit of socialist development and the collectivisation of agriculture since the end of the war. He was also loyal to Moscow, accepting Soviet leadership of international communism and acknowledging the vital contribution made by the Red Army to the defeat of Hitler. But having established their own independence by liberating themselves from German occupation, the Yugoslavs subsequently refused to accept conventional satellite status. Moreover, they resented Soviet exploitation of the Yugoslav economy and were plainly irked by the lack of Soviet support in their clashes with the West over control of Trieste and the incident in 1946 when they shot down two American planes which had violated Yugoslav airspace. Regarding communism as the wave of the future, the Yugoslavs, like the Chinese in the 50s, seemed almost to be inviting conflict with the West. Stalin for his part regarded Yugoslav behaviour, which included support for the communist rebels in Greece, as reckless in the extreme. In January 1948, presumably in an attempt to curb Yugoslav chauvinism, Moscow vetoed Tito's plans to incorporate Bulgaria and Albania with Yugoslavia in a Balkan federation. But what most concerned Stalin was the unprecedented support and popularity Tito enjoyed, not only in the party which he led, but also in the army and the country at large because of his role in the partisan movement. A nationalist leader, even one with impeccable communist credentials, enjoying widespread popular support and refusing to submit to Moscow's dictation was anathema to Stalin who decided that the Yugoslav leadership would either have to change its ways or be replaced.

The crisis intensified between March and June 1948 with an exchange of correspondence between the Central Committees of the Soviet and Yugoslav Communist Parties. In response to accusations that they had been disloyal to the Soviet Union, that their party was not run on democratic lines and that they were guilty of ideological deviations, the Yugoslavs replied with pained surprise, protesting their innocence and claiming that Moscow had been misinformed. In June, his patience evidently wearing thin, Stalin demanded that the dispute be referred to the Cominform. In a resolution expelling the Yugoslavs from its ranks, the Cominform called upon all 'healthy elements' in the Yugoslav party to replace the existing leadership if it persisted in its refusal to admit the error of its ways.

'I will shake my little finger and there will be no more Tito', Stalin is alleged by Khrushchev to have remarked at the time. A rude shock, however, awaited the Soviet dictator. Having served his apprenticeship in Moscow in the late 30s, Tito knew all about Stalin's methods of dealing with opposition. Hebrang and Zhujovil, Tito's principal opponents on the Central Committee, had already been arrested and the secret police dealt with the others. The Yugoslavs closed ranks and the leadership received an overwhelming vote of confidence from a party conference in July. The Yugoslavs were subsequently subjected to economic sanctions and a campaign of vitriolic abuse which surpassed in intensity even the diatribes leveled against the capitalist West. But force was not used. Uncertainty about how the West might react appears to have decided Stalin against military intervention to settle accounts with Tito.

The breach with Yugoslavia had immediate repercussions as well as significant long-term consequences. It precipitated the collapse of the communist rebellion in Greece. Because of their close identification with Tito, Stalin ordered a purge of the communist leaders in Greece. Yugoslavia withdrew its support from the rebels in 1949, thus depriving them of their principal sanctuary and supply base. On a wider level, to ensure that Titoism did not become contagious, Stalin launched a purge of the communist parties in Eastern Europe. Lack of popular support and the presence of Red Army divisions on their own soil made it practically impossible for communist leaders in the satellites to emulate Tito. Nevertheless, those who had incurred Moscow's displeasure became targets of suspicion and some paid a heavy price. In Poland, Wladislaw Gomulka, who had expressed scepticism about the establishment of the Cominform, was stripped of his position as Secretary-General of the Polish United Workers Party and imprisoned in 1951. Less fortunate were Kostov in Bulgaria, Rajk in Hungary and Slansky in Czechoslovakia. All three were arrested on charges of espionage, subjected to the mockery of a show trial and subsequently executed. In addition, five-year plans and intensive collectivisation drives were imposed throughout Eastern Europe in order to prevent any further heresies about 'different roads to socialism'. The Yugoslavs themselves were obliged to abandon some of their more doctrinaire measures, most notably collectivisation, and to modify their polarised view of the international situation in order to obtain much needed economic aid from the West. When the breach occurred, the Yugoslavs did not consider that questions of doctrine underpinned their differences with Moscow. But Yugoslav theorists subsequently devised a new ideological platform which was designed to demonstrate that different roads to socialism did indeed exist and that the Yugoslav model, to be based henceforth on decentralisation and on economic self-management, was still derived from Leninist principles. Finally, the conflict demonstrated Stalin's cynical disregard for the principal of equality between communist states. For Stalin, communist advancement was permissible only if Moscow retained the means to ensure absolute loyalty and unquestioning obedience. The rift with Yugoslavia can thus be seen as an ominous portent of the much greater problems in store for Moscow in its dealings with the rising power of communism in China.

THE DIVISION OF GERMANY, NATO AND WEST GERMAN REARMAMENT

Of all the problems that confronted the victorious allies at the end of the war that of Germany was the most crucial. Throughout the 50s the German question remained a major bone of contention between the great powers and the major source of friction and tension in Europe. But in the immediate post-war years, the disintegration of four-power control in Germany was a relatively gradual process. In part this was attributable to the West's strategy of concentrating initially on concluding peace treaties with Germany's allies. Equally, however, it was attributable to the nature of the issues at stake. Both sides appreciated that failure to reach agreement on Germany would have grave consequences. They therefore hesitated before making a final break.

The future of Germany hinged inevitably on the attitudes and policies of the United States and the Soviet Union.[33] At the outset American policy was designed to punish Germany. Although the more extreme Morgenthau Plan for the pastoralisation of Germany was shelved, the Americans nonetheless decided that the purpose of the allied occupation should be twofold: to bring home to the German people that they had been responsible for the war and to ensure that Germany never again threatened the peace. To these ends General Eisenhower, the American Military Governor in Germany, received instructions in May 1945 that no action was to be taken to promote an economic recovery in Germany and that no action was to be taken to promote living standards on a higher level than those existing in neighbouring United Nations countries. By 1946, however, Washington had begun to revise this approach. Reparations in particular were now viewed more as a liability than as a means to punish the Germans. Moreover, friction elsewhere with the Soviet Union began to influence American thinking on Germany. By 1947 Washington had begun formulating a strategy designed to promote, within a European context, an economic recovery in the Western zones which would enable them collectively to stand as an essential bulwark against communist inroads into Western Europe. The logical outcome of this strategy, which was also geared to giving the German people in the

Western zones more responsibility for running their own affairs, was the creation of a separate West German state. Washington did not begin with the intention of dividing Germany but it was always fully conscious of the direction in which its policy was heading.

Soviet attitudes and policies towards Germany are more difficult to fathom. Lenin was credited with the remark that whoever controls Berlin controls Germany, whoever controls Germany controls Europe. Whether Stalin intended to act upon this premise, by attempting to bring the whole of Germany under Soviet control, or whether he wanted, from the outset, to divide it, are questions which continue to intrigue historians. The evidence is full of contradictions and ambiguities. For instance, Djilas reported Stalin as having asserted in the spring of 1946 that 'all of Germany must be ours, that is Soviet, Communist'.[34] But by January 1948, only a few months before the crisis over Berlin, the same source reported that Stalin had reversed his position by stressing that Germany would remain divided: 'The West will make West Germany their own, and we shall turn East Germany into our own state'.[35] Stalin was also reported to have told Mikolajczyk, the Polish leader, that communism fitted Germany 'as the saddle of a cow'.[36] While this is hardly conclusive evidence of Soviet policy it is nonetheless undeniable that mutual animosity deriving, on the Russian side, from Nazi atrocities and theories of race supremacy, and, on the German side, from the behaviour of the Red Army forces of occupation, the severity of reparations demands and the territorial losses to Poland, made the task of communising Germany as a whole a formidable one and one which offered little prospect of immediate success. But if Stalin did not seek to communise the whole of Germany, did he want to keep it united or did he want to divide it? Both alternatives posed problems for the Soviet Union. On the one hand, a divided Germany was likely to generate German nationalist tendencies and there was no guarantee that the West might not, at some future date, rearm West Germany. On the other hand, a united and neutralised Germany would require continued four-power cooperation and control which would, in all probability, be difficult to maintain. Moreover, an economically powerful German state would probably still be anti-Russian and irredentist. Of the two, perhaps the second alternative constituted the lesser evil. Stalin's demands over reparations and his concern over Russian security would seem to suggest that it was not Soviet policy to precipitate the division of Germany. On reparations, Moscow wanted access to the resources of the Ruhr but this could be obtained only by maintaining four-power control. On security, continued four-power control again seemed the only guarantee against what the Soviet Union most feared – that the West would rebuild the economic strength, and hence the military potential, of the Western zones of Germany in order to challenge Soviet hegemony in Eastern Europe.

Beyond the elimination of Nazi influences and institutions, decentralisation was the key to the Potsdam agreements on the future of Germany in the summer of 1945. There would be no central government but essential administrative departments, headed by state secretaries, would be allowed to function under the direction of the Allied Control Council. Local self-government and democratic parties would be encouraged and, as soon as practically possible, elections would be held at regional, provincial and *Land* (state) levels. On the vital question of the economy, agreement was reached that Germany should be treated as a single economic unit. Primary emphasis would be given to the development of agriculture and peaceful domestic industries. Allied controls would be imposed on the economy to carry out programmes of industrial disarmament, demilitarisation and reparations. On the latter, Byrnes' compromise formula provided for each occupying power to take reparations from its own zone and for the Soviet Union to receive 10 per cent from the Western zones, with a further 15 per cent in exchange for food and raw materials from the Eastern zone. This formula was linked to a significant clause: 'Payment of reparations should leave enough resources to enable the German people to subsist without external assistance'.

Contrary to conventional wisdom, it was not the Soviet Union but France which constituted the first major obstacle to the implementation of the Potsdam agreements on Germany. With memories of the occupation still fresh in mind and with de Gaulle still piqued at Roosevelt's refusal to recognise him as the undisputed leader of the French nation, France used its veto on the Control Council, where decisions had to be unanimous, to oppose the creation of administrative departments, the restoration of political parties and the treatment of Germany as an economic unit. Dismemberment rather then decentralisation seemed to be the principal French objective. Their demands ranged from the annexation of the Saar, to international control of the Ruhr to French control of the entire area west of the Rhine.

Reparations, however, proved to be the major stumbling block and here the Soviet Union was just as much responsible as France. In

March 1946 agreement was reached on a Level of Industry Plan upon the basis of which it should have been possible to determine the total amount to be paid in reparations. But in May 1946 Lucius D. Clay, the American Deputy Military Governor in Germany, suspended deliveries of reparations from the American zone. Soviet and French behaviour prompted Clay's action. Both were taking goods from Germany which, according to the Americans, could either have been used to reduce the need for imports or sold as exports in order to pay for imports. Soviet policy was particularly galling. Early in 1946 the Russians stopped dismantling factories and transporting them to the Soviet Union and resorted instead to syphoning off factory output without giving an account of the amount taken. Like the British zone, the American zone in Germany was largely industrial and, under normal circumstances, dependent for its food on the regions to the east of the Elbe. Now, however, the Americans and the British found themselves obliged to provide food, at the expense of their own taxpayers, for the populations of their own zones. This situation made nonsense of the Potsdam proviso that reparations should be taken only to the extent that the Germans would still be able to subsist without external existence.

Clay's action, together with the American offer in July 1946 to unite the economy of the American zone with that of any other zone if the occupying power was willing to participate, coincided with a reassessment of American objectives in Germany. In a speech at Stuttgart in September 1946, Secretary Byrnes outlined three significant proposals. First, that Germany should be given the opportunity to export goods in order to import enough to make its economy self-sustaining. Secondly, that the Germans should be given primary responsibility for running their own affairs. Finally, that American troops should remain in Germany for as long as the occupation continued. This third proposal reversed the pledge made by Roosevelt at Yalta that American forces in Europe would be withdrawn within two years of the end of the war. The Stuttgart speech demonstrated a new American readiness to countenance the abandonment of four-power control in Germany, the premise upon which the Potsdam agreements had been based.

The first step in this direction was taken in January 1947. For the purposes of economic policy and administration, the American and British zones were merged to form a single unit – bizonia. The Russians countered with a diplomatic offensive. At the Moscow meeting of the Council of Foreign Ministers in March-April 1947, Molotov suggested that Germany should be unified once the basic aims of the Allied occupation, defined by the Russians as 'demilitarisation' and the 'firm reestablishment of the democratic system', had been achieved. Insisting that the Russians were still entitled to ten billion dollars in reparations, Molotov also proposed four-power control of the Ruhr Basin. The Western powers rejected the Russian proposals and moved ahead with further plans to integrate their own zones in Germany. In July 1947 the three Western zones were included in the Committee for European Economic Cooperation (see p. 19) for the purpose of administering the Marshall Plan.

The Soviet interpretation of the Marshall Plan, and the measures adopted thereafter for the communisation of Eastern Europe, dictated subsequent developments with regard to Germany. At London in December 1947, the final meeting of the Council of Foreign Ministers failed to reach agreement on reparations and renewed Soviet proposals for a unified Germany. As East and West grew further apart, French reluctance to associate themselves with the drift of Anglo-American policy was finally overcome. In February-March 1948, the French joined their Western allies and delegates from the Benelux countries at a conference in London to discuss the future of Germany and the establishment of an international authority for the Ruhr. At the end of March, Marshal Sokolovsky, the Soviet representative on the Control Council, demanded an account of what had been discussed at the London conference and walked out when none was forthcoming. At the beginning of June the second session of the Western-orientated London conference concluded with recommendations for six-power control of the Ruhr, a joint economic policy for the Western zones and the summoning of a Constituent Assembly with the task of preparing a constitution for Germany.

Faced with an inexorable slide towards the creation of a West German state, the Russians played their last surviving card. Located 100 miles inside the Soviet zone, Berlin represented, on a smaller scale, a mirror image of the overall German problem. The city was divided into sectors and governed by an Inter-Allied Kommandatura. Soviet recognition that the United States, Britain and France had the right to govern sectors of the city did not mean that the access rights of the three Western powers were covered by a written agreement. In the final analysis, these access rights depended upon the extent to which the Western powers were prepared to use force to maintain their position. The Americans were only too aware that Berlin posed special problems in relation to their strategy for Germany as a whole. Clay reported in January 1948: 'Anything we do to strengthen the Bizonal administration will create a hazard with respect to USSR in Berlin. On the other hand, appeasement of USSR will continue the present unsatisfactory administration of Bizonal Germany and make economic reconstruction difficult if not impossible'.[37]

The Berlin crisis began in earnest in June 1948. As part of their package for an economic recovery, the Western powers announced a currency reform for the Western zones and the Western sectors of Berlin. The Russians responded by condemning the measure as a violation of the Potsdam agreement. They announced a currency reform of their own which would be introduced, not only in the Soviet zone, but throughout the whole of Berlin. On 24 June the Russians imposed the first of the blockade measures by stopping all rail traffic between the Western zones of Germany and the Western sectors of Berlin. By 4 August canal and road traffic had also been stopped.

No formal announcement about the blockade was ever made. The first Soviet statements about the road and rail closures spoke only of 'technical difficulties'. To this day, Soviet bloc commentators deny the very notion of a blockade. They maintain that the 'restrictions' were necessary for two reasons, both of a defensive nature. First, to safeguard the economic and financial viability of the Soviet zone which was said to be in danger of being flooded by the devalued old German marks from the Western zones. Secondly, as a measure of self-defence against the creation of a 'militaristic state' in Western Germany and 'its inclusion in the military alliance of the USA, England and France'.[38] Western accounts also suggest two possible motives for the blockade. First, that Stalin intended to use Berlin as a lever with which to secure concessions from the Western powers. Conceivably, he wanted to make the West's position in Berlin conditional upon Soviet access to the industrial resources of the Ruhr. The desirability of a quadrupartite arrangement for the Ruhr was a recurrent negotiating position adopted by Soviet spokesmen during the post-war discussions on Germany. Stalin might also have seen Berlin as the means by which he could influence the Western powers to abandon their plans to create a separate West German state. This was the view of Walter Bedell Smith, the American ambassador to the Soviet Union who discussed the problem of Berlin with Stalin and Molotov and the British and French ambassadors at Moscow in August 1948. Smith argued that an agreement about Berlin could have been produced in a matter of fifteen minutes at any time during the Moscow discussions by an offer from the Western powers to abandon the decisions reached at London the previous June.[39] On the other hand, a number of Western accounts have suggested that Stalin viewed Berlin not as a lever but as a prize in itself. According to this argument, Stalin was already reconciled by the summer of 1948 to the creation of a separate West German state. The blockade was thus imposed to force the Western powers out of Berlin and to give the Russians total control of the former Reich capital.[40]

Whether Stalin viewed Berlin as a lever or as a prize, his action in 1948 still presents a problem. Although vastly superior in terms of conventional military power, the Soviet Union was at a considerable strategic disadvantage. The Russians had yet to explode their first atomic bomb. To challenge the West on such an important issue under these conditions seemed out of character with Stalin's generally prudent and cautious approach to foreign affairs. Stalin frequently resorted to military means to secure political objectives but the Berlin crisis of 1948 would appear to have entailed an unusually high degree of risk. However, it became less of a risk once account had been taken of the extent to which the American atomic monopoly constituted a real deterrent. The actual use of this deterrent was limited by three crucial factors. First, the combat radius of the American B-29 bombers was only 2,000 miles. Sustained operations from bases in Alaska, Greenland and Newfoundland would therefore have been ineffective against many important targets in the Soviet Union. The use of bases in Britain might have provided a solution but not if the Russians had air superiority over Europe. Secondly, the Americans possessed minimal delivery capability. By 1948, only 32 B29s had been modified to carry the atomic bomb. Finally, the number of assembled warheads in the American atomic stockpile was practically zero, a state of affairs which shocked Truman when he was first informed of it in April 1947. American military analysts pointed out that although the damage inflicted upon Germany by strategic bombing during the war had been the equivalent of 500 atomic bombs, Germany had still not surrendered until her armies had been defeated. They estimated that several thousand bombs would be necessary to destroy the cities and the industrial potential of a major military power such as the Soviet Union.[41]

The doubts which were being expressed in the United States about the feasibility of a campaign of strategic bombing against the Soviet Union had in all probability filtered through to Stalin. But this is not to suggest that the American atomic monopoly played no part in Stalin's military calculations. Stalin still recognised the United States as the most powerful country in the world and the mere existence of the American atomic monopoly was sufficient to ensure that the Russians would not seek to exploit their considerable advantage in conventional forces. Hence the Russians made no attempt to escalate the conflict when the Western powers responded to the blockade by airlifting supplies into their own beleaguered sectors of the former German capital. The airlift was not originally conceived by the Western powers as a solution to their problem. At the outset, in June 1948, Clay estimated that it would be possible to bring in between 600 and 700 tons of supplies a day. This was only about one-third of the normal daily food requirements of the German population, to say nothing of the 500 tons of daily supplies needed by the Allied forces in Berlin and the 4,000 tons needed to keep the economy of the Western sectors operating at a minimal level. The airlift was therefore seen at first as a way of increasing the morale of the German population. In the event, however, the Western powers surpassed their own expectations. Until the blockade was lifted in May 1949, they managed to airlift a daily average of 4,000 tons of supplies into Berlin and, on a record day in April 1949, 13,000 tons were airlifted.

The blockade was a blunder of incalculable proportions for Stalin. It not only cast the Soviet Union in an unfavourable light in the eyes of world opinion. It also produced the very political and military consequences which the Russians had worked strenuously to avoid.

Political divisions in Germany had been apparent for some time but it was the blockade which finally precipitated the creation of two German states. In July 1945 a united front of 'anti-fascist and democratic parties' had been established in the Soviet zone of Germany. It consisted of the Communists (KPD), Social Democrats (SPD), Christian Democrats (CDU) and Liberals (LDPD). Aware that the disunity of the working class had been largely responsible for the rise of fascism in the 30s, the SPD favoured a united party of the left. Led by Otto Grotewohl, the post-war SPD in the Soviet zone was in fact decidedly more Marxist than the pre-1933 party of the Weimar Republic. It called for the introduction of a socialist economy as soon as possible. But Walter Ulbricht of the KPD rejected SPD proposals for a merger and argued that the time was not opportune. The KPD was spilt into a number of factions. Ulbricht himself had spent the war years in Moscow. Other KPD members had spent the war years either in exile in the West or in concentration camps. Ulbricht wanted time in which to establish the control of the Moscow émigrés within the party. However, by the end of the year, the KPD position on merger had changed. The results of the first parliamentary elections which were held in post-war Austria in November 1945 came as a shock to the communists. They won just over 175,000 votes, compared to over 1.4 million for the socialists and over 1.6 million for the Catholic People's Party. In Germany itself, the KPD realised that it was losing out in the race with the SPD for the political support of the working class. Feeding on the resentment of the workers, who saw their factories dismantled before their eyes, the SPD had rapidly increased its membership. The KPD was handicapped by its close association with the Russian occupying power. A decision to merge the KPD and SPD in the Soviet zone was taken at a meeting of the leadership of both parties in Berlin in December 1945. At the beginning of 1946, Anton Ackermann, the communist theorist, outlined the future for a merged party in an article which proclaimed the German way to Socialism. Revolution was said to be unnecessary because the German capitalists were no longer in control. Socialism could be introduced quickly because, unlike Russia in 1917, the working class in Germany made up a majority of the population.[42]

Socialist leaders in the Western zones of Germany, particularly Kurt Schumacher, the crippled victim of a Nazi concentration camp, declared their opposition to the proposed merger. They saw it as a front for a communist takeover, a view which was shared by the Western occupying powers. In Berlin, a number of SPD officials argued that the merger issue should be decided by a referendum of all SPD members. The SPD leadership in the Soviet zone rejected this, and proposed instead a delegate conference representing all the local SPD organisations. In the event a vote was held in Berlin in March 1946. It was organised by the Western allies and confined to the Western sectors of the city. The Russians refused to permit it in theirs. Of the total 32,547 votes cast, only 2,937 were in favour of an immediate merger. But 14,763 voted in favour of some sort of alliance in order to eliminate inter-party strife and only 5,559 were against any form of alliance or fusion. Both pro and anti-mergerite socialist leaders claimed the vote as a victory. Those against pointed out that 82 per cent had rejected the proposal for an immediate merger. But

Otto Grotewohl and the SPD leadership in the Soviet zone argued that the party strength of the SPD in Berlin was 66,000 and that many of the rank and file in the Western sectors had heeded their advice not to vote at all.[43] If the vote proved anything, it was that the rank and file socialists were not opposed to a merger as such. They wanted more time to arrange it. This applied to the rank and file in both the Eastern and Western zones of Germany. The Americans conducted an enquiry in their own zone and found considerable support for some form of merger among socialist party members.[44] Conceivably, had elections been held, unencumbered by the great powers, throughout Germany as a whole, they would have been won by a united party of the left committed to parliamentary rather than Soviet-style socialism.[45]

The merger of the KPD and SPD went ahead in April 1946 when the Socialist Unity Party (SED) was established in the Soviet zone. Wilhelm Pieck of the KPD and Grotewohl of the SPD were elected joint Chairmen and Ulbricht of the KPD became General-Secretary. The Western powers refused to recognise the new party and they did not allow it to function in their own zones. In October 1946 elections were held for the five regional parliaments which had been established in the Soviet zone. The SED failed to win, as it thought it would, an overall majority. It fared even worse in the elections held in the same month for the city parliament of Berlin. The SPD, which had ceased to exist as a separate party in the Soviet zone of Germany but not in Berlin, put up its own candidates and won 48.7 per cent of the vote. The CDU won 22.2 per cent, the SED 19.8 per cent and the LDPD 9.3 per cent. The results proved that the SED had been overconfident about its ability to compete in free elections with the non-socialist parties. The SED began a programme of intensive training for its members, emphasising the experience of the Soviet Communist Party. But as elsewhere in Eastern Europe, the transformation of the SED into a Leninist party did not begin until the autumn of 1947. It was speeded up in the second half of 1948 following Stalin's break with Tito. The separate German way to Socialism was dropped and primacy given to the role of the Soviet Union and to Stalin's leadership. An SED party control commission was established to monitor and dismiss party members. A purge of 'enemies within the ranks' reduced party membership from about 2 million in June 1948 to 1.8 million in January 1949. To all intents and purposes the KPD and SED were organisationally split and the practice of joint filling of posts by members of the KPD and SED came to an end. It was retained only at the top with Pieck and Grotewohl continuing as joint Chairmen. The CDU and the LDPD, the two non-socialist parties in the original united front, were squeezed out after the creation of two new parties in June 1948. The National Democratic Party of Germany (NDPD) was set up to attract the support of former National Socialists and professional soldiers. The Democratic Peasants Party of Germany (DBD) was established to win peasant support for a programme of socialist agriculture. Both parties were led by Soviet nominees. The Christian Democratic and Liberal Parties folded. By late 1948 contacts with their counterparts in the Western zones were classified as espionage.[46]

In the Western zones of Germany, the three largest parties to emerge were the Christian Democratic Union (CDU), the Social Democratic Party (SPD) and the Free Democratic or Liberal Party (FDP). The fusion of the American and British zones into bizonia in January 1947 had a political as well as an economic dimension. As one American official put it at the time: 'It will serve the purpose of getting the United States . . . out of the red in three years in Germany, and it will give us a climate in which to plant our political ideas in Germany'.[47] In May 1947 the Americans and British established an Economic Council, consisting of members selected by the *Landtage* or state parliaments upon the basis of proportional representation, to assist in the administration of bizonia. In September 1948, following the recommendations of the London conference, a Constituent Assembly or Parliamentary Council started work in Bonn. It consisted of representatives of the political parties in proportion to their strength in the *Landtage* of the eleven *Länder* of the Western zones of Germany. Konrad Adenauer, leader of the CDU, was elected Chairman. The constitution, which provided for a federal structure of government, was approved, with certain reservations, by the Western allies in May 1949, the month the blockade of Berlin was lifted. It was known as the Basic Law (*Grundgesetz*) because it was (and still is) intended to remain in force until such time as the *Länder* of East Germany had acceded and a more permanent instrument had been drafted by a Constituent Assembly for the whole of Germany. The first elections were held in August 1949. The CDU, together with its Bavarian sister party, the Christian Social Union (CSU), won 139 seats, the SDP 131, the FDP 52 and the minor parties (which included the communists with 15 seats) 80. The Federal Republic of West Germany came formally into being in September 1949 when Adenauer, emerging with a majority of one from a vote in the *Bundestag* (lower house) in which he admitted he had voted for himself, assumed office as the first Federal Chancellor of a coalition between the CDU and FDP.

In the East, developments followed a similar pattern. The German Democratic Republic (DDR) was proclaimed in October 1949 after a People's Council (*Volksrat*) had drawn up a constitution which, like the Basic Law in the West, was also intended to apply to the whole country. Otto Grotewohl became prime minister but real power rested with Walter Ulbricht, the General-Secretary of the SED, who worked in close cooperation with the Russians. Elections for a People's Chamber (*Volkskammer*) were held in October 1950 and 99.7 per cent of voters were said to have given their approval to a single list of one-party candidates. The response from Western governments was predictable. They refused to recognise the DDR on the grounds that it had not been democratically constituted.

The military sequel to the Berlin blockade emerged in the shape of an American commitment to the defence of Western Europe. Western defence strategy began with the Dunkirk Treaty of March 1947 when Britain and France pledged mutual support against a renewal of German aggression. However, by the time of the inconclusive meeting of the Council of Foreign Ministers at London in December 1947, most Western analysts had become convinced that the Soviet Union, not Germany, constituted the principal threat to their security. Ernest Bevin, the British Foreign Secretary, broached the idea of an extended system of Western defence which would be strengthened by American participation. The initial response from Washington reflected the same approach as seen in the Marshall Plan: American involvement in support of a local or a regional initiative. Accordingly, in March 1948, Britain and France, together with the three Benelux countries, concluded the Brussels Treaty. Although it mentioned Germany by name, the Brussels Treaty was clearly devised with what was identified as the Soviet threat in mind. The treaty drew warm praise from Truman who manipulated the Czech crisis to overcome familiar Congressional reservations about American involvement. In June 1948 the Senate endorsed the Vandenberg Resolution which called for American participation in regional security pacts. The groundwork had thus been established for the North Atlantic Treaty which was signed by representatives of twelve Western governments in April 1949. Under the impact of the Korean War, the treaty became a formal alliance in 1950 when the North Atlantic Treaty Organisation (NATO) was established with an American Supreme Commander (General Eisenhower), and with a strategy of forward defence based not on the Rhine but on the Elbe. The treaty itself represented a significant point of departure for the Americans. Article 5 declared that 'an armed attack against one or more [of the signatories] in Europe or North America shall be considered an attack against them all'. Never before in peacetime had the United States entered into such a commitment.

The German story had one final twist in its tail before Stalin's death in March 1953. In June 1950 war broke out in the Far East when North Korea attacked its southern neighbour. The West interpreted the attack as the opening of a major communist offensive which highlighted the vulnerability of Western Europe. The Soviet explosion of an atomic bomb in July 1949 had upset Western calculations about defence strategy in Europe. Hitherto it had been assumed that the numerically inferior conventional forces of the West Europeans would be sufficient for defence purposes providing they had the backing of American atomic weapons. Now, however, although the Americans still outdistanced the Russians in terms of delivery capability, a semblance of atomic equality had been established. Faced with the possibility of Soviet retaliation, the American atomic deterrent was seen as a weapon of last resort.

The American response to this dilemma was twofold. First, to press ahead with plans for the development of the more powerful hydrogen bomb, and secondly, to press the West Europeans to strengthen their own conventional forces. But this second proposal was easier said than done. Public opinion in Western Europe would not take kindly to increased military expenditure at a time of pressing economic and social need. Moreover, Britain and France, the two main European powers, already had extensive overseas commitments. To the Americans, only one solution suggested itself – the rearmament of West Germany.

The idea of putting Germans in uniform again so soon after the end of the war aroused considerable and at times bitter controversy in Western Europe. The French were hardly enamoured of the idea. In West Germany the proposal was denounced by the churches and by Kurt Schumacher, the leader of the main opposition party, the Social Democrats. Both argued that rearmament would destroy any possibility of German reunification. The key figure in the debate, however, was Konrad Adenauer, the West German Chancellor. Adenauer, seized upon the issue of rearmament as a means to assert West Germany's equality with its Western neighbours. He also saw it as a means to assert his country's sovereignty by securing a relaxation of and ultimately an end to, the continuing Allied controls over various aspects of West Germany's economic and political life which were embodied in the Occupation Statute of 1949. To his SPD critics, Adenauer replied that reunification could be achieved only from a position of strength and that this in turn necessitated a policy of integration with the Western alliance. West German integration with the rest of Western Europe had begun in May 1950 when, upon the suggestion of Robert Schuman, the French Foreign Minister, France and West Germany agreed to establish joint control over their coal and steel resources. This agreement paved the way for the establishment in July 1952 of the European Coal and Steel Community (ECSC) by the inclusion of Italy and the Benelux countries.

In October 1950 Dean Acheson, Marshall's successor as Secretary of State, warned that the American commitment to the defence of Western Europe depended upon a commitment by the West Europeans to strengthen their conventional forces. In response, the French government suggested that the West Europeans should adopt the Schuman principle for coal and steel by pooling their military resources to create a West European Army. Hence was born the European Defence Community (EDC), a novel idea to enable the West Germans to make a contribution to the defence of Western Europe without the need to create a separate German national army. Two years of acrimonious debate elapsed before the Bonn and Paris Agreements, providing for the ending of the Occupation Statute and the establishment of the EDC respectively, were signed in May 1952. Both agreements required ratification by the parliaments of the countries concerned. Implementation of the first (which left the Western allies in control of their own forces in Germany and of future negotiations with the Russians on Berlin, German unification and a peace settlement) depended upon consummation of the second.

West German rearmament eventually materialised but not (see pp. 73–74) in the context of the EDC. However, the prospect of a rearmed West Germany aroused serious misgivings in Moscow. This in turn induced what was probably the most intriguing Soviet proposal of the entire Cold War period in Europe. In March 1952, Stalin handed the Western Powers the first of a series of Notes which collectively proposed a German peace treaty and a reunified Germany. The eastern frontier of the new German state would be drawn at the Oder-Neisse line. A reunified Germany would be permitted a limited degree of rearmament but it would not be allowed to join a military alliance directed against any country with which Germany had been at war between 1939 and 1945. It would be governed initially by a coalition of the two existing German governments. Within a year of the treaty, the occupation forces would be withdrawn and free elections, supervised by the allied powers and contested by all 'democratic' parties, would be held to elect a new all-German government. Moscow's proposals were clearly designed to exploit political divisions within West Germany over the issue of rearmament. They were also intended to split the Western alliance by driving a wedge between the West Europeans and the United States. But above all, they represented a belated Soviet attempt to forestall the emergence of a powerful West German state fully integrated within the Western alliance.

Western governments refused to be drawn. They wanted elections before a peace treaty and they were deeply suspicious of Stalin's motives. Washington could hardly regard the withdrawal of American and Russian forces as a comparable exercise. Bonn was fearful of how the heavily armed 'People's Police' in East Germany might be deployed. All Western governments remained convinced that Germany was too great a prize in economic and military terms to remain permanently neutral. Yet however Machiavellian the Soviet proposals might have appeared, the West failed to perceive that they were borne of a profound sense of Soviet insecurity. Under no illusions about the probable outcome of all-German elections, it seems eminently plausible that Moscow was prepared to pay dearly to prevent West German rearmament by sacrificing East Germany.[48] Far from contemplating a communist offensive in Europe, the Soviet Union was in fact acknowledging its own vulnerability. When Western statesman spoke of building positions of strength from which to negotiate with the Soviet Union, they failed to appreciate that the period between 1950 and 1952 was probably, from a Western viewpoint, the most advantageous time to conduct such negotiations. They never occurred, partly because of the mistaken belief that time was on the West's side and partly because of the political climate in the United States which rejected in advance the notion of compromise in negotiation with the Soviet Union.

Despite the continuation of problems and tensions – Germany, Berlin and the West's refusal to sanction the legitimacy of the governments in Eastern Europe – a fairly stable balance of power had been established in Europe by the time of Stalin's death in March 1953. The Berlin crisis of 1948–49, which confirmed the division of Europe, demonstrated that neither side was prepared to risk war and that both sides recognised the need to contain crises. Europe, with its unresolved problems, remained for some time the pivot of international affairs but in the early 50s attention shifted further east to Asia where new forces were beginning to make their presence felt. It is time therefore to examine the origins of the Cold War in Asia.

2 Revolution and Containment in Asia 1945–53

THE REVOLUTION IN CHINA

NOTHING demonstrates more clearly the difficulty of assessing the motives which lay behind post-war Soviet foreign policy than events in China between 1945 and 1949. Such evidence as exists, however, suggests that the advancement of communism was not the major Soviet objective.[1] Stalin's first concern was to promote Russian national, as opposed to Chinese communist, interests. The defeat of Japan opened the way for Moscow to advance traditional Russian territorial demands, most notably in Manchuria, at China's expense. Stalin may even have toyed with the idea of a divided China in which the communists in the north would be dependent upon Moscow while the nationalists of the Kuomintang in the south would lean towards the United States. What he did not anticipate, because he did not believe it possible, was an outright communist victory. It did not appear possible because it was assumed that the communists were not strong enough and that the United States would not allow it to happen. Stalin was therefore reluctant to express open support for the communists in China. Although at times the Russians played an involved game – as for instance during their occupation of Manchuria from the summer of 1945 to the spring of 1946 when they alternated between support for the nationalists by allowing them to occupy key areas, and then support for the communists by handing over captured Japanese weapons – Stalin's attitude towards China was not dissimilar to his attitude towards Greece. Stalin recognised that in Marxist-Leninist terms the end of the war would present unprecedented opportunities. But he knew also that Washington was likely to see the hand of Moscow behind local communist uprisings. Unwilling to accept responsibility for ventures which he assumed carried little prospect of success, Stalin, in the case of China, signalled to the United States his dissociation from the communists. Hence Molotov's remarks in September 1944 to General Hurley, the newly appointed American ambassador to China, to the effect that communism in China was simply a way of expressing dissatisfaction with economic conditions and that the so-called communists would 'forget this inclination when their economic condition improved'. In August 1945 a Treaty of Friendship and Alliance, incorporating the terms agreed at Yalta (see above p. 2), was concluded between the Soviet Union and the Nationalist Republic of China. Although the concessions granted to Moscow were an insult to China's pride, Chiang Kai-shek and his supporters considered them a small price to pay to gain in return a Soviet pledge to deal only with the' official republican government and to withdraw their troops from Manchuria once military operations against the Japanese had been completed. From Stalin's point of view the mere signing of the treaty demonstrated that he expected Chiang and the nationalists to remain in power for some time to come.

Two further considerations influenced Stalin's thinking on China at the end of the war. His fingers had been burned in China once already. In 1927, after the Comintern had advocated a united front strategy between the nationalists and the fledgling communists, Chiang Kai-shek's forces routed the communists in Shanghai and plunged China into the first phase of its prolonged civil war. Stalin thus had no wish to be drawn yet again into a situation which eluded his direct control. But he did not discount the communists altogether. Firmly installed in their base camp at Yenan in Shensi province, the communists ruled a significant part of the country. Their mere existence was therefore a safeguard against too great an accretion of American influence in China.

Collectively these considerations inclined Stalin to pursue a twofold China policy. First, to advise Mao Zedong and the communists to refrain from all-out civil war and to seek accommodation with the nationalists in some form of coalition, and secondly, to persuade the Americans that it was in their interests, as well as being their responsibility, to put such a coalition together. The Americans, as we shall see, were more than willing to oblige but Mao Zedong's communists were not. The civil war in China was resumed in earnest in the middle of 1946. In January 1948, with communist victories mounting steadily, Stalin reflected ruefully to Milovan Djilas: 'When the war with Japan ended, we invited the Chinese comrades to reach an agreement as to how a *modus vivendi* with Chiang Kai-shek might be found. They agreed with us in word, but in deed they did it their own way when they got home: they mustered their forces and struck.

It has been shown that they were right, not we'.[2] For Mao and the Chinese communists, Soviet attitudes and policies during the civil war were a chastening but instructive experience. Although on the eve of victory in 1949 Mao spoke of 'leaning to one side' in the struggle between the imperialist bloc led by the United States and the socialist bloc led by the Soviet Union, he could not but feel offended that fear of the American reaction had made Stalin so reticent about committing himself in support of fellow communists.

The United States was more directly involved in the Chinese civil war than the Soviet Union.[3] At Yalta, Roosevelt had been as much concerned to secure Stalin's support for a political settlement in China which would leave the nationalists as the main political force as he had to gain a promise of an eventual Soviet entry into the war against Japan. The United States was thus more than willing to assume the initiative in the peacekeeping role envisaged by Stalin. From the outset the Americans recognised, like Stalin, that the communists in China could not be overlooked. At the beginning of 1944, having been advised by his own intelligence forces that the communists represented 'the most cohesive, disciplined and aggressively anti-Japanese regime in China', Roosevelt authorised the dispatch of an American Army Observer Group, informally known as the Dixie Mission, to establish formal liaison with the communists and to explore ways of coordinating the fight against the Japanese. For members of the Mission, which arrived at Yenan in July 1944, contact with the communists was an absorbing cross-cultural experience. They could not help but admire the cohesion and discipline of their hosts and became aware of the extent to which Mao's forces had the support of the peasants in the surrounding countryside. The visit also confirmed the view that the communists were much more active in the struggle against the Japanese than the inefficient, indolent and wasteful nationalists who were the recipients of American aid.

For Mao Zedong, the significance of the Dixie Mission was not confined to the military talks which took place on the Japanese war. The communists had acquired a degree of political recognition which could not but concern the nationalists. As Mao explained to John Service, an American diplomat attached to the Mission, 'the chief importance of your coming is its political effect on the Kuomintang'.[4] In January 1945, after Yenan had made repeated requests for American military aid, Mao, in a move clearly designed to improve still further the political standing of the communists, offered to visit the

United States for exploratory talks with officials. He even offered to talk with Roosevelt should an invitation be forthcoming from the White House. One can but speculate on the intense political debate which must have taken place at Yenan before the offer was made. The communists were signalling their readiness to respond favourably to American efforts to mediate between themselves and the nationalists. For a communist party, they were also displaying a hitherto unheard of degree of independence from Moscow.

The United States did not respond to the overtures of the Chinese communists. Two factors explain why, according to some scholars and ex-foreign service officers, the Americans 'lost their chance' in China in the period between the Dixie Mission in 1944 and the onset off the civil war in 1946. First, Ambassador Hurley, although not unfavourably disposed towards the communists when he first arrived in China, became distinctly pro-nationalist after the failure of his attempts to effect a coalition between the two contending Chinese factions. When he returned to the United States after his resignation in November 1945, Hurley launched a furious campaign against China specialists in the State Department and Foreign Service, accusing them of supporting communism and undermining the nationalist government. The second factor is more fundamental. Support for or cooperation with the communists was inconsistent with an American vision of the post-war world which was based upon free trade and an 'open door' to American economic penetration. America's economic interests dictated political conditions of stability and reliability. Much as they admired the communists, the Americans concluded that their interests were safer in alliance with the conservative social forces represented by Nationalist China.

Opinion is rather more divided about the reaction of the Chinese communists to the American failure to respond to their overtures.[5] One view maintains that ideology did not play a major role in communist foreign policy and that Mao Zedong remained flexible about Sino-American relations until the eve of the proclamation of the People's Republic in October 1949. In June 1949 Leighton Stuart, the American ambassador to China, received from the communists an invitation to visit Beijing and asked the State Department for permission to go. The communists were clearly anxious for American recognition but Washington, convinced that Mao was already committed to Stalin, withheld permission from Stuart. After October the United States acquiesced in Chiang Kai-shek's efforts to blockade the coast of the mainland and his bombing of Shanghai. Mao Zedong, according to this view, drew the appropriate conclusion about American intentions and leant accordingly towards the Soviet Union. A different view emphasises that ideology was always a principal determinant of the communists' foreign policy. It suggests that Mao was willing to cooperate with the United States only because the agreements reached at Tehran and at Yalta led him to believe that Washington was prepared to support a coalition in China. His hopes were dashed in 1946 when the Americans began demonstrating their support for the nationalists. Hence, according to this alternative view, the lean to one side can be dated from the onset of the civil war.

After the Japanese surrender in August 1945, Washington claimed that American policy in China was one of strict neutrality and that it was not designed to assist any particular Chinese faction. In reality, however, during the immediate post-war years, American aid was supplied and American troops were used in an effort to alter the balance in favour of the nationalists. Washington was concerned that its intervention should not be too blatant or too costly but no American official seriously questioned the degree of commitment to the national- ist cause. Airlifts and sea transports were provided to move nationalist troops into areas (notably Manchuria) which were about to be occupied by the communists. Over 50,000 marines were landed to occupy key areas in northern China and to guard the lines of communication. They were not withdrawn until March 1947, some thirteen months after Secretary Byrnes, anxious to deflect critical publicity over the question of foreign troops in China, had ordered General Marshall to deactivate the China theatre and to withdraw the marines as soon as possible. An American Military Advisory Group was established in China in February 1946. With a staff complement of approximately one thousand, the Group trained nation- alist forces in all three branches of the services until it was disbanded at the end of 1947. Finally, in addition to military aid valued at 1,100 million dollars, an agreement was concluded in August 1946 which enabled the nationalists to make discount purchases of American surplus military equipment located in India, China itself and the Pacific Islands.

The essence of American policy in China at the time of the Japanese surrender was to give Chiang Kai-shek sufficient support to enable him to hold his own but not to the extent that he would be encouraged to embark on a self-defeating civil war. Washington never succeeded in this delicate balancing exercise. Allied to the inefficiency and corruption of the nationalist regime was Chiang Kai-shek's chauvinism. American support convinced him that he could not fail. In an attempt to curb Chiang's ambitions, the United States imposed an arms embargo between August 1946 and May 1947. Although by no means as severe as sometimes imagined, the embargo added fuel to the subsequent charge that the communists were the principal beneficiaries of America's China policy.

In December 1945, following Ambassador Hurley's resignation, President Truman sent General Marshall to China in yet a further mediation attempt. During his year-long stay, Marshall had over 50 meetings with either Zhou Enlai or his deputies but the prospect of a compromise settlement receded as the civil war gathered momentum. At the end of 1947, a year after his return from China, Marshall, now Secretary of State, made the following observation about the dilemma confronting the United States in China: '[W]e must recognise that we have the problem of prolonging the agonies of a corrupt government, and that we have probably reached the point where we will have to accept the fact that this government will have to be retained in spite of our desire to change its character'.[6] And yet, as both Truman and Marshall appreciated, to retain Chiang Kai-shek in power would involve the United States in a commitment from which it would be practically impossible to withdraw. China would, in all probability, become an area of major international conflict. But the alternative of allowing events to run their course was hardly appealing. No longer was it a case of losing an opportunity in China but rather one of losing China altogether. Washington now began to reap what it had sown. If communism was such a threat, necessitating such a far-reaching response as that laid down in the Truman Doctrine, why, the critics asked, had it become entrenched in Eastern Europe and why was it being allowed to emerge victorious from the civil war in China? The uninitiated and the diehard Republicans had a ready-made and simplistic solution. In a variation on a Soviet theme they conjured up the spectre of the enemy within and asserted that the State Department was infested with communist sympathisers.

In August 1949, in an attempt to counter such accusations, Washington published its famous China Paper. The Paper was intended to demonstrate, as Secretary Acheson wrote in a lengthy introductory Letter of Transmittal, that the outcome of the civil war in China was 'beyond the control of the government of the United States'.[7] But based as it was on a blatant contradiction, Acheson's argument did little to restore credibility to, or faith in, Washington's China policy. Acheson's Letter maintained on the one hand that the civil war in China was 'the product of internal Chinese forces, forces which this country tried to influence but could not'. On the other, it asserted that China was being exploited by a party in the interests of a 'foreign imperialism'. In this latter respect, Acheson's Letter looked forward to the day when China would 'throw off the foreign yoke' and reassert its 'profound civilisation' and 'democratic individualism'. It also maintained that the United States would encourage developments in China towards this end and concluded with a warning to the communists not to lend themselves still further to the aims of 'Soviet Russian imperialism' by engaging in aggression against China's neighbours.

The spectacle of the government of the United States baring its soul to the nation and the world was hardly an occasion for gloating on Mao Zedong's part. On the contrary, continued Soviet reluctance to accept what was happening in China and to express open support for the communists caused intense irritation. To the last, Stalin could not bring himself to believe that the Americans intended to abandon Chiang Kai-shek. Moscow continued to downplay the significance of the impending communist victory in China. The dying embers of the Greek revolt received more news coverage in the Soviet press. In April 1949 the communists captured Nanking. Most foreign ambassadors, including the American one, remained in the city but the Soviet ambassador chose to retreat with the nationalist forces to Canton.

During the civil war Chinese ideologists attempted to dispel Soviet fears that a localised conflict in China might escalate into a general war involving the Soviet Union. In an article published in January 1947, the Chief of Information of the Chinese Communist Party restated the views of Mao Zedong when he argued that the United States could not threaten the Soviet Union until it had mastered the rest of the world. 'The actual policy of the American imperialists', ran the article, 'is to attack through peaceful means the American people and to oppress all capitalist, colonial and semi-colonial countries'. Mao Zedong's analysis of the postwar international situation posited the existence of three blocs: the United States and its capitalist dependencies or satellites in Western Europe; the socialist bloc headed by the Soviet Union; and a third bloc, identified as an intermediate zone, which consisted of the countries of the Third World. The object of monopoly capitalism in the United States was not, according to the Chinese, military victory over the Soviet Union but economic domination of the entire globe. The United States could not threaten the Soviet Union before it had control of the intermediate zone. It followed, therefore, that the conflict between the United States and the Soviet Union, while not unimportant, was not the dominating feature of the post-war world. The real struggle against imperialism was, in the Chinese view, being fought out in the colonial and semi-colonial countries which included China. Mao Zedong advocated the same idea in the mid-60s when he spoke of the world's countryside (the Third World) encircling the world's cities (the capitalist bloc led by the United States). In the 40s, the Chinese maintained that revolutionary successes in the Third World involved no risk to the Soviet Union. On the contrary, they actually strengthened the prospects for peace because the Soviet Union would be able to assume a relatively passive role in the struggle against imperialism and concentrate its efforts on promoting its own internal economic development. The Chinese thus advocated armed struggle and a united front strategy which would incorporate progressive elements within the national bourgeoisie as the means to combat American imperialism.[8]

This three-dimensional Chinese view of international relations did not commend itself to Moscow. Although, at the founding conference of the Cominform in 1947, Zhadnov referred to the 'sharpening of the crisis of the colonial system', with colonial peoples offering 'increasing armed resistance' against imperialism, the Russians remained committed to their two-bloc analysis. Indeed in this respect Stalin chose to ignore the opportunities presented by the post-war retreat of European colonial empires in Asia and the rise of Asian nationalism. Presumably, he could never be sure about how the Americans might react to the provocation of armed uprisings. Nor, given the Cominform's condemnation of the French and Italian communist parties, could the Soviet Union endorse a united front strategy. Above all, however, Moscow must have found it difficult to stomach the Chinese claim to have patented a unique Asiatic form of communism. Such a claim was bound to strike a raw nerve as it challenged Soviet direction and control over other Asian communist parties.

Stalin was brought face-to-face with the realities of the new situation in China in December 1949 when Mao Zedong arrived in Moscow for negotiations intended to establish a new relationship between China and the Soviet Union. The People's Republic of China had been proclaimed in October 1949 and Chiang Kai-shek exiled to the island of Taiwan. Mao remained in Moscow for nine weeks, an unusually long stay by a visiting head of state and an indication of the tough bargaining which must have taken place between the two sides.

The talks ended with a 30-year Sino-Soviet Treaty of Friendship, Alliance and Mutual Assistance which was signed on 14 February 1950. The treaty can be interpreted in various ways. It provided for mutual assistance should Japan, or any other country in alliance with Japan (the United States?), engage directly or indirectly in acts of aggression. Beijing undoubtedly set great store by this aspect of the treaty. It provided China with an ally at a time when the revolutionary state was still vulnerable. It also enabled the Chinese to place less emphasis on military security and more on plans for national reconstruction. Equally, however, it could be argued that the chances of an attack on China from Japan were extremely remote. More likely in the circumstances would be an American-backed attack from Taiwan. In this event, it was by no means certain that the Soviet Union would fulfil its treaty obligation. The treaty also stipulated that Soviet rights over the Manchurian railways and over the ports of Dairen and Port Arthur would terminate with the conclusion of a Japanese peace treaty or, failing that, by 1952 it the latest. Stalin had thus agreed to surrender the gains made in the 1945 treaty with Nationalist China. But a peace treaty between the Soviet Union and Japan did not materialise and Stalin did not honour the 1952 deadline. The two ports were not handed over to China until after Stalin's death in March 1953. The mere mention of a deadline suggested that Stalin might still have been expecting something to happen to alter the balance of political forces in China. Finally, the treaty made provision for the establishment of joint-stock Sino-Soviet companies in China and for a Soviet loan worth 300 million dollars over 5 years at 1 per cent interest. This was an insignificant amount compared to the credits which had been extended to the Soviet satellites in Eastern Europe. Whichever view is taken of the treaty – a compromise or a compact heavily weighted in favour of the Soviet Union – the Sino-Soviet talks represented a landmark in relations between communist states. With the Yugoslav precedent to annoy him and with the Chinese proclaiming the uniqueness of their revolution, Stalin had little reason to celebrate the emergence of a communist power over which he had no direct control. Throughout the visit Mao was referred to as 'Mr' instead of 'Comrade' and when it ended *Pravda* published a picture of the treaty-signing ceremony in which Mao and Stalin appear with sombre, unsmiling faces. Both perhaps recognised that the era of Soviet domination of international communism was coming to an end.

NSC-68

As the Sino-Soviet talks were taking place in Moscow, the administration in Washington was attempting to extricate itself from the morass of its China policy. The United States had already decided to withhold diplomatic recognition from the new regime in Beijing. The Chinese were prepared to negotiate recognition but their terms for so doing – withdrawal of foreign troops, relations to be based on 'equality, mutual benefit and mutual respect of each other's independence and territorial integrity' and withdrawal of recognition from the exiled nationalist forces on Taiwan – were deemed unacceptable in Washington which insisted that Beijing should honour all agreements concluded with the former nationalist government and make no alliance with the Soviet Union. The Chinese were thus expected to shoulder the burden of debts incurred by the nationalists and to accept restrictions on the conduct of their foreign policy. Washington in fact was already seeking to 'contain' communist China, basing its strategy on trade sanctions, an indefinite military presence in Japan and, in Indo-China, on increased military aid to the French in their struggle against the Viet Minh guerrillas led by Ho Chi Minh. In two vital areas, however, American policy statements appeared, initially at least, to be somewhat ambiguous. First, in his statement of 5 January 1950, Truman declared that the United States had no intention of becoming further involved in the civil conflict in China and hence that it had no desire to obtain rights or to establish military bases on Taiwan 'at this time'. Secondly, in a speech to the National Press Club on 12 January 1950, Acheson excluded Korea from the American defence perimeter in the Pacific.[9] Following the outbreak of the Korean War in June 1950, the China lobby in the United States accused the administration of having invited communist aggression by publicly abandoning Taiwan and Korea. Yet in both cases the position was not so clear cut. On Taiwan, in addition to the qualifying phrase about the timing of the establishment of military bases, Truman maintained that the nationalist forces had sufficient resources for their own defence and that they would continue to receive economic assistance from the United States. On Korea, Acheson argued that it was not practical to guarantee areas not included within the defence perimeter. But he also maintained that should aggression occur outside it, reliance would be placed initially upon resistance by the people attacked and then 'upon the commitments of the entire civilized world under the Charter of the United Nations'. Summoning United Nations support, which in effect meant mobilising American forces, was precisely what happ-ened in the case of the Korean War. Washington had therefore resolved to stand firm against attempts at communist expansion anywhere in Asia.

But even before the outbreak of the Korean War, attempts to ostracise and contain China were not enough to silence the critics of the Truman administration in the United States. In January 1950, Alger Hiss, a former State Department employee accused of being a Communist Party agent by the House Un-American Activities Committee, was convicted of perjury by the Federal Court. In the following month Joseph McCarthy, the junior senator from Wisconsin, made the startling allegation (never substantiated and subsequently shown to be fraudulent) that he had in his possession the names of 205 State Department employees who were members of the Communist Party. Concerned at the implications of the successful testing of a Soviet atomic bomb in July 1949 and harassed, since the loss of China, by the gathering momentum of the attack of the 'primitives', as Acheson dubbed the critics, Washington was obliged to undertake a major reappraisal of the objectives of American foreign policy. The result, in April 1950, was a National Security Council Planning Paper – NSC-68.

Basing their outlook upon a polarisation of world power in which 'slave society' was said to confront the free, the authors of NSC-68 asserted that the Soviet Union was 'animated by a new fanatic faith' and that the Soviet leaders, in order to impose their own absolute authority and to eliminate any effective opposition, sought total domination of the Eurasian land mass. To resist this hegemonistic drive and to create, by way of counterforce, a functioning economic and political system in which free society could flourish, the United States was said to require sufficient military power to deter aggression against itself and to fight limited wars abroad. Only then could it be in a position to 'compel the acceptance of terms consistent with our objectives'. Specifically, NSC-68 recommended a veto on negotiations with the Russians unless they showed a change of heart. It also advocated the development of a hydrogen bomb, the rapid extension of America's conventional forces, a large increase in taxation to finance the new military expenditure, the mobilisation of American society to accept the need for sacrifice and a strong alliance system directed by the United States. Finally, it suggested a Trojan horse. In order to undermine Soviet totalitarianism from within, the Russian people were to be made 'our allies in this project'.[10]

Ironically, however, the implementation of the recommendations of NSC-68 encountered the same domestic pressures that had threatened to withhold aid to Greece and Turkey in 1947. Public opinion was likely to deem totally unacceptable a projected increase in the defence budget from 13 to somewhere between 35 and 50 billion dollars. Moreover, the more strident critics of the administration laboured under the supreme delusion that it was necessary only for the United States to exert its moral influence and to divest itself of communist sympathisers in government departments, for all the problems in its relations with the communist powers to disappear. In an election year Truman and Acheson were not inclined to force the issue but they seized upon the outbreak of war in Korea in June 1950 as an opportunity to silence their domestic critics and to regain the global initiative by implementing the strategy advocated in NSC-68.

THE KOREAN WAR

Korea at the end of the war was the mirror image of the German problem in Europe. After the Japanese surrender in 1945, Korea was divided at the 38th parallel. Soviet troops occupied the North, American troops the South. In the North the Soviet Union established a communist regime under Kim Il Sung while in the South the United States installed a non-communist regime under the presidency of Syngman Rhee. Having supplied military aid and financial support to their respective protégés, the occupying powers withdrew their troops, the former in December 1948, the latter in June 1949. They left behind two rival states, each claiming sovereignty over the whole country and each threatening military action against the other.

Two theories have been put forward to explain the outbreak of the Korean War. The first maintains that when the North initiated hostilities on 25 June 1950 by attacking the South, Kim Il Sung was obeying instructions from Moscow. The second suggests that the war was the result of a conspiracy involving Syngman Rhee, whose government had suffered a heavy electoral reverse the previous month,

General Douglas MacArthur, the American Commander-in-Chief in the Pacific and proconsul of the occupation regime in Japan, Chiang Kai-shek and John Foster Dulles, the Republican senator, who visited the region shortly before the outbreak of hostilities. The aim of the conspirators was, according to this view, to provoke the North into an attack and thus to commit the United States, first to the defence of Rhee and, secondly, by enlarging the scope of the war, to the restoration of a nationalist government in China.[11]

Those who argue Soviet responsibility maintain that Stalin viewed the question of Korea from the much wider perspective of relations with China and the future political orientation of Japan. Convinced that the United States would not intervene to prevent a communist conquest of South Korea, Stalin may well have calculated, with regard to Japan, that the Americans would be forced to choose between one of two options. First, they could cut their losses and abandon plans to rebuild Japan as a military power. A withdrawal of foreign troops would enhance the prospects of a communist takeover in Japan and leave the Soviet Union as the dominant power in the Pacific region, holding the balance between rival communist states in China and Japan. Secondly, the Americans could decide to dig in, in which case they would have to reduce their commitments in Europe. Meanwhile, in the Far East, the Chinese communists would become even more dependent on Moscow. If, as seems likely, Stalin did envisage an outcome based on one of these two scenarios, he was guilty of a grave miscalculation. The United States, acting in the name of the United Nations, intervened on behalf of South Korea. Having absented itself from the Security Council of the United Nations in protest against the refusal of that body to admit communist China, the Soviet Union was unable to exercise its veto and thus powerless to influence events in the crucial early phases of the war.

For the United Nations or, more specifically, for the United States (80 per cent of the United Nations forces were American), the objective at the outset was to reinstate the 38th parallel as the dividing between North and South Korea. The North was dubbed the aggressor and American air and naval units were ordered into action. The American 7th Fleet was sent to protect Taiwan. General MacArthur, appointed Commander of the United Nations forces in July, reversed the North's initial successes with his landing at Inchon in September and by October the dividing line was back at the 38th parallel. The United States and the United Nations now decided to enlarge their objective to achieve 'the establishment of a unified, independent and democratic government in the sovereign state of Korea'. MacArthur sent his troops across the 38th parallel and northwards towards the Yalu river, the border with China. Having already communicated a warning to the United States through the Indian ambassador in Beijing that any such action would provoke a Chinese response, China entered the war on 16 October.[12] Acting in self-defence and, at the same time, enabling Stalin to maintain his conspicuously low profile, China was the next to be dubbed an aggressor by the United Nations. MacArthur wanted to attack China. To restrain him Truman had to sack him in April 1951. The war dragged on until an armistice was agreed in July 1953. By then Stalin was dead and Truman had been replaced as president by Eisenhower. Nothing had changed in Korea. The dividing line remained at the 38th parallel.

While controversy continues to surround the outbreak and course of the war, no such doubt exists about its consequences. For both China and the Soviet Union the balance sheet of the war showed profits and losses. Faced by indefinite exclusion from the United Nations and a firmer American commitment to defend Taiwan, China had to shelve plans for economic reconstruction and military demobilisation. China also had to pay a price for having rescued the Soviet Union from Stalin's miscalculation. To acquire Soviet aid, China had to tone down the uniqueness of the Chinese revolution and its general applicability as a model which other Asian countries could follow. On the credit side, however, China had proved its worth as an ally. China's relationship with the Soviet Union, therefore, while hardly one of equality, was not one of total subordination either. Moreover, China won the sympathy and respect of Asian neutrals. Nehru's India, one of the first non-communist countries to open diplomatic relations with Beijing in December 1949, subsequently played the leading role in the negotiations over the repatriation of prisoners-of-war which preceded the Korean armistice. For the Soviet Union, the war strengthened rather than weakened the American position in Japan. A peace treaty between the United States and Japan in September 1951 was followed soon after by a security pact which gave the United States the right to maintain bases and armed forces in Japan. The repercussions of the war in Europe were likewise detrimental to the interests of the Soviet Union. Korea acted as a catalyst for West German rearmament and for the conversion of the North Atlantic Treaty from an alliance into a formal command structure. Moscow, however, was able to take some comfort from the spectacle of Western disunity. American bellicosity alarmed the Europeans. Truman's hint that the United States might use atomic weapons against China sent Clement Attlee, the British prime minister, scurrying to Washington in December 1950 seeking reassurance that they would not be deployed.

But perhaps the most significant consequence of the war lay in its impact on the American outlook. It stimulated a further debate on the objectives of American foreign policy and the means with which to secure them. At one level the debate contrasted the views of unilateralists, like the Republican senator Robert Taft, who believed that traditional areas of American influence in Asia and the Pacific should be given equal if not greater priority than Europe, with the views of administration universalists, like Truman and Acheson, who maintained that Western Europe and NATO were the pivots of American policy and that the United States would never achieve its objectives by going it alone. At another level, the debate posed yet further questions about the nature of containment. In response to those who argued that freedom was indivisible and that containment would thus, of necessity, have to be an open-ended strategy recognising no boundaries in its application, there were those, most notably Kennan, who maintained that the United States should concentrate primarily on the areas capable of producing in quantity 'the sinews of modern military strength' which were vital to American security. Viewed in these terms, Kennan believed that there were only five regions of real importance – the United States, Britain, the Rhine Valley and its adjacent industrial areas, the Soviet Union and Japan. As only one of these was already in communist hands, Kennan argued that containment's main task was to ensure that none of the others fell under communist control.[13] Kennan's outlook was based, not only on his view of Soviet communism, but also on his belief that American resources were not inexhaustable. The containment debate, however, cut across the unilateralist-universalist divide. Truman and Acheson, despite their attachment to Europe, were obliged as much by domestic pressures as by personal predilection to adopt the all-encompassing view of containment. Hence, during the Korean War, they presided over an increase in military expenditure which took the annual defence budget to 50 billion dollars.

One significant question remained. Most American officials saw the Soviet threat in ideological rather than imperialistic terms but they never made it clear how a strategy based on military containment could avert what was essentially a political danger. The American military build-up, which included the hydrogen bomb after November 1952, was designed to enable the United States, in Acheson's words, 'to negotiate from strength' with the communist world. But the object of such negotiations was not viewed as an equitable settlement of outstanding differences between Washington and Moscow. Rather, it was defined as an unconditional surrender, involving the abandonment of its post-war gains, by the Soviet Union. Such an objective, which foreshadowed a move away from the essentially defensive strategy of containment towards an offensive strategy based on 'liberation' or 'roll-back', could not be realised. It threatened areas vital to the security of the Soviet Union and, if pressed too far, ran the risk of starting World War Three. This was never Washington's intention and consequently a credibility gap was already beginning to separate American profession from American practice. And yet the alternative – recognition of East-West spheres of influence – was ruled out. As long as Washington continued to regard Soviet post-war gains as temporary aberrations capable of modification, there could be no end to the Cold War.

FRENCH INDO-CHINA

French Indo-China (Vietnam, Laos and Cambodia) was the only region in South East Asia in which a European colonial administration continued during the Second World War. Although under Japanese military control, French administration survived in Indo-China because Vichy France was not at war with Japan. Not until March 1945 did the Japanese arrest French officials and assume political as well as military control. This anomaly had important consequences, particularly in Vietnam. Free to suppress Asian nationalism in their own territories, the French were able to block the emergence of a nationalist movement similar to that led by Hatta and Sukarno in Indonesia. In consequence, at the end of the war, the Communist Party in Vietnam – led by Ho Chi Minh and better known as the Viet Minh – was much stronger than any rival nationalist movement and thus able to dominate the independence movement.

It was agreed at Potsdam that Indo-China should be divided at the 16th parallel following the Japanese surrender. The British became responsible for Cochin-China (the southern part of Vietnam) and

Cambodia; the Chinese for Annam, Tongking (the central and northern parts of Vietnam) and Laos. American support for the claims
of Chiang Kai-shek to become a new Asian policeman lay behind this
somewhat arbitrary division which enabled the two zones to develop
in opposite political directions in the crucial post-war period. In
September 1945 the Viet Minh persuaded Bao Dai, the Vietnamese
emperor, to abdicate in favour of a Democratic Republic of Vietnam
(DRV) which was established in the North at Hanoi under the
presidency of Ho Chi Minh. The DRV consolidated its position during
the Chinese occupation of the North. In the South, in the absence of
any alternative (British instructions did not go beyond securing Japan's
surrender and withdrawal) the French were allowed to resume control.
In March 1946 the French reached an agreement with the DRV
which enabled French troops to occupy the North. The DRV was
recognised as a 'free state' with its own government and army,
belonging to the Indo-Chinese Federation and French Union. France
also agreed to a referendum which would decide whether to unite the
three territorial zones of Vietnam into an independent state. 'It is
better to eat French dung for a while than to eat China's all our lives',
Ho is alleged to have remarked at the time.[14] Conscious of Sino-
Vietnamese rivalry, and at times bitter enmity which had endured
for centuries, Ho had no wish to see Vietnam become a puppet of its
great northern neighbour. British and Chinese troops withdrew from
Indo-China in September 1946 leaving the French fully in control.
Negotiations with the DRV soon broke down. France had no intention
of following the British example in India by divesting itself of its
empire in Indo-China. Fighting broke out in November 1946. Both
sides were set on a course which ended in a humiliating defeat for the
French at Dien Bien Phu in 1954.

Preoccupied with events in Central and Eastern Europe and in
China, Washington surveyed what was happening in Indo-China with
ever-increasing concern. Roosevelt had not wanted the French to
return and suggested instead an international trusteeship. He wrote
in January 1944: 'France has had the country [and its] thirty million
inhabitants for nearly one hundred years, and the people are worse
off than they were at the beginning'.[15] By March 1945 he had changed
his position slightly. France itself might become the trustee provided
the goal of independence was recognised at the outset. Ho Chi Minh
wanted the United States to use its influence for the same purpose.
Between October 1945 and February 1946, he wrote letters to Truman

and Byrnes in which he referred to the United States as the guardian and champion of world justice and called upon both the United States and the United Nations to live up to their professed ideals. His letters remained unanswered. Marshall explained why in one of his telegrams in February 1947: '[C]olonial empires in XIX Century sense are rapidly becoming thing of the past . . . On the other hand we do not lose sight fact that Ho Chi Minh has direct Communist connection and it should be obvious we are not interested in seeing colonial empire administrations supplanted by philosophy and political organisations emanating from and controlled by the Kremlin'.[16] Predating by six months Zhdanov's Comiform speech dividing the world into two camps, and by a full year the call for communist insurgencies which went out from a communist-sponsored conference of South and South East Asian youth which was held at Calcutta in February 1948, Marshall was seeing a connection which did not exist. French intransigence rather than ideological affiliation drove Ho into the Sino-Soviet camp.

By the autumn of 1948, the State Department confessed to being on the horns of a dilemma over Indo-China. In a policy statement drawn up in September, the Department admitted that it had no 'practical solution' to offer whereby America could maintain France as an ally and, at the same time, satisfy nationalist aspirations in Indo-China. The outlook seemed bleak. A succession of French puppets in the South served only to strengthen the Viet Minh in the North. The war was weakening France economically and causing irreparable damage to the West's reputation in Asia. Above all: '[W]e are all too aware of the unpleasant fact that Communist Ho Chi Minh is the strongest and perhaps the ablest figure in Indo-China and any suggested solution which excluded him is an expedient of uncertain outcome'.[17] In 1949 the French attempted to do precisely that. In an effort first to separate the nationalists from the communists, and secondly to preserve their own position in Indo-China, the French conceded qualified independence to the three Associated States of Vietnam (effectively South Vietnam, with Bao Dai returning as head of state), Laos and Cambodia. The Associated States were recognised by the United States and Britain in February 1950. A month earlier communist China and the Soviet Union had recognised the DRV. Indo-China had thus become an international problem and upon this basis France appealed for American support. After some initial hesitation, Truman and his advisers finally decided in May 1950 to extend military and economic aid to France.

Within a month, any reservations the Americans might have felt about committing themselves to the French in Indo-China had completely disappeared. Convinced that they were facing the start of a major communist offensive when war broke out in Korea in June 1950, policymakers in Washington elevated Indo-China to a front-line crisis area. What was happening in Vietnam was no longer identified as a national revolution under communist domination. Instead it was said to constitute a communist threat to the whole of South East Asia. Given the strategic importance of South East Asia, the stakes were now high. A National Security Council Staff Study on Objectives, Policies and Courses of Action on Asia, dated May 1951, outlined what these stakes were: 'The area produces practically all the world's natural rubber, nearly 5 per cent of the oil, 60 per cent of the tin, the major part of various important tropical products, and strategic materials such as manganese, jute, and economic materials'. The geopolitical stakes were just as high: 'Control by an enemy of the Asiatic mainland would deny to us the use of the most direct sea and air routes between Australia and the Middle East and between the United States and India. Such control would produce disastrous moral and psychological effects in border areas such as the Middle East and a critical effect in Western Europe'. Finally, the security of the United States itself was at risk: 'Communist control of both China and South East Asia would place Japan in a dangerously vulnerable position and thereby seriously affect the entire security position of the United States in the Pacific'. The general problems facing the United States in South East Asia were defined in equally sweeping terms. They were said to include: 'The real threat of Chinese communist invasion and subversion, the political instability and weak leadership of the non-communist governments, the low standards of living and underdeveloped resources of the area, the prevailing prejudice against colonialism and Western "interference" and the insensitivity to the danger of communist imperialism.' Threatened on such a scale, the NSC argued that the United States would have to respond in kind through military aid, collective security pacts, economic assistance, programmes of information and educational exchange (essentially anti-communist propaganda) and the encouragement of social and political reforms. For Indo-China specifically, the NSC advocated three courses of action: increasing the military effectiveness of the French army (thus obviating the need to commit American forces), continuing to encourage 'internal autonomy and progressive social and economic reforms' and continuing to promote international support for the three Associated States.[18]

An escalation of the military conflict was hardly conducive to the introduction of progressive social and economic reforms. Moreover, as the cost of the war escalated (the United States contribution had risen to over 60 per cent of the total budget by 1954), the military position of the French did not improve. On the contrary, it deteriorated rapidly. Although dependent on aid from communist China, the Viet Minh guerrillas were now more than capable of holding their own. As the French position became more serious and the war became more unpopular in France itself, international opinion, in both Western Europe and the Third World, urged a negotiated settlement. To this Washington remained resolutely opposed. An NSC Staff Study in February 1952 declared: 'Because of the weakness of the native governments, the dubious attitudes of the population even in areas under French control, and the certainty of continued communist pressure, it is highly probable that any settlement based on a withdrawal of French forces would be tantamount to handing over Indo-China to communism. The United States should therefore continue to oppose any negotiated settlement with the Viet Minh'.[19] Whatever the outcome of the present conflict, the United States had thus resolved to keep South East Asia to the forefront of the Cold War.

3 False Start: Khrushchev, Peaceful Coexistence and the Sino-Soviet Conflict 1954–65

STALIN, according to Khrushchev's retrospective account, frequently taunted his would-be successors with the comment that the imperialist powers would wring their necks like chickens when he was gone.[1] When he died in March 1953 Stalin certainly left a formidable legacy of unresolved problems. Soviet tanks were required in June 1953 to quell strikes and demonstrations by workers in East Berlin. With the Yugoslavs continuing to set an unwelcome precedent, the uprising in East Berlin demonstrated yet again that the satellites could be liabilities as well as assets. In the West, Moscow seemed unlikely to succeed with its attempt to forestall West German rearmament by offering reunification on the basis of German neutrality. In the United States a Republican president had been elected in November 1952. John Foster Dulles, Eisenhower's Secretary of State, described the conflict with communism as 'irreconcilable' and made a pointed reference to Orwell's *Animal Farm* when commenting on Soviet treatment of human beings. The conflict in the Far East provided Washington with an opportunity to flex its military muscle. Angered by Chinese intransigence over the question of repatriating Korean prisoners-of-war, Eisenhower threatened to unleash Chiang Kai-shek. Eisenhower and Dulles, the latter through India, also warned Beijing that the United States might yet resort to atomic weapons to bring the war to a speedy conclusion.

But if the outlook looked bleak for the new Soviet leaders, they soon proved that they were more than equal to the task. Having weathered the early storms they proceeded to demonstrate that they would not be handicapped by the legacy of the Stalin era. They embraced new ideas, abandoning the view that war was inevitable between states with different social systems in favour of the concept of peaceful coexistence. They also developed a completely different diplomatic style. Unlike Stalin, who had seldom travelled abroad and who viewed the outside world from the Kremlin or a country dacha, his successors were more outgoing. They acquired a penchant for foreign travel in order to gain in both prestige and influence. But unfortunately, ideas which were more flexible and a style which was more accommodating were not of themselves sufficient to guarantee success in foreign policy. Soviet ambitions frequently outdistanced Soviet capabilities. Aware of this credibility gap but not always willing to be inhibited by it, the new Soviet leadership was prepared to take far greater risks than the more dogmatic but also more cautious Stalin. Hence the paradox that during a decade when it promised peace, the Soviet Union found itself closer than at any previous time to the outbreak of a Third World War.

THE SUCCESSION TO STALIN

When Stalin died Georgi Malenkov became both Chairman of the Council of Ministers and head of the Communist Party. Within a week he had relinquished the latter position (whether by choice or by pressure is still uncertain). A collective leadership consisting of Malenkov, Molotov and Beria was then instituted but this too was shortlived. Beria, seeking to augment his personal power as head of an amalgamated Ministry of State Security and the Interior, was arrested in June and executed towards the end of the year. He was the last Soviet leader to pay the ultimate penalty for having sown fear and distrust in the minds of his rivals. Nikita Sergeevich Khrushchev was transferred to the Secretariat from his post as head of the party in Moscow and in September he became First Secretary. With the party re-emerging as an effective political force for the first time since the purges of the 30s, Khrushchev was admirably placed to mount a serious challenge to Malenkov's leadership.

The power struggle was waged over the distinct but related issues of economic and defence policy. Malenkov argued that living standards could be raised by giving consumer and light industry priority over the heavy industrial sector. On defence, he maintained that atomic weapons made war unthinkable and that the Soviet Union should therefore work for a relaxation of international tensions. Malenkov advocated coexistence and a defence policy based upon the principle of minimum deterrence. The explosion of a Soviet hydrogen bomb in August 1953 would enable Moscow to reduce the size of, and hence the spending on, its conventional forces. Khrushchev challenged Malenkov on both counts. Increased agricultural production (based on the cultivation of 'virgin lands') would, according to Khrushchev, raise living standards and leave heavy industry and hence defence intact. Khrushchev also realised that in advocating both coexistence and a reduction in conventional defence, Malenkov had moved too far too quickly. Malenkov did not have the army with him and his colleagues regarded his offer to negotiate with the West as premature. The West would be likely to regard the new regime in Moscow as being unsure of itself and vulnerable to pressure. Such considerations, allied to a bountiful harvest in 1954 for which Khrushchev took the credit, enabled the First Secretary to win the war of words. In February 1955 Malenkov was replaced by Bulganin, one of Khrushchev's supporters. Khrushchev was not as yet completely in control but he was already placing his own indelible stamp on Soviet foreign and defence policy. With Malenkov out of the way, the First Secretary began to identify himself with many of the foreign and defence policy positions which had been adopted by his erstwhile opponent.

KOREA AND INDO-CHINA

The Far East and Indo-China dominated international affairs in the months following Stalin's death. American threats and the death of Stalin brought an end to hostilities in Korea and an armistice was signed in July 1953. Representatives of nineteen countries assembled at Geneva in April 1954 and agreed to establish a five-power Neutral Nations Repatriation Commission, under Indian chairmanship, and a small Indian custodian force to supervise the delicate task of repatriating prisoners-of-war. But on the main political question of reunification, the conference failed for much the same reason as had the endless talks about Germany. The West would not agree to the communist proposal that an all-Korean government should be formed before elections were held.

Korea was one of two problems discussed at Geneva. The other was Indo-China. Here nine countries were specifically concerned – the United States, the Soviet Union, Britain, France, China, North and South Vietnam, Laos and Cambodia. The outcome of this aspect of the conference was determined by the military situation in Indo-China itself. The French, in an attempt to entice the Viet Minh into open battle, had dug in at Dien Bien Phu, their last remaining outpost in North Vietnam. Already paying 75 per cent of the cost of the war, Washington had become increasingly concerned at the military plight of the French. In March 1954 the American Joint Chiefs of Staff concluded that in the event of France opting for a negotiated settlement, the United States should dissociate itself and seek ways and means of 'continuing the struggle against the Viet Minh . . . without [the] participation of the French'. A Vietnamese partition was ruled out on the grounds that it would constitute a 'retrogressive step in the Containment Policy' and also that it would 'invite similar Communist tactics against other countries of South East Asia'.[2] At the beginning of April, Eisenhower made his famous 'domino speech' and Admiral Radford, Chairman of the Joint Chiefs of Staff, advocated air strikes against communist positions surrounding Dien Bien Phu. But fearing a repetition of Korea, Congress would not support such a move unless America acted with allies. Dulles flew to London on the eve of the conference but be was unable to convince Churchill. The conference opened on 26 April. No immediate progress had been made before the beleaguered French garrison at Dien Bien Phu surrendered on 7 May. Dulles, already incensed by the presence of communist China at the conference table, walked out leaving the diplomatic field open to the French and Chinese with, one suspects, the Russians playing a deft hand in the background. In Paris a new government under Pierre Mendès-France was pledged to resign if a settlement had not been reached in Indo-China by 20 July. As he was a vociferous opponent of the European Defence Community it was very much in Moscow's interests to keep Mendès-France in office. A private meeting between the French and Chinese premiers paved the way for the Geneva Armistice Agreement and the Geneva Accords which were concluded on 20–21 July. These two pacts collectively provided for the independence of three new states in Indo-China – Vietnam, Laos and Cambodia. Vietnam was to be temporarily divided at the 17th parallel and national elections, to be conducted by France and supervised by a neutral commission again chaired by India, were to be held within two years.

Many years later, in 1979, the government of a united Vietnam maintained that the Viet Minh could have won the war if they had carried on fighting and that it was the Chinese who put pressure on the North Vietnamese to end the conflict and to accept a compromise which gave them only half the country. This accusation was made in the Vietnamese 'White Book' of 1979. The same publication suggested that an exaggerated fear of American intervention was the reason why the Chinese, and Zhou Enlai in particular, were anxious to bring the war to an end.[3] China's reply, together with a number of other revelations prompted by the Sino-Vietnamese exchange, revealed, not only the extent to which the Viet Minh had been dependent on Chinese support (the victory at Dien Bien Phu for instance would have been impossible without Chinese advice and weaponry), but also that the strategy of compromise had been approved by all *three* communist powers involved – North Vietnam, China and the Soviet Union. Ho Chi Minh, explaining why the Geneva agreements had to be accepted, accused those who wanted to fight on of being guilty of a 'leftist deviation'. They could see 'only the trees, not the whole forest; that is, they see only the French, not the Americans'.[4] Clearly therefore, although Hanoi did not recognise the Geneva settlement as anything other than a temporary expedient, it did at least acknowledge that the struggle in the South would have to be postponed for the time being.

The Indo-China settlement at Geneva had far-reaching consequences. Neither the United States nor South Vietnam signed the pacts and they did not consider themselves bound by them. In Washington, the National Security Council produced a speedy assessment which regarded the settlement as a 'loss of prestige' for the United States and as one which had given the communists 'an advance salient in Vietnam from which military and non-military pressures can be mounted against adjacent and more remote non-communist areas'.[5] To enable the United States to protect its position and to recoup its prestige, the Council recommended the immediate negotiation of a regional alliance which duly emerged in September 1954 in the shape of the South East Asia Treaty Organisation (SEATO). Within Indo-China itself, the Geneva provision for elections in Vietnam presented the United States with a dilemma. Washington could hardly oppose elections but Eisenhower admitted that Ho Chi Minh would probably win 80 per cent of the vote. The National Security Council advocated a duel strategy of, on the one hand, economic and military aid to South Vietnam, and, on the other, support for elections to a Constituent Assembly. Provision would be made for the government of South Vietnam to reject the constitution if it were deemed unacceptable.[6] In the event, France did not remain to conduct the elections and the elections themselves did not take place. Instead, as American military advisers began training a South Vietnamese army and Eisenhower pledged economic aid, Washington moved in behind the scenes in support of the government of Ngo Dinh Diem in Saigon.

The principal beneficiary of the Geneva settlement was undoubtedly

in each other's affairs; equality and mutual benefit; and peaceful coexistence. Sino-Indian friendship was cemented further in June 1954 when, during a break in the Geneva conference, Zhou Enlai paid a three-day visit to India on his way back to Beijing. The stage was thus set for an Afro-Asian conference of 29 nations which was held at Bandung in Indonesia in April 1955.[7] Beyond colonial subjugation in the past and a determination to resist imperialism in the future, the participants had little in common. Nevertheless, Bandung provided a forum within which to discuss common problems and to promote solidarity. Zhou Enlai enhanced his own personal reputation for moderation by assuring the leaders of South and South East Asia that China would not use the millions of overseas Chinese as instruments for the expansion of communism. He also used Bandung as a forum to propose bilateral Sino-American talks to defuse the Taiwan Straits crisis. The crisis had begun in September 1954 when, in response to the threat allegedly posed by SEATO and also to rumours that the nationalists were contemplating an offensive against the mainland, the communists began shelling the offshore islands of Quemoy, Matsu and the Tachens which lay between the mainland and Taiwan.

The significance of China's diplomatic manoeuvres between 1954 and 1955 was not lost on the new leaders in the Kremlin. It made them aware that they had to make up for lost time. Stalin had failed to exploit the advantages enjoyed by the Soviet Union in Asia at the end of the war. The Soviet Union was not burdened with a colonial past and the nationalist leaders of Asia distrusted Moscow less than they did the West. Reluctant at first to antagonise his wartime allies, Stalin appeared disinterested in what Zhdanov described as the 'crisis of the colonial system'. As the Cold War gathered momentum after 1947, Stalin modified his position. But when, in 1948, communist parties were ordered on to the offensive, their targets included non-communist nationalist leaders as well as the colonial powers. Zhadnov's 'two-camp' prognosis denied the possibility of a neutral third force. Nationalist leaders were regarded as part of the imperialist camp. This analysis displayed a woefully inadequate appreciation of the relative strengths of communism and nationalism in Asia at the end of the war. The results were predictable. Militant communism in countries such as India, Burma, Malaya (now Malaysia), Indonesia and the Philippines foundered on the rock of popular support for nationalist governments or movements. Only in Vietnam, Laos and Cambodia, where the nationalist movements were led by communist leaders who recognised the tactical advantage of retaining the support of non-communist nationalist forces, did communism itself make significant gains. Elsewhere, communist leaders found themselves isolated. In some cases (Burma and Malaya), they were arrested and their movements driven underground. In others (India, Indonesia and the Philippines), communist leaders took heed of local conditions and began to explore the possibility of pursuing the parliamentary road to socialism.

It was not only local communist leaders who found themselves isolated and without influence in Asia. So too did the Soviet Union and it was this position that the new leaders in the Kremlin set out to rectify. Taking their cue from Zhou Enlai, the Russians realised that if they built bridges to the neutral countries of the Third World, it would enable them to leapfrog the barriers of containment erected by the United States. The Soviet leaders concentrated their efforts on Egypt and India, negotiating with the former an arms deal through Czechoslovakia in 1955 and agreeing to build a steel plant at Billai in the latter in the same year. The task of the Soviet Union was made that much easier by the attitude of the United States. Like Zhdanov in the 40s, Dulles refused to accept neutrality as a legitimate policy. He described neutrality as 'immoral and shortsighted' and extended the ring of containment by persuading Britain, Turkey, Iran and Iraq to establish the Baghdad Pact in 1955. Intended to keep communist and Soviet influence out of the Near and Middle East, the Pact served only to offend nationalist sentiment throughout Asia and the Middle East.

THE THAW IN EUROPE

Soviet initiatives in Asia and the Middle East coincided with equally significant moves in Europe. Here Moscow ultimately failed in its efforts to prevent the rearmament of West Germany. In August 1954 the French National Assembly rejected the agreement reached at Paris in May 1952 to establish a European Defence Community. The French decision invalidated the Bonn agreement of the same date which was intended to restore sovereignty to the Federal Republic. Amidst an unprecedented display of Western disunity, Britain rescued the situation by proposing that West Germany and Italy should become members of a new West European Union, an extended version of the 1948 Brussels Treaty. Upon this basis, with the Germans contributing twelve divisions, West Germany and Italy became members of NATO in May 1955. In the same month the Warsaw Pact was established. Article five of the Warsaw Treaty made provision for joint command of the Eastern bloc's armies while article six established a Political Consultative Committee to coordinate foreign policy. Politically, economically and now militarily, the East-West divide in Europe was complete.

In a sense, the extension of NATO and the formation of the Warsaw Pact were out of step with the prevailing climate of opinion. Relations between East and West in Europe had never been better since the end of the war. As in Asia, the Soviet Union assumed the initiative. Having previously insisted that an Austrian peace treaty would have to await a settlement of the German problem, Moscow consented to an Austrian State Treaty in May 1955. The occupying powers withdrew their forces and the Austrian government pledged its neutrality. In Northern Europe, the Soviet Union returned the naval base at Porkkala to Finland. Moscow's diplomatic offensive extended into Eastern Europe. In May 1955, against the wishes of Foreign Minister Molotov, Bulganin and Khrushchev visited Belgrade in an attempt to make peace with Tito's Yugoslavia. Khrushchev admitted that Moscow had been at fault in the original dispute but chose at this time to blame Beria rather than Stalin. Tito was wary and agreed only to the re-establishment of diplomatic but not inter-party relations. Nonetheless, a communiqué issued at the end of the visit clearly showed the train of thought of some at least of Moscow's leaders. In pledging 'mutual respect and non-interference' in domestic affairs, both sides agreed that 'questions of the internal structure, differences of social systems and differences of concrete form in developing socialism are exclusively a matter for the peoples of the different countries'.[8]

The thaw for which Moscow had been responsible culminated in July 1955 with a big four summit at Geneva, the first of its kind since Potsdam in 1945. The Soviet delegation was led by Bulganin but he was clearly only a front man for Khrushchev. Neither side came anticipating significant breakthroughs. The inevitable discussion on Germany produced a predictably ambiguous outcome. 'The reunification of Germany by free elections', read the final communiqué, 'shall be carried out in conformity with the national interests of the German people and the interests of European security'. On disarmament, Eisenhower's 'open-skies' proposal that each nation should make available plans of its military facilities and allow aerial surveillance of its military installations evoked an indignant rejection from Khrushchev. In time-honoured diplomatic fashion, the leaders called upon their foreign ministers to reassemble to consider further such matters as European security, Germany, disarmament and the means to encourage greater contacts between East and West. That the summit had assembled at all, however, was more important than the absence of concrete results. A dialogue of sorts had been resumed. Tensions had been lifted and a new spirit – the spirit of Geneva – was in the air. For the Russians the summit had been a test of their character and leadership. As Khrushchev admitted in his memoirs, the Soviet delegation had arrived at Geneva, quite literally, with an obvious sense of inferiority. The aeroplanes carrying the other delegations had four engines; that of the Soviet delegation had only two. 'All things considered, I would say we passed the test', was Khrushchev's verdict.[9] That the Soviet Union would emerge as the main beneficiary from such an open-ended summit had been clear to Dulles from the outset. He advised Eisenhower to maintain 'an austere countenance' when being photographed with Bulganin. The president could not keep a straight face and the famous Ike grin duly appeared on the front pages of the world's newspapers.

THE TWENTIETH PARTY CONGRESS AT MOSCOW, FEBRUARY 1956

In their relations with Eastern Europe, the Western powers and nationalist forces in Asia and the Middle East, the new Soviet leaders had introduced fundamental changes in Soviet foreign policy during the three years since Stalin's death. Such major deviations required theoretical underpinning. A new 'correct line' in ideology had to be established. This was the task of the Twentieth Congress of the Soviet Communist Party which met at Moscow in February 1956.

The Congress marked a seminal point in the post-war history of the Soviet Union. Khrushchev used it as platform from which to promote de-Stalinisation both at home and abroad. A selective indictment of Stalin in the 'secret speech' was accompanied by a theoretical justification for the changes which had been introduced in foreign policy. Peaceful coexistence and the concept of different roads to socialism were the two major doctrinal innovations.[10] Different roads to socialism implied that there was no single path of development which all socialist countries should follow and also that socialism itself could be achieved by means other than revolution. The possibility of a parliamentary road to socialism was thus endorsed. Peaceful coexistence, however, became the cornerstone upon which the edifice of Soviet foreign policy was now to be built. Lenin had advocated 'cohabitation' with imperialism as a defensive mechanism to protect the infant Soviet state at a time when socialism as a world system was non-existent. For Lenin, such cohabitation could not but be a temporary phenomenon. War was always inevitable while imperialism continued to exist. Khrushchev's concept of peaceful coexistence differed in the sense that it was envisaged as a long-term policy. Circumstances were now different. Not only was the Soviet Union a great power, there was also now a 'world camp of socialism' which, supported by the Third World and the anti-war forces in the capitalist countries, possessed the material and moral means to resist aggression. War for Khrushchev was thus no longer 'fatalistically inevitable'. But peaceful coexistence did not mean the end of the ideological struggle between socialism and capitalism. It did not imply a rejection of the basic Marxist belief that capitalism was doomed. Khrushchev, no less than Stalin, believed in the final victory of socialism. The question was how to achieve that victory. The destructive power of modern weapons ruled out war because the danger of mutual destruction was too great. The main struggle now would be economic. Better and closer relations with the West would bring not only peace but also access to scientific and technological know-how. As the contradictions within capitalist society propelled the advanced industrial nations towards a final and catastrophic slump, the Soviet economy would catch up and then surge ahead. The rest of the world would be convinced, as Isaac Deutscher once put it, 'through their stomachs' of the merits of socialism.[11]

So much for the theory. In reality, as Khrushchev was well aware, there were serious practical problems to be overcome. Two in particular loomed large: the German question and the danger of an uncontrolled arms race. On the first, now that West Germany was part of NATO, Moscow switched emphasis. Instead of advocating a reunified but neutral German state, the Soviet Union recommended a European security agreement which would put the seal of legitimacy on the post-war divisions within Europe. An essential ingredient of such an agreement would be Western recognition, not only of East Germany as a sovereign state, but also of Poland's Western frontiers. On the second, in seeking agreement with the West to limit the growth of nuclear weapons, Khrushchev was influenced by a number of considerations. His personal fear of nuclear war had been reinforced in 1957 by an explosion at an atomic plant in the Urals. In order to demonstrate the superiority of socialism, he wanted to spend less on defence and more on agriculture and the consumer industries. Finally, Khrushchev was anxious to avoid a situation in which, as a consequence of an escalated arms race, the United States might provide West Germany with nuclear weapons. West Germany would then be able to intimidate East Germany and Poland and this in turn could lead to full-scale war between the United States and the Soviet Union.

SOURCES OF OPPOSITION TO KHRUSHCHEV

The problems in themselves were difficult enough but in attempting to solve them to Moscow's satisfaction Khrushchev faced opposition from at least four quarters. First, he had to contend with American intransigence.[12] Dulles had condemned the containment strategy of the Truman administration as 'negative, futile and immoral'. Containment, he argued, had surrendered the initiative to the communists who were in consequence free to attack targets which stretched Western resources to the limit. The Republicans had achieved office upon the basis of an improbable promise – to pursue an offensive policy designed to 'liberate' or 'roll-back' communist influence and yet, at the same time, to reduce expenditure on defence. They were thus committed to the NSC-68 diagnosis of a worldwide communist threat but not to its prescribed remedy of a vast American military establishment financed by budget deficits and punitive levels of taxation. The strategy of 'massive retaliation' was the means chosen by the Republicans to resolve these contradictions. The United States would not fight any more Korean Wars. It would reduce spending on conventional forces and rely instead on the threat of instantaneous nuclear retaliation at the first sign of communist aggression. The problem with this strategy was one of credibility. Given the new outlook in the Kremlin, communist aggression in Europe was hardly likely. It was more probable in peripheral areas such as the offshore islands separating Taiwan from mainland China. But would the United States seriously consider using nuclear weapons to defend such places as Quemoy and Matsu? Moreover, when Beijing launched its bombardments of these islands in 1954 and again in 1958, Washington's sabre rattling served only to alarm its European allies. Within

Europe too the problem was one of credibility. The hollowness of liberation was soon exposed. Washington confined itself to verbal protests when Soviet tanks intervened in East Berlin in 1953 and again in Budapest in 1956. Dulles was aware of the limitations of his own rhetoric and the call for liberation seemed calculated to roll-back the Democrats in the United States rather than the Red Army in Eastern Europe. Dulles appreciated that the public mood in the United States was in favour of a more vigorous policy which would bring about an end to the Cold War. He therefore argued that the United States should seek, not coexistence with the communist menace, but the elimination of that menace. Yet words alone would not eliminate any Soviet satellite. To achieve this, the United States would have to accept the risk of war with the Soviet Union. This was a risk that the American people were not prepared to take. They were, however, prepared to convince themselves that the United States was once again pursuing a moral and righteous policy which would somehow force communism into retreat. In this sense, liberation served, for a time, its domestic purpose admirably. But abroad, as events in East Germany and Hungary demonstrated, liberation was no different to containment. From a Soviet viewpoint, Khrushchev's task was not made easier by the incompatibility between America's professed aims and its actual policies. Washington was hardly likely to enter negotiations with Moscow with a view to recognising the permanence and legitimacy of communist rule in Eastern Europe.

Communist China constituted a second source of opposition.[13] The Sino-Soviet conflict had roots which extended far beyond ideological differences. Equally important were disputes over matters of state interests and, from the Russian perspective at least, fear and distrust based on centuries of historical experience.

At the level of state interests, relations between Beijing and Moscow were plagued by a longstanding border dispute. In the nineteenth century, during the twilight years of the Manchu dynasty in China, the great powers of the world infringed the sovereignty of the Chinese state by securing economic concessions and extra-territorial rights. China was obliged to sign treaties which ceded substantial frontier regions to the Russian empire. Although inhabited by non-Chinese ethnic groups, these regions had long been ruled by China and were recognised as part of the Chinese state. The post-revolutionary leadership of communist China described these treaties as 'unequal' in the sense that they had been forced on China at a time when the country had been weak. In consequence, Beijing refused to acknowledge the legitimacy of long stretches of the Sino-Soviet border and demanded that the treaties be renegotiated upon the basis of equality. The Russians, however, considered the border to be legitimate as it stood. They feared that border concessions would encourage China to make greater demands as it became stronger. Moreover, Moscow worried that concessions to China might encourage other nations, like Japan and Romania, to press their own territorial claims. The prospect of a surge of irredentism in the Soviet bloc could not be discounted.

On a more fundamental level, the Russians found it impossible to overcome their own psychological barrier in dealing with the Chinese. During Khrushchev's visit to China in 1954, Mao treated his Russian guest to a poolside discourse on war, peace and the atomic bomb. Incapable of comprehending what he described as the 'Oriental' cast of mind, Khrushchev recalled the occasion in his memoirs as a 'nauseating' experience. His revulsion reflected a deep and abiding fear about the age-old 'yellow peril'. In the popular Russian mind, China presented – and still does – a menace of incalculable proportions. Any aversion the average Russian citizen might have for the 'Western imperialists' is far outweighted by his fear and distrust, even hatred, of the Chinese. This cultural paranoia, which equates the teeming millions of China today with the predatory instincts of the Mongol warlords of the eleventh and twelfth centuries, is deeply rooted in Russian history. One historian of contemporary Russia depicts Russian feelings towards China in the following terms:

China, whether metaphorically perceived as the 'yellow menace' or the 'red dragon', is in itself an image of menacing power for the Russian reader. Russian racial feeling about 'Orientals' – though often repressed, sometimes successfully, and publicly of course unacknowledged – is strong and widespread. It applies to Chinese, to Japanese, to Uzbeks and other Turkic peoples, and it is sometimes passionately reciprocated. No doubt such feelings go back to the days of the Mongol conquest, the Muscovite princely wars for independence, the imperial expansion of Russia and the subjugation and attempted integration of Asiatic populations. Russia's defeat at the hands of the Japanese in 1904 may have played a certain role here.[14]

The Soviet leadership under Khrushchev shared these sentiments. Khrushchev recalled in his memoirs:

> You might say that China is both close to us and far from us. It's close in that it's our next-door neighbour and shares a long border with our country. At the same time, China is far away in that the Chinese have little in common with our people.... It's always difficult to know what the Chinese are really thinking.... It's impossible to pin these Chinese down. There is, however, one thing I know for sure about Mao. He's a nationalist, and at least when I knew him, he was bursting with an impatient desire to rule the world. His plan was to rule first China, then Asia, then ... what? There are seven hundred million people in China, and in other countries like Malaysia, about half the population is Chinese.... His [Mao's] chauvinism and arrogance sent a shiver up my spine.[15]

At the level of ideology, the Chinese entertained serious reservations about the proceedings at the Twentieth Party Congress in Moscow. Although at the time his criticisms remained muted, Mao resented the fact that he had not been consulted in advance. He believed that the attack on Stalin ran the risk of bringing the entire international communist movement into disrepute and he also took exception to the doctrinal innovations. On coexistence, the Chinese adhered to the Leninist view about the inevitability of war. They argued that the nature of imperialism had not changed and that the threat of nuclear war was therefore irrelevant to the unchanging structure of class forces and antagonisms in the post-war world. For Beijing, coexistence was possible only between socialist countries and the non-aligned countries of the Third World. It could not be accepted as a basis for relations between socialist and imperialist countries. The Chinese also had reservations about the achievement of socialism by peaceful or parliamentary means on the grounds that it would retard the anti-colonial struggle in the Third World. This argument did not necessarily conflict with Beijing's Bandung strategy of promoting good relations with nationalist governments in Asia and Africa. Beijing always made a distinction between countries, like China itself, which had achieved 'national liberation' (a term which implied a socialist dimension to the process) and countries, like India, which had achieved only 'national independence'. For the Chinese, therefore, if a revolutionary situation developed in a country of the Third World, then it became the duty of the socialist camp to lend all possible support to that struggle, irrespective of the possible reaction in the West.

Pursuing a moderate line themselves at home and abroad in the mid-50s, the Chinese did not immediately take issue with their Soviet comrades. At a meeting of the Chinese Politburo in April 1956, Mao coined the slogan, 'Let a Hundred Flowers bloom and a hundred schools of thought contend.' The 'Hundred Flowers' campaign was an attempt to revitalise the revolution in China by inviting criticism and popular debate in the certain belief that, the virtues of Marxism being self-evident, the party would emerge with stronger roots amongst the mass of the people. The experiment did not last long. Mao called a halt in June 1957. Intellectual criticism had gone much further than anticipated and had called into question the entire fabric of socialist society. Mao reverted to the politics of thought control and launched the Great Leap Forward in 1958. People's communes were established to facilitate a rapid push towards the development of a fully socialist society. In the absence of a technological base, Mao placed supreme confidence in the two assets which China possessed in abundance – manpower and, given the necessary level of party exhortation, the revolutionary enthusiasm of the population.

A radical shift within China was automatically thought at the time to have induced a hardening of the Chinese attitude towards the outside world. The Bandung era was assumed to have been one of the first casualties. But in fact the Bandung era survived the launching of the Great Leap Forward. That relations did ultimately cool between Beijing and a number of nationalist governments in Asia was more often the result of specific disputes over matters of national interest in which questions of ideology played little part. The Tibetan rebellion of 1959 and the subsequent Sino-Indian border dispute are cases in point.

Nonetheless, the Great Leap Forward did have an external dimension. What concerned China in 1958 was that just when it appeared that imperialism had entered an aggressive phase, the Soviet Union seemed least inclined to do anything about it. Moscow delivered only mild protests when, following the successful revolution against the pro-Western monarchy in Iraq in 1958, American and British forces intervened to prop up the pro-Western governments in the Lebanon and Jordon respectively. Similarly, when in 1958 the Chinese resumed their bombardment of the offshore islands in the Taiwan Straits and Washington again threatened to use nuclear weapons, Moscow remained silent. Only when the bombardment ceased did Khrushchev see fit to remind the United States that 'an attack on the People's Republic of China ... is an attack on the Soviet Union'. At this juncture, Khrushchev was attempting to force a settlement with the West over Berlin. He ignored Chinese strictures that it was time the Soviet Union exploited its technological advances in order to compel the West to retreat over areas such as the Middle East, Taiwan and Berlin. The Soviet Union had tested the first intercontinental ballistic missile and launched the first space satellite, Sputnik 1, in 1957. Khrushchev certainly fed the 'missile gap' scare which these developments created in the West but he remained acutely aware that the Soviet Union could not compete in delivery terms with America's long-range bomber force.

To silence Chinese criticisms, Khrushchev attempted to compel Beijing to toe the Soviet line. Moscow requested but was refused permission to station troops and weapons on Chinese soil as a safeguard against the outbreak of war in the Taiwan Straits. In 1959 the Soviet Union unilaterally abrogated an agreement to supply technical assistance to China which included plans to develop a Chinese atomic bomb. Adam Ulam has suggested (see below p. 95) that Khrushchev was manoeuvring for an agreement with the West on Berlin which would be underpinned by a joint Soviet-American understanding that if Washington withheld nuclear weapons from West Germany, Moscow would do likewise in respect of China.[16]

The Chinese drew their own conclusions about the drift of Khrushchev's policies. The Great Leap Forward became for the Chinese the means to remove their dependence on Soviet support and technical aid. Beijing, however, went further, accusing Moscow of revisionism. Khrushchev in turn poured scorn on the Great Leap Forward ('samovar industrialisation' was how he described it) and accused the Chinese of dogmatism. Clearly irked by the manner in which the Chinese quoted from Lenin to prove their view about the inevitability of war, Khrushchev declared: '[O]ne cannot mechanically repeat now on this question what Vladimir Ilyich Lenin said many decades ago on imperialism'.[17] The Sino-Soviet quarrel simmered in print until the first head-on confrontation occurred at a Congress of the Romanian Communist Party at Bucharest in June 1960. It was broadcast to the rest of the world at the Twenty-Second Congress of the Soviet Communist Party at Moscow in February 1961. Other communist parties were obliged to take sides. With the exception of the Albanians, the ruling parties in Europe sided with Moscow although the Romanians saw in the quarrel an opportunity to pursue an independent line of their own. Elsewhere, however, and particularly among the non-ruling communist parties in Asia, the Middle East and Latin America, there was a tendency to identify with the Chinese position. Khrushchev was thus faced with the unpalatable truth that as a consequence of his pursuit of coexistence with the West, the communist movement was in danger of fragmentation. For the first time, Moscow's leadership of the worldwide communist movement had been brought into question.

The West German attitude was another problem for Khrushchev. Adenauer had visited Moscow in August 1955 with the twofold aim of securing the release of German prisoners-of-war still detained in the Soviet Union and exploring for himself the real motives behind the Kremlin's peace overtures. Although agreement was reached on the return of some of the prisoners, in return for which Adenauer agreed to establish diplomatic relations with Moscow, the visit merely confirmed the West German Chancellor's deepest suspicions about Soviet intentions.[18] Immediately after his visit, an East German delegation arrived in Moscow to conclude a treaty whereby the Russians formally restored sovereignty to East Germany and authorised the government in East Berlin to open diplomatic relations with other states. West Germany countered in December 1955 with the Hallstein Doctrine which declared that Bonn would regard recognition of East Germany by any other state as an 'unfriendly act'. The Doctrine, named after the then State Secretary in the West German Foreign Office, was enforced twice – in 1957, when Bonn broke off diplomatic relations with Yugoslavia, and in 1963, when relations between West Germany and Cuba were severed. Adenauer's critics maintained that his policy served only to tighten Moscow's grip on its satellites in the sense that it made East Germany and Poland still more dependent on Soviet protection. Adenauer, however, regarded all Soviet proposals about Germany and Central Europe as attempts to reduce American influence in Europe, to weaken NATO and to entice West Germany out of the Atlantic Alliance. Maintaining that Western Europe would thus be left at the mercy of Soviet pressure and propaganda, Adenauer refused to enter serious negotiations with Moscow over the German question.

Finally, Khrushchev had to contend with his domestic critics.[19] In the aftermath of the upheavals in Poland and Hungary in the autumn of 1956, Khrushchev survived an attempt to relieve him of his position as First Secretary. Returning from a visit to Finland in June 1957, he was summoned to a meeting arranged by a number of his colleagues on the Presidium.[20] Led ostensibly by Bulganin, but with Molotov the real architect of the plot, the 'anti-Party group' as they became known launched a bitter attack on Khrushchev's policies and recommended that he should be transferred to the Ministry of Agriculture. Khrushchev, however, reacted quickly and with the help of Marshal Zhukov, the Defence Minister, he summoned a meeting of the Central Committee. Here the tables were turned and the accusations flowed the other way. Molotov soon found himself as ambassador in Outer Mongolia. Malenkov, another member of the group, found himself in charge of power stations in Central Asia. Bulganin survived a little longer but in March 1958 he was relieved of his position and Khrushchev became Chairman of the Council of Ministers as well as First Secretary. Yet Khrushchev did not acquire from his victory the commanding position once occupied by Stalin. He could not alter the composition of the Presidium without the consent of his colleagues upon whose support he was now dependent. Indeed in this respect it was now clear that Khrushchev was on trial. Support would be forthcoming only if his policies paid dividends. Increasingly, however, Khrushchev met with setbacks which raised ever-increasing doubts about his credibility as a leader. At home, his agricultural reforms and his decentralisation of the economy did not produce the anticipated increases in food consumption or the projected increases in industrial growth. Moreover, the very concept of de-Stalinisation within the Soviet Union was seen by many as a threat to communist orthodoxy. Success abroad was the only means by which Khrushchev could re-establish his domestic credibility. In the final analysis, the 1963 Test Ban Treaty was meagre reward when set against the upheavals in Eastern Europe, the continued presence of the Western powers in Berlin, the fragmentation of the communist world and the utter humiliation of the Cuban missile crisis. It was not surprising therefore that Khrushchev failed to survive a second attempt to force him from office in 1964.

YEARS OF CRISIS, 1956–65

De-Stalinisation opened up a veritable Pandora's box in Eastern Europe for the repercussions of which a solitary visit to Belgrade by

Bulganin and Khrushchev had been wholly inadequate preparation. Why, if Stalin had been dethroned, should his minions in Eastern Europe, who were so closely identified in the popular mind with the repression of the Stalin era, be allowed to survive? Unrest began in Poland in July 1956 among factory workers at Poznan. In October the Central Committee of the Polish United Worker's Party appointed Wladyslaw Gomulka as First Secretary and dismissed Marshal Rokossovsky, a Russian, who had been Poland's Defence Minister since 1949. Moscow was alarmed. Gomulka was identified as the symbol of Polish resistance to Soviet domination. Khrushchev and three of his colleagues flew to Warsaw for a stormy meeting with their Polish counterparts but the Soviet Union did not act over Poland. However unwelcome the changes were in Moscow's eyes, communist government in Poland was not in question. The same could not be said of Hungary where, in October 1956, Imre Nagy was recalled as prime minister. Nagy replaced Gerö who only three months earlier had been Moscow's choice to replace the Stalinist Rakosi. In November Nagy announced plans to end the one-party system and to withdraw Hungary from the Warsaw Pact. The Hungarian Revolution, or counter-revolution depending on one's point of view, represented a direct threat to Moscow's interests – militarily, to its security; politically, to the very basis upon which communist rule in Eastern Europe had been established. Soviet tanks were moved into Budapest. Amidst bitter fighting, over 30,000 Hungarians were killed and 180,000 fled to the West which remained passive throughout. Janos Kádár was installed in place of Nagy who had taken refuge in the Yugoslav Embassy. Enticed out on the strength of a guarantee of his personal safety, Nagy was promptly arrested and taken to Romania where he was executed in 1958.

The Soviet Union escaped universal condemnation before the court of world opinion because the invasion of Hungary followed hard on the heels of a crisis in the Middle East. Regarding Israel rather than communism as his principal enemy, Colonel Nasser, the Egyptian leader, had no desire to become one of the West's Cold War camp-followers in the Middle East. Instead he sought the best of both worlds, negotiating with the West a loan to finance the building of an irrigation dam at Aswan on the Nile and accepting modern weapons in an arms deal with the Eastern bloc. In July 1956 the United States attempted to persuade Nasser to come off the fence by withdrawing the American offer of a loan. Nasser retaliated by nationalising the

Suez Canal, incurring in so doing the wrath of the British and French governments. Nasser's name was anathema in London and Paris. Anthony Eden, the British prime minister, regarded him as a latter-day Hitler, while in Paris French opposition was based on Nasser's support for the rebels in Algeria. In October 1956, in collusion with Israel, Anglo-French forces attacked Egypt in an operation designed to regain control of the Suez Canal. Washington, however, refused to condone the invasion and supported instead a resolution passed by the General Assembly of the United Nations which called for a cease-fire and a withdrawal of foreign troops. Western prestige throughout the Middle East was seriously damaged by the Suez crisis. Egypt and Syria, the leading Arab opponents of continued Western influence, turned increasingly to Moscow for their military and economic aid. Washington countered in January 1957 with the Eisenhower Doctrine which offered economic and military aid to all countries in the Middle East and which emphasised that such assistance might include the use of American military forces. The Eisenhower Doctrine, which was invoked for the first time in the Lebanon crisis of 1958, ensured that the Middle East would remain in the front line of East-West confrontation.

If Suez spared the Soviet Union strict censure, the invasion of Hungary still had some undesirable consequences from Moscow's point of view. It ended what slender prospects remained of effecting a permanent reconciliation with Yugoslavia. Tito regarded the invasion as a necessary evil but argued that it could have been avoided if his advice had been followed at an earlier stage. The upheavals in Eastern Europe also provided the Chinese with an opportunity to make capital out of Moscow's difficulties. Zhou Enlai's efforts at mediation between Moscow and Belgrade in 1957 set an unwelcome precedent for Chinese intervention in communist affairs in Europe. In November 1957, at a conference of communist parties which was held in Moscow, Mao Zedong delivered his famous 'east wind prevailing over the west wind' speech and stunned his audience by suggesting that the cause of socialism would be advanced if, as a result of a nuclear war, half of mankind died.[21] The declaration issued at the end of the conference was a compromise between conflicting Soviet and Chinese ideological points of view. The declaration endorsed coexistence and described the Soviet Union as 'the first and mightiest socialist power'. But the Chinese challenge was also evident in the section which dealt with revisionism and dogmatism. Although the declaration condemned dogmatism and maintained that it was up to individual communist parties to decide which of the two heresies threatened them more at any given time, it was nonetheless quite specific when it asserted: '[T]he communist parties believe that the main danger at present is revisionism .... The existence of bourgeois influence is an internal source of revisionism, while surrender to imperialist pressure is its external source'.[22]

Between the Moscow conference in 1957 and the Cuban missile crisis in 1962, the problem of Berlin ranked equally with that of China in Khrushchev's foreign policy initiatives. In November 1958 Khrushchev delivered an ultimatum over Berlin. In a note to the three Western powers, he demanded that they should remove their troops from West Berlin and convert West Berlin into a 'free city' under the auspices of the United Nations. If agreement were not reached within six months, Khrushchev threatened to hand over to East Germany certain functions previously exercised by the Soviet Union. These included control over the West's access routes into West Berlin. The motives which prompted the ultimatum are discussed in detail below (pp. 93–97). Suffice it here to say that the West reacted firmly to Khrushchev's threat. In December 1958 the three Western powers, with full NATO backing, rejected the Soviet repudiation of their obligations and reaffirmed their commitment to remain in West Berlin. But the ultimatum did have the effect of concentrating minds in the West. Britain and America, particularly after Dulles' retirement in April 1959, seemed more willing to contemplate negotiations with the Soviet Union. Already, in February and March 1959, Harold Macmillan, the British prime minister, had visited Moscow. Between May and August a conference of foreign ministers was held at Geneva with German representatives present. Here it was suggested that Khrushchev should visit the United States.

The Berlin ultimatum was now, for the time being, conveniently forgotten. In June 1959 the Soviet Union secretly renounced the agreement to provide Beijing with atomic technology and in September Khrushchev made his first visit to the United States. With Khrushchev describing Eisenhower as a man of peace, the 'spirit of Camp David' seemed to suggest the possibility of a major breakthrough in East-West relations. In reality, however, although the talks were a useful exercise in public relations for Khrushchev, little of substance was actually agreed. The two leaders arranged a further summit in Europe and signed a communiqué on Berlin. Eisenhower described the

West's position in Berlin as 'abnormal', an inappropriate expression. Khrushchev had frequently referred to the West's position in Berlin as 'abnormal'; by using the same word Eisenhower had unwittingly strengthened Khrushchev's hand. If the West's position was abnormal, then the Russian demands seemed reasonable and, by implication, it was up to the Western powers to alter their position to normalise the situation.

The spirit of Camp David did not impress the Chinese, as Khrushchev himself found out when he visited China at the end of September 1959 immediately after his American visit. Khrushchev was prepared to sanction an intensification of the revolutionary struggle in South Vietnam but in other parts of the world his policy in this respect continued to be one of restraint. In the Middle East, the Soviet leader continued to support Kassem (the new ruler of Iraq) and Nasser in Egypt, despite the fact that both had declared war on communists within their own countries. In order to curry favour with de Gaulle, who had returned to power as president of France in December 1958 and whose anti-Americanism was still as strong as ever, Khrushchev counselled caution to Ferhat Abbas, the leader of the National Liberation Front in Algeria. The Soviet Union also chose not to take sides in the 1959 Sino-Indian border dispute. More galling still to Beijing was Khrushchev's hint, dropped during an address to the Supreme Soviet in October 1959, that China should reconcile itself for the time being to the loss of Taiwan.

Impervious to Chinese criticism, Khrushchev pressed ahead on the assumption that agreement with the West was in his grasp. In January 1960 he announced to the Supreme Soviet that the Soviet armed forces would be reduced by one-third, a cut of about 1.2 million men. Confident that war was less likely, Khrushchev was in any case preparing to switch the emphasis in Soviet defence policy from the conventional to the strategic. But as the big four summit which had been fixed for Paris in May 1960 drew closer, it became evident that Khrushchev had assumed too much of the Western powers. In West Germany, Adenauer had become increasingly concerned by what he regarded as a dangerous trend in American and British policy. The West, Adenauer stressed, had to maintain its rights and obligations in Berlin. He warned that a demonstration of Western weakness in Berlin would have serious consequences for the whole of Europe. France supported West Germany. Always ready to argue that the United States was an unreliable ally, de Gaulle envisaged Europe as a world power in its own right. Believing that France and the Federal Republic would play the most important roles, de Gaulle was unwilling to contemplate changes that might endanger West Germany's security.[23] With the Western alliance divided, Eisenhower was in no position to deliver what Khrushchev wanted. A fortnight before the Paris summit was due to convene, the Chinese added to Khrushchev's difficulties by commemorating the 90th anniversary of Lenin's birth with a series of articles entitled 'Long Live Leninism'.[24]

Khrushchev arrived in Paris anxious to find a means to extricate himself from his dilemma. Such an opportunity presented itself when the Soviet delegation was informed that an American U-2 spy plane had been shot down some 1,300 miles inside Soviet territory. The U-2 flights were not new and had been going on for years. However, this was the first occasion upon which the Soviet Union had fired a missile high enough to bring one down. The Eisenhower administration responded at first by claiming that the plane had been engaged in meteorological observation and that it had strayed off course. It then had to admit the truth when Khrushchev revealed that the pilot had been captured. After a series of acrimonious exchanges, with Khrushchev demanding an apology which Eisenhower refused to give, Khrushchev stormed out of Paris, flew to East Berlin and threatened to sign a peace treaty with East Germany. The threat came to nothing but Khrushchev delivered a personal insult to Eisenhower by declaring that another summit would have to be postponed for six to eight months, by which time Eisenhower would no longer be president.

The collapse of the Paris summit was Khrushchev's most serious setback to date. It was followed by bitter exchanges within the communist world. The Third Congress of the Romanian Communist Party in June 1960 was the scene of a heated verbal confrontation between the Soviet and Chinese delegates. Khrushchev himself was reported to have attacked Mao Zedong by name. In August the Russians unilaterally withdrew aid to China and recalled nearly 1,400 industrial and technical advisers with their blueprints. Advisers from Eastern Europe were also withdrawn. In November, at a meeting in Moscow attended by representatives of 81 communist parties, an attempt was made to paper over the ideological cracks. The ensuing conference statement was a collation of Soviet and Chinese views which were hardly compatible. Support for the national liberation struggle was endorsed but so too was the idea of a peaceful transition to socialism. The monolith, however, had been broken. For the first time, the Russians attended a communist party conference not to dictate their will but to defend and explain their policies against severe criticism.[25]

With the arrival of John F. Kennedy in the White House in January 1961, the pendulum of American foreign policy swung back once more to the outlook of NSC-68. To the Democrats, the Eisenhower administration had been languid, inactive and prone to compromise. For all the bold talk, the previous eight years had done little more than expose the shallowness of Republican rhetoric. Eisenhower had accepted that there were limitations to America's world role. Kennedy did not. The new president was ready to take up the challenge of communist support for wars of national liberation. 'The great battle ground for the defence and the expansion of freedom today', he declared, 'is the whole southern half of the globe . . . the lands of the rising people'. In another memorable speech Kennedy argued that the people of Latin America, Africa and Asia should 'start to look to America, to what the President of the United States is doing, not to Khrushchev or the Chinese Communists'.[26] Convinced now that the main communist threat would take the form of support for insurgency wars, the Kennedy administration strengthened America's conventional forces. A 15 per cent defence budget increase in 1961 enabled the army to double the number of combat divisions in its strategic reserve, the navy to add 70 vessels to the active fleet and the air force to add a dozen more wings to its tactical forces. Special emphasis was placed on the training of elite counter-insurgency forces like the Green Berets. Conventional defence spending was not introduced at the expense of the strategic defence of the United States. Aware by now that the alleged missile-gap in favour of the Soviet Union was pure fiction, the Kennedy administration nevertheless began to implement a strategic programme designed to achieve a clear American superiority. This was deemed essential, not only to guard against a Soviet strategic build-up, but also to demonstrate American superiority to the rest of the world. The Kennedy administration inherited from Eisenhower 200 intercontinental ballistic missiles. By 1964, a year after Kennedy's death, the number had risen to 834. Expanding means to safeguard interests in classic NSC-68 style, Kennedy's defence budget soared to 56 billion dollars.

Vietnam became the test-case of the administration's resolve but not before Kennedy had suffered a sharp reverse in the Caribbean. The new president inherited from Eisenhower a CIA-backed plan to provide logistical support for an invasion of Cuba by a group of Cuban exiles in the United States. The Cuban revolution of January 1959 had brought Fidel Castro to power in Havana in place of the dictator, General Batista. Castro's land reform and nationalisation programmes threatened American interests in Cuba which included ownership of about 80 per cent of the public services and 40 per cent of the sugar crop, Cuba's principal export. In February 1960 Castro signed a trade agreement with Moscow and by December 1961 he was openly declaring that he had become a Marxist-Leninist. Having insisted upon the non-involvement of American troops, Kennedy approved an invasion of Cuba in the area of the Bay of Pigs in April 1961. The operation went disastrously wrong and Kennedy had to accept responsibility.

The Cuban fiasco might well have persuaded Kennedy to stay his hand in a crisis which had arisen over Laos. Here, twice in recent years (1958 and 1960), the United States had conspired to overthrow Prince Souvanna, the head of the Laotian government whose attempts to pursue a course of neutrality had at times led him to form coalitions with the communist Pathet Lao. The coup of 1960 and subsequent American support for a new right-wing government provoked a major Pathet Lao offensive and the possibility of Chinese intervention. At a reconvened Geneva conference in May 1961 the United States accepted in principle the neutralisation of Laos, an agreement which enabled Prince Souvanna to return in 1962 at the head of a precarious coalition with the Pathet Lao.

No such accommodation was possible in Vietnam. Here the growing Sino-Soviet rift presented Hanoi with an opportunity to resume the pressure on the regime of Ngo Dinh Diem in Saigon in a manner which was designed to avoid compromising the Soviet policy of attempting to reach agreement with the West in Europe. At the beginning of 1959 Hanoi decided to renew the struggle against Diem, not by frontal attack, but by insurrection in the South. The National Front for the Liberation of South Vietnam (NFLSV) was established in December 1960 after the Moscow conference had endorsed support for wars of national liberation. The subsequent communist claim that the NFLSV was a purely Southern movement, acting independently of the North, was part of a deliberate deception. The tactics of the NFLSV were determined by the Vietnamese Workers' Party in the North. The decision to separate the two halves of the Vietnamese revolution was taken by Hanoi to give the struggle in the South the appearance of a separate liberation movement and hence to make it more acceptable to Moscow. Khrushchev was fully aware of Hanoi's strategy. The opening shots in the Southern campaign coincided with the Camp David visit in September 1959 and in November Moscow agreed to assist Hanoi's three-year economic plan without imposing any restraint on its policy towards the South. With China having already decided to abandon the Bandung strategy in relation to those countries of South East Asia which had become militarily as well as politically committed to the United States, Moscow had no option, if it wanted to avoid Beijing seizing the initiative, but to support a more active revolutionary line in Indo-China whilst still pursuing agreement with the West in Europe.[27] It has become customary to attribute the renewal of the struggle in South Vietnam to a spontaneous popular revolt against the repression of the Diem regime. Diem's government was undoubtedly repressive but the revolt in the South was not spontaneous. Pursuing its own strategy of Vietnamese reunification, North Vietnam became the principal beneficiary of the Sino-Soviet conflict in the sense that some of the constraints which had been imposed on Hanoi by the 1954 Geneva settlement had now been lifted.

The American response to these developments was initially divided between those who saw the problem in political terms and who were worried about Diem's inefficiency and growing unpopularity as a leader, and those who interpreted what was happening as a grave military threat which demanded unconditional support for Diem even at the risk of creating political unrest in South Vietnam. After an abortive army coup against Diem in November 1960 the second view prevailed. This was the situation inherited by Kennedy. The president sent two fact-finding missions to Vietnam. The first, in May 1961, was led by Vice-President Lyndon Johnson. The second, in October 1961, was led by General Maxwell Taylor and State Department official Walt Rostow. Both missions reported back that the Diem government warranted increased American aid. With his own perception of a communist threat to the whole of the free world, Kennedy was convinced that the crisis in South Vietnam was not one that could be solved by negotiation. When Eisenhower left office at the beginning of 1961, there were 500 American military advisers in South Vietnam. At the end of 1963, by which time both Kennedy and Diem had been assassinated, the latter being replaced by the first in a series of right-wing military leaders, there were about 16,000.

Kennedy had only one meeting with Khrushchev during his shor-tlived administration. This took place at Vienna in June 1961 when Kennedy was still reeling from the Bay of Pigs débâcle. Clearly seeking to intimidate his inexperienced opposite number, Khrushchev was in menacing form. The conversation turned on communist support for national liberation wars and the danger of a nuclear war between the United States and the Soviet Union arising from a miscalculation. On the first, Khrushchev argued that wars of national liberation were inevitable and that socialist countries had a duty to support them. He was, however, prepared to compromise on Laos by agreeing to reconvene the Geneva conference. But on the dangers of nuclear war, Khrushchev resorted to bullying and flew into a rage. 'Miscalculation! Miscalculation! Miscalculation!', he thundered, 'All I ever hear from your people and your correspondents and your friends in Europe and every place else is that damned word, miscalculation. You ought to take that word and bury it in cold storage and never use it again! I'm sick of it!'[28] The meeting ended with another threat (which once again remained unfulfilled) that the Soviet Union would sign a peace treaty with East Germany if agreement on Berlin had not been reached by the end of the year. Kennedy departed Vienna forecasting a long cold winter. In the meantime, the summer and autumn became decidedly hot. On 13 August 1961 units of the East German People's Army, People's Police and factory militia began taking up positions at various crossing points between the sectoral borders of Berlin and the borders between West Berlin and East Germany. Under the supervision of these armed units, East German workers began placing barbed wire and other light obstacles at the crossing points. By 15 August the barbed wire obstacles were being replaced by prefabricated concrete blocks. The second Berlin crisis had begun.

Before examining precisely what induced Khrushchev to sanction the building of the Berlin Wall it is necessary to comment on a number of Western misconceptions about Soviet actions and policies.[29] First, it has been suggested that the crisis over Berlin, which began with the ultimatum of 1958 and culminated with the construction of the Wall in 1961, constitutes evidence of a wide gap between ideology and practice in Soviet foreign policy. The Twentieth Party Congress of 1956 had, according to this argument, ushered in a series of moderate policies in the Soviet Union in the form of de-Stalinisation, reductions in the armed forces,[30] more emphasis on consumer goods and commit-ments to a strategy of coexistence abroad. As Khrushchev wanted to stand by these policies, his pressures on the Western powers over Berlin and his emphasis on threats and military power are said to be entirely out of keeping with the general ideological line.

But this reasoning is in itself flawed. Khrushchev's manoeuvrings over Berlin were very much in keeping with the current ideological stance which was stated in two important documents in 1961. First, Khrushchev's report on the 1960 Moscow conference which he read at a joint meeting of the party organisations of the Higher Party School, the Academy of Social Sciences and the Central Committee's Institute on Marxism-Leninism in January 1961; secondly, the Draft Programme of the Soviet Communist Party which was adopted at the June 1961 plenary meeting of the Central Committee. Both documents dealt with the questions of the likelihood of war and the means to avert it. In this respect, they refined the ideological basis of peaceful coexistence as formulated at the Twentieth Party Congress. Three kinds of war were identified. First, world wars among capitalist or imperialist powers into which socialist countries might be drawn. These were considered improbable although Khrushchev did concede that the imperialist powers might be preparing for wars against socialist countries. Secondly, local wars. The Western powers viewed local wars as conflicts between 'third actors' in the sense that they did not involve the United States and the Soviet Union or their allies. Examples would be the Arab-Israeli conflicts in the Middle East or the conflicts between India and Pakistan on the Indian subcontinent. Khrushchev, however, had a different view which suggested that a local war involved one of the great powers or one of its closest allies in a conflict which was limited in geographical scope and in the nature of the weapons used. Examples according to this Soviet view would be Korea, Vietnam and the Anglo-French attack on Suez. The third and final category involved wars of national liberation. Such wars, according to Khrushchev, were not only probable but also inevitable.[31]

Upon the basis of this Soviet analysis, national liberation wars were inevitable, local wars were probable and the risk of escalation in both cases was high. How, therefore, might it be possible to avoid a world war? Khrushchev's report on the Moscow conference and the Draft Programme of the Soviet Communist Party were quite clear on this point. 'Peace', it was argued, 'cannot be begged for. It can be safeguarded only by an active purposeful struggle.' The elements of such a struggle were outlined as follows: (1) to strengthen the economic and military potential of the socialist camp; (2) to strive for greater unity of action among communists (an appeal to China to toe the line); (3) the enlargement of the 'zone of peace', including both socialist and non-socialist 'peace-loving' states in Europe and Asia; (4) to exploit the contradictions among imperialist countries; (5) to sharpen the awareness of the 'masses' and the political leaders in the capitalist countries about the consequences of nuclear war; and (6) to use threats in order to 'sober up' Western political leaders and to 'bring them to their senses'. Points 1, 5 and 6 in this programme would seen to invalidate the argument that Khrushchev's aggressive stance over Berlin contradicted the theoretical under-pinning of peaceful coexistence.[32]

A second misconception in the West concerns the bearing which Sino-Soviet relations had on the Berlin problem. As noted above, Adam Ulam believes that a settlement over Berlin was the means by which Khrushchev hoped to prevent both West Germany and China acquiring nuclear weapons. Isaac Deutscher adopted a similar view, suggesting that Khrushchev was hamstrung in his negotiations with the West about Berlin by his need to compete with Mao for leadership of the communist camp. This, according to Deutscher, made it difficult for Khrushchev to engage in genuine diplomatic bargaining and also imposed upon him the diplomatic rigidity which so surprised Kennedy at Vienna in June 1961.[33] Plausible in theory, both arguments are based on conjecture. Such indicators as exist point to different conclusions. Ulam's argument about West Germany acquiring nuclear weapons is difficult to square with the fact that the issue was *not* raised at Khrushchev's Camp David meeting with Eisenhower in September 1959. According to Eisenhower's own account: 'Numerous problems were brought up somewhat haphazardly, but again and again we seemed to come back to Berlin and the latest Soviet ultimatum'. The gist of Khrushchev's ideas about an East German peace treaty was that, in Eisenhower's words, 'the existence of West Berlin as an unwelcome irritant in the body of "peace-loving" East Germany was becoming intolerable'. Kennedy met with the same response at Vienna. Similarly, it seems difficult to reconcile Deutscher's belief that the growing Sino-Soviet rift limited Khrushchev's room for manoeuvre with the fact that the one compromise agreement reached at Vienna was on an issue of direct concern to China, namely Laos.[34]

The Berlin crisis from 1958 to 1961 has been interpreted too narrowly by most Western observers. Khrushchev had not one, but a range of objectives. The first, and the most unlikely, was that the

Western powers would surrender their position in West Berlin. The other objectives were rather more realistic. Khrushchev wanted to enhance the domestic stability and international status of East Germany. To achieve this, he had to limit the influence of West Berlin as a showcase of the West by increasing its sense of vulnerability and possibly decreasing its ties with West Germany. Above all, Khrushchev wanted to secure a final and irrevocable acceptance of the post-war political and social order in Europe by neutralising West Germany's policy of non-recognition of East Germany and Bonn's expressed goal of German reunification.[35]

Seen from this perspective, Khrushchev's threats over Berlin were part of a broad strategy which embraced questions of ideology, economic performance and Soviet state security. At issue here, during a period of perceived Western aggression, were questions concerning the cohesion and stability of the 'Socialist Commonwealth'. A crucial factor undermining the desired cohesion and stability was the parlous state of the East German economy, a condition manifested above all in an acute labour shortage. According to West German statistics, in the period between the end of the Second World War and 1961, 3.8 million people had migrated to West Germany from the East but only 565,000 had migrated in the opposite direction. This represented a net loss to East Germany of about 3.3 million people. Over a narrower period, from 1949 to 1961, the population of East Germany had declined from just over nineteen million to little more than seventeen million. Fifteen per cent of the working population had been lost, including a disproportionately high share of young people and skilled workers. The East German economy faced other problems, notably a lack of capital for investment and a severe decline in agricultural production caused by a collectivisation drive which had been mounted between 1958 and 1960. Overall growth rates had fallen from 12 per cent in 1958, to 11 per cent in 1959, to 6 per cent in 1960 and finally, in the year of the Berlin Wall, to a mere 4 per cent. These figures had serious implications for the economy of the Soviet Union. In 1960, 34.5 per cent of the Soviet Union's total imports of machinery and equipment originated in East Germany. The Soviet Union depended on East Germany for high technology products and equipment such as machine tools, chemical products, optical instruments and electrical appliances. In turn, East Germany depended on the Soviet Union for raw materials, energy and semi-finished products. A trade imbalance between the two countries had developed. Soviet exports to East

Germany rose in value from 1051.7 million dollars in 1960 to 1209.1 million in 1961 but the value of imports from East Germany fell from 929.3 million dollars to 875.9 million. Over the same period, Soviet imports of East German machinery and equipment fell from the above-mentioned 34.5 per cent to 28.4 per cent.[36]

Emphasising the view that the Berlin Wall must be seen primarily as a move to strengthen the cohesion and stability of the socialist bloc, Hannes Adomeit, author of one of the most comprehensive accounts of both Berlin crises of 1948 and 1961, has written: 'To that extent the Berlin crisis of 1961 underlines the importance of ideology for Soviet security; and at the same time it makes a nonsense of a rigid dichotomy between ideology and national interests'.[37] It is impossible to divorce Soviet ideological from Soviet state interests in the crisis of 1961. Both, according to Adomeit, 'reinforced each other and formed a unified entity'. East Germany's labour shortage problem was not simply an ideological embarrassment. On account of East Germany's deepening economic crisis, it was also a serious setback to the ambitious targets of the Seven Year Plan (1959–65) in the Soviet Union and a severe handicap in the main declared area of East-West competition, namely economic performance.

As in the case of the 1948 Berlin crisis, the crisis of 1961 was carefully managed. The balance of military advantage was more equally divided than it had been in 1948. America's strategic superiority was balanced by Soviet superiority in conventional forces and in intermediate missiles capable of hitting targets in Western Europe. Stringent limits were thus set to the use of force by both sides. Moscow did not attempt to interfere with the West's rights of access to West Berlin and Washington did nothing to challenge the unilateral action taken on 13 August. For the West, the Berlin Wall was seen as an admission by the Soviet Union that Soviet-style socialism in Eastern Europe was a failure. The Wall was therefore hailed in the West as a propaganda victory. Kennedy exploited the symbolic significance of the Wall during his visit to Berlin in the summer of 1963. He sent a huge crowd into raptures when he proclaimed, 'Ich bin ein Berliner'. In fact the animal behaviour of the crowd frightened the president. He felt sure he would have been obeyed had he given the order to charge the Wall.[38] Retrospective Western accounts of the crisis have also questioned what they see as a lack of realism in Soviet policies. While challenging the West on a vulnerable and important issue in Central Europe, Khrushchev still thought that it would be possible to gain access to Western credits and technology and to expand East-West trade.

Soviet and East German interpretations of the significance of the Berlin crisis differ substantially from those put forward in the West. They do not see it as a defeat. A Soviet account published in 1974 emphasised that as a result of the Berlin crisis, the attitude of the Western powers towards the German problem changed. They no longer supported demands for free elections and reunification and they dropped their previous insistence that the fulfilment of these demands was a prerequisite for a settlement of other international problems. The same source also emphasised that the crisis played its part in altering the balance of political forces within West Germany. The loss by the CDU/CSU coalition of its absolute majority in the *Bundestag* in September 1961 was said to indicate that the Adenauer era was about to come to an end. Henceforth the West Germans were forced to abandon their positions on the German problem to which they had clung for so long. A collective East German account, published in 1968, made much the same point by emphasising that East Germany was now in a position to win acceptance of the principle of peaceful coexistence, and hence more normal relations, between the German states.[39] Such arguments carry justification, but only from a long-term perspective. At the time, the act of dividing Berlin by a concrete wall, and then the shooting of people trying to escape or emigrate across it, retarded the process of normalisation and made it even more difficult for the West to establish relations with Ulbricht's regime at any level. If anything, the crisis gave new impetus to West Germany's claim to be the sole representative of the German nation. In terms of the immediate effects of the crisis, Soviet and East German sources are on firmer ground when they argue that it represented the opening of a new chapter in the history of East Germany. It made it possible for East Germany to begin the task of the 'large-scale construction of socialism', to introduce a new system of economic planning and to develop its economy at a faster rate.

In his own retrospective account, Khrushchev emphasised the same arguments. Also, while admitting that a German peace treaty would have represented a 'moral' victory for the socialist bloc, Khrushchev believed that greater material gains had been made without a treaty. A treaty, he argued, would have entailed concessions to the West, particularly with regard to the movement of people across the border. Khrushchev also believed that the Soviet Union had survived an important test of character. Commenting on the tense days in October 1961 when American and Soviet tanks squared up to each other at Checkpoint Charlie, he wrote: 'Thus the West had tested our nerve by prodding us with the barrels of their cannons and found us ready to accept their challenge. They learned that they couldn't frighten us. I think it was a great victory for us, and it was won without firing a single shot'.[40]

Hannes Adomeit attaches particular significance to Khrushchev's analysis that a victory had been won without recourse to open hostilities. Inferior in a strategic sense, the Soviet Union, by careful planning and by a determination not to be forced into retreat, had successfully taken unilateral action and presented the West with a *fait accompli*. If such were the conclusions drawn by Khrushchev from the Berlin crisis, Adomeit argues that they would go a long way towards explaining the origins of the Cuban missile crisis. John Erickson, a leading Western authority on the Soviet military, supports this view. He believes that the logistical preparation for the Cuban operation began in the autumn of 1961 when the Soviet Union began moving supplies, particularly of oil, to its Black Sea ports.[41]

Khrushchev did not remain in office long enough to take the credit for the part eventually played by the Berlin crisis in persuading the Western powers to adopt a more accommodating attitude towards the German problem. The crisis imposed an enormous strain on both leaders of the East-West divide. Kennedy, we are told, fought shy of having a book written about his first year in office because he felt it would be a story of one disaster after another. But the pressures on Khrushchev were much greater. Setbacks both at home and abroad had resulted in increasing criticism of his leadership. His agricultural reforms, upon which Khrushchev had staked his personal reputation, had failed to make good his 1957 boast that within five years the Soviet Union would overtake the United States in *per capita* production of milk, butter and meat. Abroad, coexistence had yet to produce tangible results and it had also split the communist world. Militarily, the United States already possessed a three-to-one superiority over the Soviet Union in intercontinental and submarine-launched ballistic missiles. Khrushchev realised that the first casualty of any Soviet attempt to close this new and more realistic version of the strategic missile gap would be the Soviet economy. A combination of these circumstances compelled Khrushchev to press ahead with his greatest gamble to date.

Although the Russians began planning the Cuban operation in 1961, it did not assume the proportions of a crisis in Washington until 14 October 1962 when a U-2 flight produced irrefutable evidence that missile installations were being constructed on Cuba. The crisis was broadcast to the world in a televised address by Kennedy on 22 October. The details of the drama need not be recounted. At issue here is the question of Khrushchev's motives. In his memoirs, Khrushchev claimed that in the aftermath of the Bay of Pigs the missiles were necessary to defend Cuba against another American-backed invasion. His reasoning was hardly convincing; 20,000 troops armed with conventional weapons would have sufficed for this purpose. The missiles, which were of intermediate-range, were intended by Khrushchev to kill several birds with one stone. Success in this venture would bring inestimable benefits. The United States' strategic superiority would be neutralised at a stroke because the Soviet Union would have missiles on Cuba, just 90 miles off the coast of Florida. The Soviet Union would be spared an expensive intercontinental missile programme. Khrushchev would be in a position to bargain over Berlin or over the question of American missile bases in Turkey. Finally, in personal terms, Khrushchev's prestige would be increased enormously. What better way of vindicating his policies and silencing his domestic and Chinese critics?[42] But the gamble did not pay off. When confronted by an American naval 'quarantine' (a euphemism for blockade), Khrushchev had to back down. The Soviet Union possessed neither the strategic nor the conventional means to force the issue. Amidst Chinese criticism that the Russians had been guilty of both 'adventurism' and 'capitulationism',[43] it was cold comfort for Khrushchev to be informed by Kennedy that in future the United States would respect the independence of Castro's Cuba.

In the aftermath of the missile crisis, when the United States and the Soviet Union had come closer than ever to war, saner counsels prevailed. Two positive agreements were reached. In June 1963 the Hot Line was established, linking by telex the Kremlin and the White House. In August 1963 the United States and the Soviet Union, together with Britain, a junior third party in the nuclear club, initialled a Test Ban Treaty prohibiting the testing of nuclear weapons in the atmosphere, outer space and underwater but permitting continued underground testing. Both agreements, but particularly the Test Ban Treaty, were based on the assumption that the search for a safer world had, of necessity, to be led by the United States and the Soviet Union.

This concept of bipolarity implied that the respective allies of the two most powerful countries in the world would continue to play a subordinate role. But in fact, the missile crisis and the Test Ban Treaty added further fuel to controversies which were already threatening to fragment both Eastern and Western blocs. It was not only the Soviet Union that found its leadership under challenge. In Europe, France, aided and abetted by West Germany, was beginning to assert a degree of independence from the United States. The result was a gradual weakening of the two blocs and a significant shift away from bipolarity. In the long-term, as we shall see in the next chapter, détente in Europe was made possible as a result of new initiatives taken by one of the subordinate allies of the Western alliance.

The controversy in the West initially revolved, as had so many in the past, around the question of West Germany's military contribution to NATO. Since 1955 it had become clear that Bonn would not be able to fulfil the promise made by Theodor Blank, Adenauer's first Defence Minister, that West Germany would provide 500,000 men. Blank's successor, Franz-Josef Strauss, the bombastic leader of the Christian Social Union, the ruling party in Bavaria, argued instead that West Germany should be given part control of an allied nuclear force. He made it clear that he was not suggesting that West Germany should become an independent nuclear power like Britain. He did, however, argue that West Germany should not be left in a position of permanent inferiority in the alliance and he also maintained that the American deterrent would be that much more effective if it were linked to a nuclear force under a high degree of European control.

Although supported by General Norstad, the American Supreme Allied Commander in Europe at the end of the Eisenhower administration, Strauss's arguments did not find favour with Robert McNamara, Kennedy's Defence Secretary. McNamara maintained that NATO's nuclear deterrent should be kept under unified, in other words American, control. McNamara's views fell foul, not only of Strauss but also of de Gaulle. The missile crisis over Cuba rekindled de Gaulle's worst fears about the United States. He resented the manner in which he had simply been kept informed and not consulted by the Kennedy administration. Officials in Paris now feared that the United States might drag the European allies into a nuclear exchange without consulting them. De Gaulle therefore argued in favour of a joint NATO directorate for control of military strategy. Failing this, he was determined that France should have its own nuclear deterrent.

Matters came to a head at the end of 1962. Following Washington's cancellation of the Skybolt missile upon which Britain had intended to base its own nuclear strike force, Macmillan met Kennedy at Nassau in December 1962 and accepted as a replacement American Polaris missiles which could be launched from British-built submarines. A similar American offer to Paris was scornfully rejected by de Gaulle who had no desire to see France become dependent upon the United States for its missiles. For de Gaulle, the solution to the cancellation of Skybolt should have been a Franco-British effort to develop a European deterrent. Macmillan's acceptance of Polaris convinced him that in a crisis Britain would always support Washington. Having already withdrawn the French Mediterranean fleet from NATO command in March 1959, de Gaulle was now determined to press ahead with the development of a French *force de frappe*. He retaliated against the Nassau agreement in three ways. First, in January 1963, he vetoed Britain's entry into the European Economic Community. De Gaulle believed that Britain's membership of the Common Market would be a superficial veneer to maintain American influence in Western Europe. Secondly, again in January 1963, he negotiated with Adenauer a Franco-German Treaty of Friendship and Cooperation. This for de Gaulle was to be the beginning of a truly independent Europe. Finally, like China, he refused to sign the Test Ban Treaty. France's treaty with West Germany undermined Kennedy's 'grand design' for Europe which envisaged a degree of European interdependence while preserving overall American leadership of the Western alliance. Having been forced to resign in the autumn of 1962 over the manner in which he had attempted to stop criticism of himself in *Der Spiegel*, the West German news magazine, Strauss was no longer in office. Nonetheless, with Adenauer supporting de Gaulle over the Berlin and Cuban crises, Washington was now concerned that a German version of Gaullism might emerge and demand a German national nuclear force. To counter this possibility the United States proposed the creation of a multilateral nuclear force (MLF), the very idea of which McNamara had previously rejected. It would be owned and managed by those NATO countries which wanted to participate. The MLF never got off the ground. France regarded it as a yet further attempt to maintain American domination of the alliance. Britain was content to rely on its own Polaris submarines. Looking increasingly like a bilateral arrangement between Washington and Bonn, President Johnson, Kennedy's successor decided to shelve it. Western Europe, as even de Gaulle was aware, remained heavily dependent on the American nuclear deterrent for its defence against the Soviet Union. But the points on the political compass had shifted decisively. It could no longer be assumed that American and West European interests would always converge.[44]

In the East, the Test Ban Treaty landed Khrushchev in hot water with the Chinese who regarded the agreement as the ultimate sellout. In June 1963 Beijing had published a 25 point indictment of the Soviet Communist Party. In July, as the Test Ban Treaty was being negotiated, a Chinese delegation visited Moscow to discuss ideology. By now incensed with China's opposition, Khrushchev was determined to go ahead with the treaty irrespective of Beijing's views. When members of the delegation began distributing Maoist leaflets they were ordered to leave Moscow.[45] The Sino-Soviet breach had become public property. In January 1964 France recognised the People's Republic, a considerable diplomatic coup for Beijing and a blow for Khrushchev. In order to exploit the widening gulf between de Gaulle and Washington, Khrushchev had been prepared to withhold recognition from the radical provisional government of Ferhat Abbas in Algeria. China's recognition of the Abbas government in 1964 was a considerable embarrassment for the Soviet Union because it had to follow suit. Khrushchev's difficulties reached their inexorable climax in October 1964. Summoned to attend a Presidium meeting from his Black Sea vacation, Khrushchev was unable to repeat the tactics which had saved him in 1957. The conspirators against him had done their homework and he was dismissed. On 14 October Leonid Brezhnev became First Secretary. A day later Alexei Kosygin became prime minister. On 16 October, having already made it clear that they would not sign the Test Ban Treaty, the Chinese successfully tested an atomic bomb.

THE KHRUSHCHEV ERA: AN ASSESSMENT

Khrushchev's downfall in October 1964 can be attributed to his failures in domestic and foreign policy. In foreign policy, the Soviet Union had been humiliated at the time of the missile crisis, coexistence had yielded only the Hot Line Agreement and the Test Ban Treaty, and the communist monolith under Soviet control and leadership had been shattered. In Europe, certain Eastern bloc countries began to take advantage of the Sino-Soviet rift to assert their independence. By

1964, Romania and Albania, in addition to Yugoslavia, were no longer reliable from the Soviet point of view. Elsewhere, 1963 saw the beginning of the development of pro-Chinese splinter communist parties in countries such as Belgium, Ceylon (now Sri Lanka), Australia, Peru and India, while some major communist parties, such as the Indonesian one, took up the Chinese stance in the Sino-Soviet dispute.[46] By 1963–64, anyone who talked about a monolithic communist threat was discussing a world that no longer existed.

In domestic affairs, the new Soviet leadership made some important changes after 1964. Khrushchev's more 'liberal' policies were abandoned in favour of a return to communist orthodoxy. In economic terms, this meant an end to decentralisation and a return to an economic strategy based upon centralised planning. In foreign policy, the new leadership made an attempt to repair the breach with China. In February 1965 Kosygin visited Beijing but the Chinese terms for a reconciliation were unacceptable. One reason for this was that the Soviet leadership was still interested in agreements with the West about European security and limiting nuclear weapons. In other words, from the Soviet point of view, Khrushchev had failed but his policy objectives were still valid. But an important qualification should be noted. The Soviet military build-up can be traced to the postmortems which inevitably followed the Cuban confrontation. Without the appropriate military strength, the Soviet Union would never be able to compete on equal terms with the United States or make its influence felt on a global basis. For Brezhnev and Kosygin, therefore, negotiations to limit the growth of nuclear weapons could only begin in earnest when the Soviet Union was within sight of strategic parity with the United States. This military consideration, together with the growing American involvement in Vietnam, meant that the dialogue between the United States and the Soviet Union could not be resumed immediately after Khrushchev's downfall.

4 A Decade of Detente 1966–76

AT first glance, the mid-to-late 60s present a picture of unremitting international conflict and tension. Dominated by the war in Vietnam, these years also witnessed major conflicts on the Indian subcontinent between India and Pakistan in 1965 and in the Middle East between Israel and three of her Arab neighbours in 1967. The Cultural Revolution, a renewed bout of communist self-examination which was launched in 1966, plunged China into turmoil and left Beijing isolated from the outside world, its foreign policy scarcely recognisable. The war of words between China and the Soviet Union escalated into serious border clashes in 1969. In Eastern Europe, an attempt to liberalise the communist regime in Czechoslovakia was ruthlessly crushed when, following the pattern of East Berlin in 1953 and Budapest in 1956, Soviet tanks appeared on the streets of Prague in August 1968. At the beginning of the 80s such a constellation of forces would have been more or less guaranteed to find politicians and analysts alike on both sides of the East-West divide dusting down their Cold War dictionaries. At the time, however, the reverse was the case. The tensions and conflicts sowed the seeds of détente. Détente emerged first in Europe. The groundwork was laid by President de Gaulle of France and then, on a more lasting basis, by the West German *Ostpolitik*. It was subsequently elevated to the international level, embracing the United States, the Soviet Union and China. In this chapter we shall look first at the emergence of détente through Gaullism and the *Ostpolitik* and through the policies of the superpowers and China. We shall then consider what détente achieved and what its limitations were.

GAULLISM AND THE *OSTPOLITIK*

Konrad Adenauer resigned as Chancellor of the Federal Republic in October 1963. His resignation occurred at a time when the ruling Christian Democrats were divided over the question of the Federal

Republic's external alignment. Adenauer himself, who remained an influential figure as chairman of the Christian Democrats, together with Franz-Josef Strauss, the former Defence Minister, headed a 'Gaullist' faction which maintained that Europe should become a third force in world affairs, independent of the United States. Having freed France of the burden of the Algerian war in the summer of 1962, de Gaulle was now anxious to restore France to what he regarded as her rightful role as a major European power. He refused to accept the prevailing assumption that the responsibility for easing the tensions and negotiating the agreements which were necessary to make the world a safer place devolved exclusively on the United States and the Soviet Union. Aware that he could not entirely eliminate American-Soviet influence within Europe, de Gaulle sought nonetheless to reduce it as much as possible. For the West Europeans, this would mean reducing their dependence on the United States. With this aim in view, in 1966, the year in which he made a much-publicised visit to Moscow, de Gaulle ordered France's withdrawal from the military wing of NATO. In consequence both the military and political headquarters of NATO were transferred from Paris to Brussels. De Gaulle's vision of a Europe liberated from the bloc-mentality of the Cold War stretched, in his own words, 'from the Atlantic to the Urals'. He saw the ending of Franco-German enmity as the essential prerequisite for the fulfillment of his grand design. Hence the simultaneous veto of Britain's entry into the European Economic Community and the negotiation of the Friendship Treaty with West Germany at the beginning of 1963.[1] Adenauer shared some of de Gaulle's doubts about American reliability. Moreover, as a Catholic and a Rhinelander possessing thereby a closer cultural affinity with Paris than with Berlin or East Germany, Adenauer was attracted by de Gaulle's vision of a new and independent Europe based upon friendship and cooperation between France and West Germany.

In opposition to Adenauer's outlook stood Dr Ludwig Erhard, Adenauer's successor as Chancellor, and Dr Gerhard Schröder, Erhard's Foreign Minister. Erhard and Schröder led an 'Atlanticist' faction which wanted a foreign policy based firmly upon the Western alliance. Assuming the position adopted by Adenauer in the mid-50s, the Atlanticists maintained that American influence in Europe was an essential guarantee of both West German and West European security. Erhard and Schröder favoured some improvement in relations with Eastern Europe. In an effort to take the sting out of

Gaullism, a strategy of bridge-building was being advocated on the other side of the Atlantic, first by Kennedy and then by Johnson. In consequence the Federal Republic opened trade missions in Poland and Romania in September and October 1963. In December 1963, agreement was reached with the East German government on Christmas visits to East Berlin by West Berliners. In July and October 1964 further trade missions were opened in Hungary and Bulgaria. Schröder described this policy as one of 'small steps' in the direction of a more flexible West German attitude towards Eastern Europe. But there was no question as yet of abandoning the Hallstein Doctrine. Hence the opening of trade missions instead of embassies.[2]

The year 1966 marked a watershed in West German politics. For the first time the Social Democrat entered the government in coalition with the Christian Democrats. Willy Brandt, the leader of the SPD, became Vice-Chancellor and Foreign Minister of a new government led by Kurt Kiesinger. The price which Kiesinger had to pay for SPD support was the sacrifice of a number of CDU sacred cows, the most notable being policy towards Eastern Europe. With his youthful and progressive Kennedy-image, Brandt, a former mayor of West Berlin, believed the time had arrived to place West Germany's relations with Eastern Europe on a more realistic footing. In a memorandum written in August 1964 and published at the beginning of the following year in the *Frankfurter Allgemeine Zeitung*, Brandt argued that it was in Western interests to support what limited independence the countries of Eastern Europe possessed. Such a policy, while respecting the military and ideological ties which bound together the countries of the Eastern bloc, should concentrate on building economic and cultural links. To promote more human contact between East and West was a desirable end in itself but particularly important for West Germany. Brandt's memorandum stopped short of advocating recognition of East Germany as an independent state. It did, however, express the hope that increased contact between East and West in Europe would also extend to what West Germany still described as the 'Soviet zone' of Germany.[3] Implicit in Brandt's argument was the recognition that the Hallstein Doctrine hindered rather than aided the freedom of manoeuvre of both West Germany and the countries of Eastern Europe. Hence it was set aside. In 1967 the Federal Republic opened diplomatic relations with Romania and in 1968 diplomatic relations were established with Yugoslavia.

Brandt's view that it was necessary to improve relations with

Eastern Europe was accepted by the Western alliance as a whole. In December 1967 NATO replaced the strategy of 'massive retaliation' with one of 'flexible response'. In the event of Soviet aggression in Europe, the new strategy was designed to enable NATO to respond at an appropriate level on an escalating military scale. No longer would it be necessary to rely at the outset on an irretrievable strategic response. Instead, conventional forces would be used first, followed by theatre-based or intermediate nuclear weapons and then, as a last resort, by strategic or intercontinental nuclear weapons. Flexible response posed special problems for West Germany. It envisaged a scenario in which Soviet aggression would be well-advanced before strategic weapons were brought into play. West Germany would bear the brunt of the Soviet attack. Its cities would either be destroyed or occupied by Soviet forces. NATO acknowledged this problem by adopting the recommendations of the Harmel Report, again in December 1967. The work of a committee of experts under the chairmanship of Pierre Harmel, the Belgian Foreign Minister, the report maintained that the purposes of the Western alliance included not only military defence but also détente with the countries of the Warsaw Pact.[4] NATO as a whole therefore recognised the importance of reducing the possibility of a war in Europe which would engulf West Germany as its first victim.

The Warsaw Pact invasion of Czechoslovakia in August 1968 did not deflect the West from this objective. Under the popular leadership of Alexander Dubček, who replaced Antonin Novotny as First Secretary of the Czech Communist Party in January 1968, Czechoslovakia enjoyed a brief 'Prague Spring' in which freedom of speech flourished as part of a campaign to present 'socialism with a human face'. The leaders of neighbouring Poland and East Germany feared that the Czech experiment might become infectious. Hence Moscow was faced with a potential 'domino' situation of its own in Eastern Europe. Pressure was brought to bear almost immediately on Dubček to change course. That the invasion was delayed until August suggested a division of opinion within the Soviet leadership. The West roundly condemned the invasion and the subsequent 'Brezhnev Doctrine' of 'Limited Sovereignty' which was used to justify it. Speaking at a Congress of the Polish Party in November 1968, Brezhnev declared:

When internal and external forces, hostile to socialism, seek to reverse the development of any socialist country whatsoever in the direction of the restoration of the capitalist order, when a threat to the cause of socialism arises in that country, a threat to the security of the socialist commonwealth as a whole – this already becomes not only a problem of the people of the country concerned, but also a common problem and the concern of all socialist countries.[5]

But as in the cases of East Germany in 1953 and Hungary in 1956, the West confined its condemnation of the invasion to verbal protests. Western leaders recognised that they had no alternative but to accept the division of Europe if they wanted to make it less harsh in the long term.

This was certainly the view of Willy Brandt who became the Chancellor of a coalition between his own Social Democrats and the Free Democrats (FDP) as a result of the West German election in 1969. Upon the basis of a slender majority in the *Bundestag* (one of only twelve seats), Brandt resolved to press ahead with his *Ostpolitik* or Eastern policy.[6] The *Ostpolitik* was a pragmatic strategy based on the realisation that West Germany had to balance two key factors in devising its foreign policy. First, for its defence and national security, the Federal Republic had to look west to the NATO alliance. Secondly, to ensure that it remained out of the firing line, and also to promote greater economic and human contacts, the Federal Republic had to look east to the Eastern bloc and in particular to the governments of the Soviet Union and East Germany. To the West Germans, peace in Europe could be preserved only if both sides had a vested interest in maintaining it. It became the principal task of the *Ostpolitik* to construct such vested interests.

Brandt was not prepared to abandon the West German ideal that one day it might be possible to reunite the two halves of Germany. Domestic political considerations as much as his own personal views dictated his stand on this issue. The Preamble to the Basic Law of 1949, which to this day constitutes the West German constitution, asserts that the Law will remain in force until Germany is reunited. For a West German leader to contemplate amending the Basic Law would mean almost certain political suicide. However, Brandt was prepared to go further than the leader of any previous West German government in acknowledging the post-war divisions of both Germany and Europe. In return, he anticipated that West Germany would gain in three ways. First, in terms of defence and security, by ending the chronic East-West crises over Berlin. Secondly, in terms of economic relations, by extending the trading links with Eastern Europe which had been established in the early 60s. The value of West Germany's exports to East Germany had risen from 228.4 million dollars in 1960 to 584.1 million dollars in 1969. Over the same period, West Germany's exports to Poland had risen from 72.1 to 157.2 million dollars, to Czechoslovakia from 65.2 to 210.7 million and to the Soviet Union from 185.3 to 405.7 million.[7] Between 1958 and 1969, only Britain of the other countries of Western Europe enjoyed a greater volume of trade with the countries of the East. This was largely because Britain was not subject to the same agricultural import restrictions which had been agreed by member states of the European Economic Community. In this respect, the position changed dramatically in West Germany's favour after Britain's entry into the EEC in 1972. All East European countries ran up trade deficits with West Germany, despite an overall increase in the value of their own exports to the Federal Republic. For Brandt, however, the political benefits of trade outweighed any considerations of indebtedness and the Chancellor never hesitated to authorise fresh and cheap loans as and when they were required by West Germany's trading partners in the East. Finally, Brandt anticipated that West Germany would gain in humanitarian terms through increased East-West contacts. The continuing importance of this to the West Germans cannot be overstated. They were, and still are to a large extent, estranged from their seventeen million fellow-countrymen and women in East Germany. There are also thousands of Germans still living in Poland and the Soviet Union. But the position had improved during the 60s. From 1964, the East German government had permitted 4-week visits by East German pensioners (women over 60 and men over 65) to their relatives in West Germany. According to West German statistics, over six million such visits had taken place in the period down to 1969 although clearly many of the people involved were making the same trip several times. During the same period, over 100,000 East Germans travelled to West Germany for business trips, scientific and cultural conferences and sporting exchanges. Between 1967 and 1969 over one million West Germans visited East Germany although West Berliners were allowed only occasional holidays.[8] The maintenance and extension of these contacts have remained priorities for successive governments in Bonn.

Brandt launched his *Ostpolitik* in the autumn of 1969 by outlining the principles upon which West Germany was prepared to negotiate treaties with Poland and the Soviet Union. Force would be renounced as a means of settling disputes. The territorial integrity of the countries involved would be respected – an implicit offer on Brandt's part to recognise the Oder-Neisse line as Poland's eastern frontier. Finally, assurances would be given about non-interference in the domestic affairs or the alliance relationships of the opposite side. At the same time, Brandt offered to establish a dialogue with East Germany on the basis of equal rights. He also offered a trade agreement to Czechoslovakia and compensation for the victims of Nazi persecution. In order to demonstrate to the Eastern bloc that West Germany's intentions were peaceful, Brandt signed the Non-Proliferation Treaty in November 1969. The treaty had been negotiated by the United States, the Soviet Union and Britain in July 1968. They pledged themselves not to transfer nuclear weapons to other countries or to assist other countries in the manufacture of nuclear weapons.

Brandt's initiatives met with a mixed response in Eastern Europe. After the hiatus over the invasion of Czechoslovakia, the reaction in Poland and the Soviet Union was favourable. West German readiness to recognise the Oder-Neisse line and the prospect of increased trade with the country possessing the strongest economy in Western Europe were welcomed by the governments in Warsaw and Moscow. However, the response from East Germany was one of caution and suspicion. East Germany had its own equivalent of the *Ostpolitik* – a *Westpolitik* or Western policy. Ulbricht, the party leader, argued that West Germany should first extend full diplomatic recognition to the German Democratic Republic before there could be any genuine détente.[9] This position had in fact been adopted at a conference of European communist parties which convened at Karlovy Vary in Czechoslovakia in April 1967 to discuss problems of European security. At the time, West Germany had just opened diplomatic relations with Romania and Moscow was clearly on its guard against any attempt by the Federal Republic to drive a wedge into its Eastern glacis.[10] Brandt, however, was not prepared to extend full diplomatic recognition to East Germany. His nearest approach was to propose the formula that Germany consisted of 'two states within one nation'.[11] This did not satisfy Ulbricht but the East Germans agreed to negotiate. In March 1970 an historic meeting took place at Erfurt in East Germany between the two German heads of government – Brandt and Willi Stoph, the East German prime minister. To the embarrassment of his hosts, Brandt was greeted by large crowds of enthusiastically cheering East Germans. The talks were conducted in a sombre atmosphere and achieved little beyond an agreed date for a further meeting which took place at Kassel in the Federal Republic in May 1970. The importance of these meetings lay not in what was discussed but in the fact that they took place. Although the East Germans were reluctant to talk the meetings indicated they were prepared to do so under obvious Soviet pressure.

In August 1970, Brandt visited Moscow and signed a Non-Aggression Treaty between West Germany and the Soviet Union. In December 1970, he visited Warsaw and signed a similar treaty with Poland which included West German recognition of the Oder-Neisse line.[12] There remained the problem of East Germany. Aware that Ulbricht represented an obstacle to further progress in improving relations in Europe, Moscow engineered his dismissal in May 1971. He was replaced by Erich Honecker, a man more likely to follow Moscow's wishes. Ulbricht's departure paved the way for a series of agreements on Berlin and Germany. The Quadripartite Agreement of September 1971 confirmed as unchanged the individual and joint rights and responsibilities of the four occupying powers. The Agreement conceded the Soviet argument that West Berlin was not part of West Germany but also confirmed the Western view that the city should have close links with the Federal Republic. Separate agreements on transit rights were reached between the two German governments. These were highly technical and complex matters. Egon Bahr, Brandt's chief negotiator, and Michael Kohl, his East German counterpart, had over 70 meetings between November 1970 and December 1972 before they reached agreement on transit traffic between West Germany and West Berlin and travel and visitors' traffic between West Berlin and East Germany.[13] These agreements improved the position for West Berliners by making it easier for them to travel to East Germany to visit their relatives. The framework for the conduct of future intra-German relations was established in a Basic Treaty which was signed by the two Germanies in December 1972. It provided for 'good neighbourly' relations through increased trade and increased cultural and personal contacts and through mutual respect for the frontiers and alliance obligations of both signatories. When the treaty was signed, Bonn sent a letter to the East German government stating that the treaty did not conflict 'with the political aim of the Federal Republic of Germany to work for a state of peace in Europe in which the German nation will regain its unity through free self-determination'.[14] Within nine months, both Germanies had been admitted to the United Nations and, at the end of 1973, the remaining gaps in Bonn's new relationship with Eastern Europe were filled when West Germany signed a treaty with Czechoslovakia, declaring void the Munich Agreement of 1938, and then established diplomatic relations with Bulgaria and Hungary.

The *Ostpolitik* was pursued in the face of vigorous and at times bitter criticism from the CDU opposition within the Federal Republic. The opposition argued that Brandt had conceded too much and they found it difficult to accept the Chancellor's view that, in the long-term, West Germany would benefit from improved relations with the Eastern bloc. The charge was made that the reconciliation with East Germany was unconstitutional in the sense that it legitimised the government in East Berlin and thus made the achievement of self-determination more difficult. In 1970 the defection of three Free Democrats reduced Brandt's majority from twelve to six and it was not until May 1972 that the *Bundestag* ratified the Chancellor's treaties with the Soviet Union and Poland. The West German election of November 1972, the first premature election in the history of the Federal Republic, was dominated almost entirely by the issues raised by the *Ostpolitik*. The result, however, recorded an overwhelming majority in favour of Brandt's diplomacy.

The significance of the *Ostpolitik* is that it represented the first concrete steps towards détente in Europe. It opened the way for a whole series of agreements on European Security and Cooperation, the first round of talks on which began at Helsinki in July 1972. Much of the credit rests with Brandt and Egon Bahr. However, the *Ostpolitik* should not be viewed in isolation. It succeeded to the extent that it did because the United States and the Soviet Union had begun to reappraise their own positions and policies. Without support from Washington and Moscow, the four-power agreement on Berlin would not have been possible. In order therefore to place the *Ostpolitik* in context, it is necessary to examine the changing perceptions of the United States and the Soviet Union.

AMERICAN *REALPOLITIK*: NIXON AND KISSINGER

American foreign policy in the mid-and late-60s was dominated by the war in Vietnam.[15] Under Lyndon Johnson, Kennedy's successor, American support for South Vietnam escalated from the provision of military advisers to a full-scale military commitment. Bombing raids against North Vietnam began in 1965. By 1968 there were nearly 550,000 American combat troops in South Vietnam. The crucial turning-point, and one which precipitated the beginning of the American withdrawal, occurred in January and February 1968. During the Buddhist festival of Tet, the South Vietnamese communists, known now as the Vietcong, launched a major offensive in the South. During a four-week onslaught, when even major cities such as Hué and Saigon came under attack, the Vietcong lost nearly 50,000 men. But a military defeat was turned into a psychological victory for the communists. The scale of the Tet offensive, and the sacrifice involved, exploded the myth of American invincibility. In America itself, as Henry Kissinger observed, 'Public support was ebbing for a war we could not win but also seemed unable to end'.[16] Johnson decided to quit. In March 1968 he ordered a partial halt to the bombing of North Vietnam. In May, tentative peace talks with representatives from Hanoi began in Paris. At the same time Johnson announced that he would not stand as a candidate in the November presidential elections. Set against the background of mounting and increasingly violent opposition to the war on university campuses in America, Vietnam seemed to be indicative of a deep malaise in American society. Richard Nixon, the new Republican president, recognised this upon entering the White House. He knew also that Vietnam was a bottomless pit draining vital resources. Together with Henry Kissinger, his National Security Adviser who became his Secretary of State in 1973, Nixon resolved to end the war –'peace with honour' were the words he used – in order to reverse the decline of American morale and prestige. Nixon and Kissinger were both secretive, suspicious, egocentric and power-orientated. Under their influence and guidance America moved towards its first attempt at global accommodation with countries previously regarded as sworn enemies.

The erosion of America's economic and military superiority, which had formed the basis of America's omnipotence in international affairs since the end of the Second World War, was the principal consideration which prompted Nixon and Kissinger to reassess the aims and methods of American foreign policy. Between 1964 and 1972 America had switched from a 7 billion dollar trade surplus to a 7 billion dollar trade deficit. The overall balance of payments deficit, which averaged 1.5 billion dollars in the late 50s, had risen to 8 billion dollars by 1970 and to 30 billion dollars by 1971. The cost of oil imports was one cause of this decline. America itself produced 11.2 million barrels of

oil per day but consumed 17.4 million. Other causes were the cost of
the war in Vietnam and increased economic competition from America's allies in Europe and Japan. In consequence the dollar came under
pressure. At the end of the 60s, there was a rush to convert dollars
either into gold (the value of the dollar had been fixed in terms of
gold at Bretton Woods in 1944) or into the stronger Deutschemark or
Japanese yen. For some time de Gaulle had been exchanging every
35 dollars in his reserves for an ounce of gold, arguing in justification
that he did not trust the dollar because America's balance of payments
was so deeply in the red. To halt the decline of the dollar and to
remedy the balance of payments deficit, Nixon took an economic
decision in August 1971 for political reasons. Anxious for re-election
at the November 1972 presidential election, Nixon was determined
not to raise taxes. Instead he imposed severe import controls and
suspended dollar convertibility. The dollar itself was not revalued;
instead other countries were obliged to revalue their currencies in
relation to it. Nixon's economic package, and particularly the brusque
manner in which it was implemented, came as a shock to America's
allies in both Europe and the Far East. Japan, enjoying a four billion
dollar trade surplus with America alone, suddenly found the yen
forced up almost 20 per cent in value.[17]

The relative decline of American power was not confined to the
economic sphere. The military omnipotence enjoyed by the United
States since 1945 was rapidly becoming a thing of the past. As the
following figures demonstrate, Washington entered the 70s facing
major changes in the nuclear balance:[18]

		1964	1966	1968	1970	1972	1974
USA	ICBM	834	904	1054	1054	1054	1054
	SLBM	416	592	656	656	656	656
	LR Bombers	630	630	545	550	455	437
USSR	ICBM	200	300	800	1300	1527	1575
	SLBM	120	125	130	280	560	720
	IC Bombers	190	200	150	150	140	140

The apparent Soviet gains are misleading. The figures take no account
of warheads or the development of new weapons systems. In both
areas the United States had a clear superiority. One of the main aims
of the détente strategy of Nixon and Kissinger was the preservation

of this superiority in an arms control agreement with the Soviet Union.

In conventional terms, the war in Vietnam demonstrated that America was overextended in its global commitments. Nixon therefore decided that America's role as the 'world policeman' would have to be scaled down in the future. The new president served notice of America's intentions with the Nixon Doctrine of July 1969. America would use air and naval power to fulfil its treaty commitments in the Western Pacific, but henceforth Asian troops would have to carry the burden as Americans withdrew from the mainland. Next, Nixon introduced the concept of 'Vietnamisation' – training South Vietnamese troops to defend themselves while American forces returned home. From 1969 to mid-1972, American troops in Vietnam were reduced from 550,000 to 50,000.[19] The withdrawal, however, exposed the central problem of Vietnamisation. The regime in South Vietnam grew weaker as it lost the essential American military protection. Consequently, in 1969, Washington authorised secret bombing raids against Vietcong sanctuaries in the neighbouring regions of Eastern Cambodia. In 1970, the United States connived at the coup which overthrew the neutralist Cambodian government of Prince Sihanouk and installed in its place the pro-American military regime of Marshal Lon Nol. In their efforts to end the war, Nixon and Kissinger had in fact escalated it.[20]

But it was not only secrecy which made an escalation of the war possible. Nixon and Kissinger viewed the triangular game of relations between America, Russia and China as the diplomatic means by which the United States could extricate itself from Vietnam with a minimum loss of face. The American opening to China in 1971–72 (Kissinger's secret visit to Beijing in July 1971 paved the way for Nixon's state visit in February 1972) was designed to isolate and put pressure on Hanoi. It was assumed that Beijing would stop supporting the North Vietnamese because of its fear of Moscow. Sino-Soviet border clashes in 1969 had been followed by rumours that the Russians were contemplating a preemptive strike against China. If Beijing needed a Sino-American dialogue to ward off the Russians, there was every reason to believe that the Chinese would be prepared to pay the American price over Vietnam. Similarly, it was assumed that the prospect of a Sino-American rapprochement would be sufficient to persuade Moscow to refrain from aiding Hanoi. A repeat of the 1954 Geneva conference scenario was thus on the cards. Hanoi would have no alternative but to accept a cease-fire agreement backed by the two communist giants. Meanwhile, with both Moscow and Beijing competing for American favour, they would be unlikely to oppose America's own escalatory moves which were designed to bring a speedy conclusion to the war in Vietnam.[21]

Kissinger had written a book and several articles on European diplomacy in the nineteenth century. His aim had been to understand the processes which had enabled post-Napoleonic Europe to establish a peace that lasted for nearly a century. He attributed this to the classic notion of a balance of power. Denying that the strategies or designs of previous periods could be literally applied to a different age, Kissinger nonetheless admitted that he entered office convinced that the past could teach some important lessons. 'If history teaches anything', he wrote in the first of his two-volume memoirs, 'it is that there can be no peace without equilibrium and no justice without restraint'.[22] But the United States had yet to come to terms with what Kissinger regarded as these self-evident truths. He discerned in American foreign policy an idealistic tradition which viewed international relations as a contest between good and evil. There was also a pragmatic tradition which sought to resolve problems as and when they arose. There was even a legalistic tradition which treated international issues as juridical cases. But there was no geopolitical tradition which sought to base American foreign policy on a 'sober perception of permanent national interest'. In the past, America's participation in the world had oscillated between the extremes of 'overinvolvement and withdrawal . . . between optimistic exuberance and frustration with the ambiguities of an imperfect world'. Equally, Americans had yet to come to terms with the fact that American power, while vast, also had its limits. As Vietnam demonstrated, American resources were no longer infinite in relation to America's problems. Priorities had to be set, 'both intellectual and material'. In the 50s and 60s the United States had attempted 'ultimate solutions to specific problems'. The challenge now, according to Kissinger, was to 'shape a world and an American role to which we were permanently committed, which could no longer be sustained by the illusion that our exertions had a terminal point'.[23] This new age of realism had implications for the traditional values and principles which Americans held so dear. The ideals of democracy and freedom would still 'inspire our efforts and set our direction' but Americans would have to learn to reconcile themselves to 'imperfect choices' and 'partial fulfilment'.

In the nuclear age especially, diplomacy involved the compromise of clashing principles. As Kissinger wrote in the second volume of his memoirs: 'Diplomacy may be, in Clausewitz's terms, the continuation of war by other means, but it has its own appropriate tactics. It acknowledges that in the relations between sovereign states, even the noblest ends can generally be achieved only in imperfect stages. Prophets are needed to raise sights; yet the statesman cannot always live by their principles'.[24]

The opening to China and the SALT negotiations with the Soviet Union were two examples of the new balance of power *Realpolitik* in American foreign policy. Kissinger and Nixon had not, as some of their critics later charged, abandoned containment. Instead, they had refined it.[25] Writing in the second volume of his memoirs, Kissinger rejected the view that the United States could fulfil its aims 'either in an apocalyptic showdown or in a final reconciliation'. 'Détente', he wrote, 'was built on the twin pillars of resistance to Soviet expansionism and a willingness to negotiate on concrete issues, on the concept of deterrence and a readiness to explore the principles of coexistence'.[26] Kissinger believed that the threat posed by Soviet Union was one of 'ruthless opportunism'. Confident that the flow of history was on their side, the Russians sought to 'promote the attrition of adversaries by gradual increments, not to stake everything on a single throw of the dice'.[27] To curb their adventurism, Kissinger wanted to lock the Russians into a collaborative pattern of international behaviour which would give them a vested interest in maintaining the status quo. This was to be achieved through linkage, essentially an old-fashioned carrot and stick approach.[28] There would be penalties for adventurism and rewards for responsible behaviour. Trade agreements, arms limitation, technology transfers and credit arrangements were the means by which the White House assumed it might be possible to induce the Kremlin to forswear its allegiance to what the Americans regarded as destabilising national liberation movements.

Kissinger's grand strategic scenario was flawed in many respects, not least in its assumption that relationships between the major powers were all that mattered and that the countries of the Third World were significant only to the extent that they could be manipulated by the countries of the First. It was equally flawed in its assumption that the Soviet Union was ready for global accomodation on American terms. Détente for the Russians meant something quite different.

THE SOVIET PERCEPTION OF DETENTE

In a military sense, it was particularly important to the Soviet Union that the arms race should be stabilised. Virtually defenceless against an American first strike since the end of the Second World War, the Russians now commanded what seemed to be strategic parity with the United States. The growth of the Soviet nuclear arsenal, together with the development of Soviet conventional forces and the emergence of the Soviet navy, were all a direct consequence of the Cuban missile crisis. But such a concerted effort had important consequences for the domestic economy. According to one estimate, Soviet defence expenditure for the year 1969–70 was the equivalent of 53 billion dollars, while the United States, with a gross national product (GNP) over twice that of the Soviet Union, spent an estimated 78 billion dollars on defence of which 25–30 billions were attributable to the Vietnam war. At the same time the Soviet GNP had actually declined, from a growth rate of 6.4 per cent in 1958, to 5.3 per cent in 1967, to 3.7 per cent in 1973.[29] A high level of military expenditure was not the only reason for the economic difficulties of the Soviet Union but it did mean that both the agricultural sector and the consumer industries had been starved of investment. The leaders in the Kremlin were thus faced with an awkward decision. To sit back and do nothing was to court disaster. In neighbouring Poland, economic mismanagement had produced food shortages and high prices which in turn led to riots in the Baltic cities and ultimately, in 1970, to the replacement of Gomulka by Edward Gierek. To embark on a root and branch reform of the Soviet economy, decentralising industrial management and introducing incentive schemes, was hardly likely to commend itself to such an orthodox and essentially conservative team as that of Brezhnev and Kosygin. Fortunately, a third option suggested itself. Stepping up trade with the West would enable the Soviet Union to compensate for its domestic shortcomings by obtaining credits from Western banks, surplus grain from the farmers of the American midwest and Western technology and management techniques. Furthermore, the growth of foreign trade would provide the right climate for an agreement to check the growth of nuclear weapons. This in turn would spare the Soviet Union the cost of an unrestrained arms race and thus enable it to divert scarce resources to the agricultural and consumer sectors of the Soviet economy.

Above and beyond questions of the military balance and the

performance of the Soviet economy, two further considerations influenced the Russians when they embraced détente. The first was strategic. Soviet policies in relation to West Germany were designed to pull the Federal Republic towards neutrality and eventually perhaps still closer relations with Moscow. Although they acknowledged that the Federal Republic belonged to the West, the Russians emphasised that Moscow was Germany's natural and historic economic partner. West Germany's *Ostpolitik* made it possible for the Russians to argue that Moscow, not Washington, held the key to West German aspirations about improving contacts with East Germany[30]. Moreover, the *Ostpolitik*, and in particular Bonn's treaties with Poland and the Soviet Union, were seen as an important step towards something the Russians had long since wanted – an East-West security agreement on Europe according to which both sides would recognise the inviolability of the post-war frontiers and the legitimacy of the existing governments. The security that such an agreement would afford to the Soviet Union in the West was of no little consequence given the problems that the Russians were facing with China in the East.

The fall of Khrushchev had brought no improvement in relations between Moscow and Beijing. The war in Vietnam heightened the tension between the two communist giants[31]. Moscow did not accept the Chinese view that the war was attributable to monolithic American imperialism. Conscious in the mid-6os of their nuclear inferiority and hence anxious to avoid provoking the Americans, the Russians held a different view. Kremlin ideologists attributed the war to American shortsightedness. They identified two groups in America – those seeking global dominance and the rather more restrained isolationists – and concluded that the war was evidence, for the time being at least, that the first group was in control. President Johnson's announcement in April 1968 that Washington would enter into unconditional peace-talks with the North Vietnamese received a cautious welcome in Moscow. China, on the other hand, denounced the talks when they opened at Paris in May 1968 and accused the Russians of colluding with the Americans in order to encircle China. Russian military aid to the North Vietnamese, which included the latest surface-to-air missiles, was of much more use to Hanoi than the small arms being offered by China. As Hanoi became more dependent on Soviet aid, Beijing began to fear that if the Americans withdrew from Vietnam they might be replaced by the Russians. The Soviet Union had no direct frontier with Vietnam and needed Chinese cooperation to supply Hanoi. Predictably, the Soviet request for an air corridor across China was rejected. The Soviet invasion of Czechoslovakia in August 1968, and the subsequent Brezhnev Doctrine which was used to justify it, provoked Beijing into a fresh bout of ideological polemics. As well as being revisionists, the Russians were now said to be hegemonists or social imperialists. Professing socialism in theory they had become imperialist in practice[32]. For China, the invasion of Czechoslovakia was also evidence of Soviet-American collusion to preserve superpower hegemony. The American failure to deliver more than verbal protests suggested to China that the Soviet Union and the United States considered themselves free to do as they pleased in their respective spheres of influence. The invasion of Czechoslovakia was followed by an increase in the number of incidents along the 11,000 kilometre Sino-Soviet frontier. Moscow made extensive military preparations. Between 1968 and 1971, the number of Soviet divisions in the Far East was increased from 15 to 33. Over 1.2 million troops were deployed along the frontier. The border incidents culminated in a serious clash on Damanski Island, a small uninhabited region on the Ussuri River which demarcates part of the Far Eastern Sino-Soviet frontier. China had thus become a major military problem for the Soviet Union. Notwithstanding the continued exchange of ideological polemics, the nature of the Sino-Soviet conflict had undergone a significant qualitative change. As William Hyland observed:

> Whereas Khrushchev brought primarily political and psychological pressures on China, without any real threat of military action, the Brezhnev regime began building up its military forces, with the implicit threat of intervention. Where Khrushchev wanted to win over the majority of the Communist movement and reestablish Soviet preeminence, the Brezhnev regime came to see the contest more in conventional power terms. . . . The conflict was transformed from an ideological contest to a power struggle between two potential enemy states.[33]

Under these circumstances, American diplomacy towards China in 1970-71 undoubtedly came as an unpleasant shock to the Russians. Worse followed. China moved next to improve relations with Japan, inviting Prime Minister Tanaka to Beijing in 1972. Moscow viewed these developments with mounting concern. With its deep-seated fear of encirclement, the Soviet Union began to see the spectre of an anti-

Soviet coalition in the Far East based on the United States, the People's
Republic of China and Japan. Détente with the West thus became an
essential means by which Moscow attempted to ensure that the
Sino-American rapprochement did not develop beyond the stage of
symbolic gestures.[34] The playing of the 'China card' had certainly
worked from the American point of view. Kissinger noted in his
memoirs how the Russians were 'suddenly anxious to create the
impression that more serious business could be accomplished in
Moscow than in Peking'.[35] Henceforth, one of the yardsticks by which
Moscow would judge the success of détente was in the extent to which
it kept the United States and China apart.

The final consideration for the Russians in pursuing a strategy of
détente concerned their own status as a great power. Having achieved
strategic parity with the United States and with the capacity now to
extend its influence beyond the Eurasian land mass, the Soviet Union
had become a force to be reckoned with in international politics. The
official *History of Soviet Foreign Policy* described the Soviet Union in
1971 as 'one of the greatest world powers, without whose participation
not a single international problem can be solved'.[36] The Russians
expected regular consultation with the United States, particularly in
the field of crisis management, and cited the role that they had played
at the Geneva conference on Indo-China in 1954 as the pattern for
the future. But contrary to expectation in the West at the time, this
did not mean that Moscow was prepared to forgo ideology as a
principal determinant of its foreign policy. As in the case of Khrushchev's peaceful coexistence in 1956, so now in the case of Brezhnev's
détente in the 70s, an era of superpower accommodation did not in
Moscow's eyes mean an end to competition between capitalism and
socialism. Détente differed from coexistence only to the extent that it
envisaged a much closer relationship with countries previously
regarded as enemies in areas such as arms control, trading links and
scientific and technological exchange. On the fundamental question,
nothing had changed. For the Soviet Union, coexistence and détente
meant only an undertaking not to commit nuclear suicide. Moscow
did not consider itself constrained by any other ground rules. If the
United States considered that it was in American interests to maintain
close political economic and military ties with right-wing regimes in
Latin and Central America, Southern Africa and South West and
South East Asia, then, by the same token, the Soviet Union considered
that it was in Soviet interests to pledge support for national liberation

movements whenever opportunities presented themselves. As one Soviet analyst put it in 1975: 'Peaceful coexistence is a principle of relations between states which does not extend to relations between the exploited and the exploiters, the oppressed peoples and the colonialists'.[37] Kissinger's concept of linkage had, in consequence, no validity in Soviet eyes.

THE RE-EMERGENCE OF CHINA

A reorientation of China's foreign policy completed the realignment of international relationships which made détente possible. A number of Western analysts maintain that the Soviet Union contemplated a pre-emptive strike against China soon after the border clashes in 1969. The Chinese, it is said, were driven in consequence to make overtures to the United States. The Soviet threat was indeed real. According to Arkady N. Schevchenko, an experienced Soviet diplomat who defected to the United States in 1978, the Soviet Defence Minister, Andrei Grechko, actively advocated a plan to 'once and for all get rid of the Chinese threat'.[38] Grechko was overruled by the Politburo but the military tension remained high. In June 1969 Soviet bombers ran mock attack exercises in north-west China, the locus of China's nuclear production facilities. In August and September, observed Henry Kissinger, 'we detected a standdown of the Soviet air force in the Far East. Such a move, which permits all aircraft to be brought to a high state of readiness simultaneously, is often a sign of a possible attack; at a minimum it is a brutal warning in an intensified war of nerves'.[39] The problem with this argument, however, concerns the Chinese reaction. Had the Soviet threat been sufficient, on its own, to prompt the Chinese to seek improved relations with the United States, the Sino-American démarche should have taken place in 1969 when the threat was at its greatest. Instead, the dialogue between China and the United States was established in 1970–71, when the Soviet threat had receded. Clearly, therefore, there was more to China's position than simply fear of the Soviet Union.

China's foreign policy in the mid-60s was intended to encourage the formation of a united front in the Third World against both imperialism and revisionism. In 1965, a year before the beginning of the Cultural Revolution, Lin Biao, the Chinese Defence Minister, published an article entitled 'Long Live the Victory of the People's War'.[40] Lin Biao's essay reaffirmed Mao Zedong's theory of the world's countryside encircling the world's cities. Unless directly threatened, China would not engage the imperialist powers itself. Instead, it would provide moral and, where possible, material support to Third World revolutions. But this united front strategy paid few dividends. True, one area of the world's countryside (Vietnam) was weakening one of the world's principal cities (the United States), but elsewhere, particularly in Africa and Latin America, two regions upon which the Chinese had pinned high hopes, the prospects for successful revolutions seemed to be receding. Moreover, the Cultural Revolution estranged China from the outside world. All but a handful of communist parties were hostile to China and several states severed relations with the People's Republic. China's friends abroad were dwindling. In Africa, the influence China had gained by agreeing to build the Tanzam railway was in part nullified by the overthrow of President Kwame Nkrumah of Ghana while he was on a visit to Beijing in 1966. That the Soviet Union was equally discomforted, Nkrumah having been one of Moscow's earliest clients in Africa, seemed small consolation. An even greater setback for China occurred in Indonesia. The abortive Indonesian coup of October 1965 led not only to the downfall of President Sukarno, whose persistent anti-Westernism China had always encouraged, but also to the liquidation of the Indonesian Communist Party, the second largest in Asia and hitherto China's most consistent supporter.

But if the People's War strategy had failed to produce results, the changing international environment at the end of the 60s suggested an alternative course for China to pursue. The two main power blocs were riven by dissension. American policy in Vietnam drew criticism from the NATO allies in Europe. By 1969, when the worst excesses of the Cultural Revolution were over, Canada, Italy and Belgium opened negotiations with the People's Republic with a view to establishing diplomatic relations. The Soviet Union, which now ranked equally in China's eyes with the United States as a principal adversary, was in trouble in Eastern Europe. With Romania pursuing an independent foreign policy and the invasion of Czechoslovakia weakening rather than strengthening the Warsaw Pact, Soviet control in Eastern Europe was slackening. If, as the Chinese believed, the United States and the Soviet Union collaborated with one another in order to protect their hegemony within their respective power blocs, it made little sense for China to continue to regard them both as undifferentiated enemies. Mao Zedong and Zhou Enlai saw the opportunity to escape from their own isolation by exploiting the differences between the United States and the Soviet Union and between each of them and their respective allies. To achieve this, a dialogue had to be kept going between China and the Soviet Union and new lines of communication had to be opened between China and the United States. Hence, while exploring the possibility of talks with Moscow on the border dispute, China put out feelers, through Romania, for the reopening of the ambassadorial talks in Europe which had been an intermittent feature of Sino-American relations since the mid-50s. The American bombing of Cambodia made this impossible in 1970 but the visit by an American table-tennis team to China in April 1971 opened the way for Kissinger's secret visit in July. China had little difficulty in explaining the apparent about-turn in its relations with the United States. The situation in 1970–71 was said to parallel that in the 1940s. Once the major enemy (Japan then, the Soviet Union now) had been identified, it became a question of coming to terms with the power or powers (the United States in both cases) which posed the lesser threat. The alleged Soviet threat was therefore useful to Mao Zedong and Zhou Enlai in that it enabled them to pursue a course which they already wished to explore. Seen from this perspective, it was not so much China's fear of the Soviet Union as American weakness in Asia that made the Sino-American rapprochement possible.[41]

DETENTE 1: THE ACHIEVEMENTS

The differing American and Soviet perceptions of détente did not become immediately apparent. With each superpower anxious for its own reasons to make headway in negotiation with the other, détente in the early 70s appeared to make spectacular progress. Four key areas were involved: Sino-American relations; the ending of the Vietnam War; Soviet-American relations; and East-West relations in Europe.

Détente in Asia produced first the rehabilitation of China. Nixon's much-publicised visit to China in February 1972 ended with the Shanghai communiqué on Taiwan. China claimed in the communiqué that the People's Republic was the only legal government for China, that the liberation of Taiwan was an internal Chinese affair and that all American forces and military installations on Taiwan should be withdrawn. In reply, Nixon declared that there was but one China, that Taiwan was part of that China and that the ultimate objective of the United States was a military withdrawal. He was not, however, prepared to concede the Chinese claim that Taiwan should be governed from Beijing. Nonetheless, the American recognition of one China enabled the People's Republic to gain admission to the United Nations in October 1971. Taiwan lost its membership and became increasingly isolated. Simultaneously, China used its membership of the United Nations to promote a new Third World identity. Lin Biao's strategy of People's War became obsolete and Lin Biao himself was allegedly killed in a plane crash attempting to escape to Moscow after an abortive coup in 1971. The united front strategy still applied but in place of revolution China now attempted to counter superpower hegemony by establishing state-to-state relations upon the basis of mutual equality between nations. Between 1971 and 1976, more than 60 countries established diplomatic relations with China.

Détente in Asia also brought about an end to the war in Vietnam. The cease-fire agreement reached at Paris in January 1973 between the United States and North and South Vietnam provided for the withdrawal of all remaining American troops and for the release of all prisoners-of-war. The 17th parallel was restored as a provisional demarcation line. Military movements across the line were prohibited and civilian movements required the agreement of both Vietnamese governments. Hanoi agreed to withdraw its forces from Laos and Cambodia and pledged that it would not use the territory of either of these two countries for military action against South Vietnam. The future government of South Vietnam was left to be negotiated between Hanoi and Saigon. Kissinger's critics condemned the agreements as a sell-out but Kissinger argued that they were the best that could be obtained under the circumstances. At least Le Duc Tho, Hanoi's principal negotiator, had dropped his previous insistence that no agreement was possible with the existing government in Saigon. Kissinger subsequently claimed that he had been under no illusions about the ultimate intentions of North Vietnam. He attributed the final collapse of South Vietnam in 1975 to the Watergate scandal in the United States which effectively paralysed American power.[42]

Détente achieved what appeared to be its most spectacular successes in the field of relations between the United States and the Soviet Union. Between 1972 and 1974 no less than four summit meetings were held between Brezhnev and his opposite numbers in the White House.[43] Nixon made history twice by becoming the first American president to visit the Soviet Union. His first in May 1972 was the most important. For two years, American and Soviet experts had been engaged in Strategic Arms Limitation Talks at Vienna. At the Moscow summit the first SALT agreement was signed by Brezhnev and Nixon. SALT 1 consisted of two parts. First, an interim agreement imposing a five-year freeze on American and Soviet missile launchers at their existing levels. Intercontinental ballistic missiles (ICBMs) were frozen at 1,054 for the United States and 1,618 for the Soviet Union; submarine-launched ballistic missiles (SLBMs) at 656 for the United States and 740 for the Soviet Union; and long-range bombers at 455 for the United States and 140 for the Soviet Union. The American superiority in warheads was Nixon's principal justification for the apparent inequality of SALT 1. Having already deployed missiles which carried several warheads and which were capable of hitting several targets – multiple independently targetable re-entry vehicles (MIRVs) – the United States was estimated to have a three-to-one superiority in numbers of warheads. The second part of SALT 1 consisted of an Anti-Ballistic Missile (ABM) Treaty. Both sides were permitted two ABM screens, one for their respective capitals and one for a major missile site, each consisting of 100 anti-ballistic missiles. This was the ultimate in nuclear deterrence. Both sides were left virtually defenceless against attack. Hence MAD – Mutual Assured Destruction.

Nixon's first Moscow visit also produced a Joint Declaration on the Basic Principles of Relations between the United States and the Soviet Union and a series of commercial agreements. The Joint Declaration acknowledged that, in the nuclear age, superpower relations could be conducted only in accordance with the principles of peaceful coexistence. To this end, the two sides pledged that they would consult one another to avoid military confrontations and to prevent the outbreak of nuclear war. They also pledged that they would not seek to obtain unilateral advantages at each other's expense. The commercial agreements provided for an arrangement which enabled the Soviet Union to purchase American grain (worth 750 million dollars) over 3 years, and for the establishment of a Joint Trade Mission. The ground had thus been laid for the October 1972 Soviet-American Trade Agreement, under the terms of which Congress granted Most Favoured Nation Status to the Soviet Union. In June 1973, when Brezhnev visited the United States for the second summit, no less than eleven new agreements were signed. Three of the most important covered nuclear matters. They provided for the peaceful use of atomic energy, an agreement on the prevention of nuclear war and an agreement to impose permanent limitations on strategic weapons in a SALT 2 treaty. The third summit took place in June and July 1974 when Nixon made his second visit to Moscow. This meeting was overshadowed by the Watergate crisis and the president was only six weeks' away from resignation. Nonetheless, agreement was still reached that the number of ABM screens under the 1972 ABM Treaty should be one instead of two and also that the testing of underground nuclear weapons having a yield in excess of 150 kilotons should be prohibited. The final summit, between Gerald Ford, Nixon's successor, and Brezhnev was held at Vladivostok in November 1974. An interim agreement was reached on the outline of a SALT 2 treaty which recognised the principle of parity. The American Senate had insisted upon this when it ratified the SALT 1 agreement. The Vladivostok outline suggested that both sides should have a maximum of 2,400 strategic launchers of all kinds (ICBMs, SLBMs and bombers) of which not more than 1,320 were to be fitted with MIRVs.

In Europe, détente set in motion a series of military and political discussions which were designed to reduce tension and improve East-West relations. In July 1972 the first round of talks on European Security and Cooperation opened at Helsinki. In October of the following year, talks aimed at the reduction of conventional forces in Europe – Mutual Balanced Force Reductions (MBFR) – opened at Vienna. The security conference ended in August 1975 with an agreement which became known as the Helsinki Final Act. A 30,000-word document signed by 33 European countries (excluding Albania), the United States and Canada, the Final Act was not a peace treaty and hence it had no legal sanction.[44] It was similar to the Joint Declaration on Basic Principles of Relations between the superpowers in that it represented a statement of intent. The Final Act consisted of four headings, colloquially known as baskets. Under basket 1, which dealt with the political principles of security, the signatories pledged themselves to recognise the inviolability of Europe's frontiers. Frontier changes were not ruled out but they would have to be implemented by agreement, by peaceful means and in accordance with the principles of international law. The signatories also pledged themselves to refrain from interference in the affairs of other countries, to recognise the right to belong (or not to belong) to international organisations, including treaties of alliance, to renounce force and to respect minority rights. Provision was made for a number of confidence-building measures, notably the requirement to give advance notice of military manoeuvres involving more than 25,000 troops. Basket 2, which dealt with cooperation in the fields of economics, science, technology and the environment, made provision for exchanges of statistical information and trade agreements based on Most Favoured Nation Status. Basket 3, on cooperation in the humanitarian and cultural fields, dealt with such matters as freedom of movement, the reunification of families, the exchange of books, films and periodicals, visas for journalists and cultural, artistic and sporting exchanges. Finally, basket 4 made provision for a follow-up or review conference to be held at Belgrade in 1977.

Many in the West were sceptical about the Helsinki conference. Their criticisms were heard before the ink was dry on the Final Act. Some Western leaders, most notably Gerald Ford, were criticised for even attending the signing ceremony. The critics found it difficult to square the provisions of baskets 1 and 3 with the invasions of Hungary and Czechoslovakia, the Brezhnev Doctrine and the dismal record on human rights throughout Eastern Europe.[45] The provisions of basket 3 had not been part of the original Soviet agenda for the Helsinki conference. Moscow had to accept basket 3 in order to obtain under basket 1 Western recognition of the post-war governments and frontiers in Eastern Europe. The critics in the West argued that while their own governments had paid in hard cash at Helsinki, Moscow had simply issued promisory notes which were not worth the paper they were written on. Nonetheless, basket 3 provided the West with an institutionalised forum within which it could pass judgement on human rights practices within the Eastern bloc. It also gave encouragement to human rights activists (dissidents in Soviet parlance) throughout Eastern Europe. Monitoring groups, such as Charter 77 in Czechoslovakia, were set up. But if Western governments ever seriously anticipated that the provisions of baskets 1 and 3, and the incentives of basket 2, would persuade the communist regimes of the Eastern bloc to relax their controls voluntarily, they were soon disillusioned. One of the great paradoxes of the détente era, but one which nonetheless had a perverse logic to it, was that as Moscow moved to liberalise its contacts abroad through the importation of trade, science and technology, it moved also to tighten the ideological reins at home to ensure that the Soviet Union and Eastern Europe did not become infected with the germ of Western political ideas. In 1970, Alexander

Tvardovsky was dismissed from the editorship of *Novyi Mir*, the influential Soviet literary journal. Alexander Solzhenitsyn, author of such masterpieces as *One Day in the Life of Ivan Denisovich* and *The Gulag Archipelago*, was deported in 1974. Andrei Sakharov, the distinguished Soviet scientist and leader of the first unofficial civil rights movement in the Soviet Union, became the target of official harassment and abuse. The Soviet position on such matters was made clear by Brezhnev in his speech at Helsinki: 'No one should try to dictate to other people, on the basis of foreign policy considerations of one kind or another, the manner in which they ought to manage their internal affairs'.[46]

DETENTE 2: THE LIMITATIONS

Although détente had derived from sober perceptions of individual national interests, it was, as we have seen, based on a number of false premises and misconceptions. Helsinki should have been the highpoint of détente. Instead it marked the beginning of a steep downward curve. The false premises and misconceptions began to make their presence felt in three key areas – SALT, Sino-American relations and linkage. In each case the problems became magnified because of the crisis surrounding the American presidency.

Watergate and the war in South East Asia combined to destroy, not only Richard Nixon, but also the domestic consensus upon which the American strategy of détente had been based. The peak years of détente –1972–74 – were also the key years in the Watergate scandal. Henry Kissinger has penned a typically eloquent statement of the impact made by Watergate on American foreign policy: 'With every passing day Watergate was circumscribing our freedom of action. We were losing the ability to make credible commitments, for we could no longer guarantee Congressional approval. At the same time, we had to be careful to avoid confrontations for fear of being unable to sustain them in the miasma of domestic suspicion .... Deprived of both the carrot and the stick, we could only watch with impatient frustration as first Hanoi and then Moscow began to exploit our discomfiture'.[47] Within the United States, détente came under increasing attack from conservatives who opposed the agreements with the Soviet Union on ideological grounds and who, according to Kissinger, wanted to maintain a posture of 'uncompromising verbal hostility'. It was also opposed by liberals who were outraged when they found out about the secret bombing raids in Cambodia and then critical of the administration for not having been more forceful on the issue of human rights. These two strands of opposition were united in the person of Senator Henry Jackson, a mainstream Democrat from Washington with progressive views on domestic policy but hardline views on defence, communism and Vietnam. The campaigns of the opposition had important consequences. In August 1973, angered by the indiscriminate bombing of South East Asia, Congress passed a War Powers Act. The Act required the president to report back to Capitol Hill within 48 hours of sending new or additional troops to foreign countries. He was also obliged to end hostilities after 60 days unless Congress specifically authorised continued commitment and to withdraw troops within a 90-day period if Congress instructed him to do so. The Act effectively paralysed the administration in relation to the events which took place in Vietnam and Angola in 1975. On the question of human rights, the Jackson-Vanik amendment to the 1974 Trade Reform Act was an attempt to make the expansion of Soviet-American trade conditional upon a relaxation of the Soviet Union's emigration policies, particularly with regard to Jews. The publicity given to the campaign eventually persuaded Moscow to cancel the 1972 Soviet-American trade agreement. It also had the opposite effect to that intended. As Kissinger pointed out, quiet diplomacy through informal channels had enabled the numbers of Jews allowed to emigrate from the Soviet Union to rise from 400 a year in 1968 to nearly 35,000 in 1973. By 1975 the figure had been reduced to 13,200.[48]

The crumbling of presidential authority under Nixon was an important factor in the retreat from détente but others were equally decisive. By 1973, an essential flaw in the SALT negotiations had been exposed. By imposing limits on launchers, and none on what was launched, SALT 1 was seen in Washington as the means to restrict the growth of ICBMs and SLBMs at a time when MIRVs had given the United States a clear advantage in warheads. Also, as Kissinger admitted, the freeze gave the United States the opportunity to develop other systems – the Trident nuclear submarine, the MX missile and the cruise missile – which were not covered by the SALT 1 treaty. The view from Washington was that it would take the Russians many years to master the technology of MIRVs. But in 1973 the Russians confounded the experts in America by successfully testing a new range of MIRVed missiles. At a stroke, the justification for the inequality of SALT 1 had been wiped out.[49] In this respect, SALT 1 demonstrated

a problem which has become all too familiar in arms control negotiations. Political relations between the superpowers invariably fail to
keep pace with technological developments. The SALT talks had
opened at Vienna in 1970, by which time the United States was already
deploying MIRVs on its Minuteman 3 ICBMs. The implications for
the strategic balance of MIRVed missiles might have been considered
by the negotiators on both sides had the SALT talks opened, as
originally planned, in 1968. The invasion of Czechoslovakia, however,
made this impossible. The problem of MIRVs was dealt with in the
Vladivostok interim agreement for a SALT 2 treaty but by then a
new generation of weapons systems, particularly the American cruise
missile and the Soviet backfire bomber, were emerging to threaten
the strategic balance. Endless wrangling over these new weapons
made it impossible to reach agreement on a SALT 2 treaty before the
1976 American presidential election. The delay in negotiating one
SALT agreement had therefore served only to complicate the negotiations for the next.

Sino-American relations had also begun to falter. In part this was
caused by the leadership crises on both sides. The crisis of Watergate
in America was paralleled in China by the deaths of Mao Zedong
and Zhou Enlai in 1976 and the subsequent power struggle between
the left-orientated Gang of Four and the centre-modernising faction
led by Deng Xiaoping. Of much greater significance, however, was
China's criticism of the West's strategy of détente with the Soviet
Union. Aided by détente in Europe through Helsinki, and détente
with the United States through SALT, China feared that the Soviet
Union would be increasingly free to move more of its forces to the
east. The humiliating circumstances of the American collapse in South
East Asia also impeded progress on the normalisation of Sino-American
relations, particularly over Taiwan. Domestic pressures in America
meant that President Ford had nothing further to offer on Taiwan
when he visited Beijing in December 1975. This, together with the
Helsinki and Vladivostok agreements, explained why Ford received
such a cool reception during his visit. Ford's reception contrasted
visibly with the warmth of the welcomes extended to a number of
right-wing West European politicians – Edward Heath, Margaret
Thatcher and Franz Josef Strauss – who also visited China and who
were more inclined to emphasise the potential Soviet threat to Western
Europe.

For the United States, the erosion of linkage and the undermining of the assumptions upon which it had been based constituted the principal casualties of détente. The 70s began well for Washington in this respect. While urging restraint upon the Soviet Union in the Third World, Nixon and Kissinger were waging a programme of economic warfare designed to undermine the Popular Unity government of Salvador Allende which had been elected in Chile in 1970. Allende was overthrown and replaced by the military junta of General Pinochet in September 1973. Similarly, on their way back from the SALT negotiations at Moscow in 1972, Nixon and Kissinger stopped off in Tehran and pledged support to the Shah in his efforts to destabilise the neighbouring state of Iraq which was allied to Moscow.[50] The outcome of the Arab-Israeli war of October 1973 also worked to the advantage of the United States. The 1967 Arab-Israeli War had been disastrous for the Arab states. It demonstrated that they were in urgent need of advanced military technology and trained personnel who could operate it. With the United States preoccupied in Vietnam, the Soviet Union was able to ingratiate itself with the Arab world and to acquire in the process air bases and naval facilities in Egypt. In 1970, upon the death of Colonel Nasser, Anwar Sadat became president of Egypt. Sadat announced that 1971 would be a 'Year of Decision' for the Arabs and a Soviet-Egyptian Treaty of Friendship and Cooperation was signed. Moscow viewed the treaty, and the arms which were supplied in consequence, as the means whereby the Arab states would gain the necessary bargaining strength in negotiation with Israel. But the Arabs, and Sadat in particular, saw them as the means whereby Egypt, Syria and Jordan would be able to recover the territory lost in 1967. Having adopted a warlike stance, Sadat was frustrated to find that the progress of détente between Moscow and Washington made it less likely that the Soviet Union would support a bellicose policy in the Middle East. In a move that shocked Moscow but which came as an unexpected and welcome surprise in Washington, Sadat took the drastic step of demanding the withdrawal of an estimated 21,000 Soviet military and economic advisers from Egypt in July 1972. When war broke out in 1973, the Russians were anxious to restore their damaged reputation. Hence they threatened unilateral action to halt the Israeli advance on the Suez Canal. Washington accused Moscow of having violated the recently-negotiated agreement on the prevention of nuclear war and American nuclear forces were put on worldwide alert. Henry Kissinger's subsequent shuttle diplomacy confirmed the marginalisation of Soviet influence in the

Middle East. Sadat became even more hostile to Moscow and in 1976 he tore up the 1971 Friendship and Cooperation Treaty. The Soviet Union had thus been deprived of one of its principal air and naval bases in the Third World.[51]

However, these American gains were more than offset by a number of serious reverses. Two conditions in particular undermined the concept of linkage. First, Washington assumed that the inducements of SALT and economic and technological exchange, together with a period of international stability, would be sufficient to persuade the Soviet Union to behave with restraint in the Third World. But linkage had to contend, not only with a presidential crisis in America, but also with a decade of international instability.[52] Within the Third World a process of revolutionary upheaval, which began with the deposition of Emperor Haile Selassie of Ethiopia in September 1974, was repeated on no less than thirteen occasions within the next six years. Among the casualties were South Vietnam, Laos and Cambodia in South East Asia, Portugal's colonial possessions in Southern Africa, the hitherto impregnable Shah of Iran who had acted as the West's policeman in the Persian Gulf and the Somoza regime in Nicaragua. The Sandinista victory in Nicaragua brought the revolutionary spiral to America's backdoor and unrest began to develop in El Salvador. The winds of change also swept through Southern Europe.[53] In Portugal, a left-wing armed forces movement overthrew the military dictatorship of Dr Caetano in April 1974. Washington watched in consternation as a new left-wing government under General Goncalves improved relations with Moscow. Rumours began to circulate that Portugal, a NATO country, was about to offer port facilities to the Soviet navy. The election of April 1975, which gave victory to Dr Mario Soares' Socialists and which pushed the communists into third place, removed such fears and set Portugal on the road to parliamentary democracy. The United States and NATO were further discomforted in 1974 by the overthrow of the Greek junta and the subsequent clash between Greece and Turkey (both NATO members) over Cyprus. The Greeks were left with a grudge against the Americans and a less than wholehearted commitment to NATO. Elsewhere in Europe, there were fears, again misplaced, that Spain might turn to the left after General Franco's death in 1975. Finally, the invasion of Czechoslovakia stimulated the development of Eurocommunism. Communist parties in Western Europe condemned the invasion, distanced themselves from Moscow and asserted their independence. In consequence, they grew in popularity and acquired substantial electoral followings in France and Italy. Eurocommunism was a disturbing phenomenon for the United States. It threatened to undermine the West's solidarity.

The second condition which undermined linkage concerned the response of the Soviet Union, particularly in South East Asia and Southern Africa. Linkage angered the Russians. They felt that it was an insult to their status as a great power and that it contradicted their internationalist duty to aid progressive and fraternal allies. But part of their anger stemmed from their own impotence. The Americans consistently exaggerated the extent to which Moscow could exert leverage in its dealings with its Third World clients. Soviet influence over the radical Arabs in the Middle East was never as great as the Americans assumed. Witness the débâcle of the Russian expulsions from Egypt in 1972. The same was true of Soviet relations with North Vietnam.

The role played by Moscow in inducing Hanoi to accept the 1973 cease-fire in Vietnam remains a matter of speculation. The critical year was 1972 when the stakes for Nixon and Kissinger were particularly high. In May of that year, just two weeks before Nixon's scheduled summit visit to Moscow, the Americans mined the North Vietnamese harbour at Haiphong and resumed heavy bombing raids over Hanoi. American actions posed a dilemma for the Soviet leadership. Should it stand by its Vietnamese ally, condemn American aggression and call off the summit? Or, given what was in the offing in the Nixon visit, should it turn a blind eye and allow the summit to proceed? Hardliners on the Politburo were reported to have urged that the summit be cancelled.[54] But Brezhnev, conscious perhaps of his role in history, argued against them and won the day. The Moscow summit became the scene of protracted discussions about Vietnam. The Russians denounced the bombing. But in response to a fresh American initiative about elections in South Vietnam, which made provision for the Vietcong to be represented on a tripartite electoral commission, Moscow agreed that President Podgorny should travel immediately to Hanoi to convey the new American proposals. Precisely what Podgorny told the North Vietnamese remains uncertain. The same applies in the case of any pressure brought to bear by the Chinese, Kissinger having flown direct from Moscow to Beijing to enlist the support of Zhou Enlai. But when peace negotiations were resumed at Paris in July 1972, Kissinger noted that Le Duc Tho had moderated his tone. In August, American military intelligence reported a slow-down in the delivery of Soviet and Chinese supplies to North Vietnam. A year later, during his visit to the United States, Brezhnev appeared on American television and stated, with reference to the cease-fire agreement concluded at Paris in January 1973, 'The improvement of Soviet-American relations has undoubtedly played a part in helping to end the long Vietnam war'. In private conversation with Nixon and Kissinger, Brezhnev remarked that the Soviet Union had stopped military deliveries to North Vietnam after the signing of the Paris accords. 'There may be rifles', he said, 'but nothing of considerable significance. We will urge them [the North Vietnamese] to adhere to the Paris Agreement'.[55]

But this last was easier said than done. Any pressure brought to bear by the Soviet Union on the North Vietnamese to accept a cease-fire was probably resented in Hanoi. Although dependent on Soviet military supplies, North Vietnam had no intention of becoming a Soviet puppet. Hanoi had successfully resisted Soviet pressure to declare itself on Moscow's side in the quarrel with Beijing. The North Vietnamese exploited the conflict between the Soviet Union and China, accepting aid from both but siding with neither. Hanoi's studied neutrality in this respect irritated Moscow. A further source of irritation stemmed from Hanoi's tendency to be secretive. North Vietnam's strategic planning – as well as its dealings with the Chinese – were occasionally concealed from the Russians. During the Paris peace talks, the Russians often found that Henry Kissinger was a better source of information about progress than their North Vietna-mese ally.[56] Moreover, North Vietnam showed every intention of asserting its independence. Neither side in Vietnam respected the 1973 cease-fire and fighting was resumed. Moscow's previous talk of showing solidarity with fraternal allies, together with its suspicion of how China might react, meant that the Soviet Union had no option but to support North Vietnam. Soviet backing for Hanoi was not matched by a comparable American commitment to the forces of President Thieu in Saigon. The result was inevitable. On 30 April 1975, Saigon fell to communist forces. A fortnight earlier Phnom Penh, the capital of Cambodia, fell to the communist Khmer Rouge. Lon Nol fled Cambodia, soon to be renamed Kampuchea, as the Khmer Rouge made plans for the most horrific act of genocide since the holocaust of the Second World War. The communist triangle in South East Asia was completed at the end of 1975 when the Pathet Lao assumed effective control of Laos. The communist victory in Vietnam did not smooth relations between Hanoi and Moscow. Fresh problems emerged as the two sides haggled over the question of Soviet aid to rebuild Vietnam's devastated civilian economy.[57]

Before the 70s, Soviet efforts to gain influence in Africa had brought little reward. Black Africa had few indigenous communist movements. But it abounded with radical nationalist politicians leading independence movements against the White colonialists of Western Europe. The Khrushchev reassessment of the mid-50s recognised the anti-Western political and economic potential of African nationalism. A beginning was made in West Africa. Soviet embassies were established in Ghana and Guinea in 1958. Of the two, the latter seemed to be the more promising. When it became independent from France in 1958, Guinea opted out of French plans to merge the former French colonies in a French African Community. Guinea needed friends and expertise for its economic planning and the socialist bloc in Eastern Europe was soon providing 85 per cent of the capital for the country's development plans. Building on this experience, Soviet analysts developed the theory that socialism could be introduced into Africa from the top down. By cultivating the friendship of those nationalist leaders who were not Marxist but who showed a ready inclination towards socialism, Soviet analysts argued that it would be possible for the socialist camp to facilitate the emergence of an African proletariat.

Soviet relations with West Africa were not an unqualified success. There were some embarrassing moments, particularly when a shipment to Guinea was unloaded and found to include a large crate containing a snowplough. Sékou Touré, the leader of Guinea, proved to be a prickly client. In 1961, he dismissed the Soviet ambassador for becoming too closely involved in a teachers' strike and during the Cuban Missile crisis in 1962 he refused to allow Soviet jets to refuel at Conakry airport. At the wider continental level, Soviet influence in Africa suffered a setback as a result of Moscow's ill-fated attempts to provide military support for the militant nationalist leader Patrice Lumumba during the crisis which arose in the Belgian Congo (now Zaire) in 1960. The crisis in the Congo taught two important lessons. First, that the Russians had yet to acquire the influence, or indeed the logistical capability, which would enable them to intervene decisively in an African country. Secondly, that there were considerable risks involved in making heavy investments in countries where the nationalist politicians were so unpredictable and the state of post-independence politics so volatile. This last point was emphasised when two Soviet backed African leaders – Nkrumah of Ghana and Modibo Keita of Mali – were overthrown in 1966 and 1968 respectively. Thereafter, Moscow became rather more selective in choosing its friends in Africa. Less emphasis was placed on the ideological potential of any faction or political leader and rather more on the strategic value of individual countries. During the Nigerian civil war in 1970, Soviet analysts regarded the leaders of the break-away province of Biafra as being more progressive but Moscow supplied military aid and diplomatic support to the central government in Lagos. The prospect of gaining influence in one of the largest, wealthiest, and most strategically important African countries carried more weight for the Russians than any question of ideological affiliation. One further factor influenced Soviet strategy in Africa. The Chinese-backed Tanzam railway project, which was designed to enable Zambia to circumvent Rhodesia and gain an outlet to the sea through Tanzania, demonstrated to the Russians the need to act where possible to check the growth of Chinese influence.[58]

Turning now to the crises of Southern Africa in the mid-70s, Soviet strategy was influenced by the same strategic and political calculations. The crises were facilitated by the revolution in Portugal in 1974 which in turn precipitated the collapse of Portugal's African colonial empire. In Portugal's five colonies – Angola, Cape Verde, Guinea-Bissau, Mozambique and São Tomé – guerrilla movements seized power. The revolutions in Angola and Mozambique, the two largest countries involved, were the most important. Angola's mineral resources and strategic location made it a tempting prize. Mozambique, although one of the poorest countries in Africa, offered the prospect of port and naval base facilities at Lourenco Marques and Beira. The geopolitical implications of the revolutions were equally significant.[59] With Soviet-aided and Marxist-orientated governments in Luanda and Maputo, Angola and Mozambique were now seen as frontline Black African states from which further national liberation struggles could be launched against White-dominated governments in Rhodesia (now Zimbabwe), South-West Africa (now Namibia) and South Africa itself. When Portugal withdrew from Angola in 1975, the country was gripped by a civil war in which there were three competing factions: Agostinho Neto's Popular Movement for the Liberation of Angola (MPLA), which had been receiving Soviet help since the mid-60s; Holden Roberto's National Front for the Liberation of Angola

(FNLA), which was aided by the West and China; and Jonas Savimbi's National Union for the Total Independence of Angola (UNITA), which was backed by South Africa and Zaire. The South Africans were the first to intervene, ostensibly to protect their stake in the Cunene Dam project, but also to attack the guerrilla bases of the South West African People's Organisation (SWAPO) which had been set up in Angola. Close to defeat, the MPLA was saved by Soviet arms deliveries and about 17,000 Cuban troops who began arriving, with Soviet logistic support, in November 1975. Although it was not recognised in the West at the time, it seems likely that the need to check the growth of Chinese influence in Southern Africa was a major factor in Moscow's increased support for the MPLA. In Washington, the Ford administration was rebuffed by Congress in its efforts to secure increased aid for the FNLA and also UNITA. Already licking its wounds, Congress was in no mood to contemplate another commitment along the lines of Vietnam. Angola was not the first occasion upon which Cuban troops had intervened as Soviet proxies in Africa, nor was it to be the last. They had already been used in Guinea, Congo (Brazzaville) and Guinea-Bissau and they were to be used again, in 1977–78, in Zaire's Shaba province and in the Ogaden War between Ethiopia and Somalia. Their presence in these regions bore dramatic testimony to the fact that Moscow had overcome the limitations to its capabilities which had thwarted its ambitions in the Congo in 1960 and over Cuba in 1962. The Soviet Union was now not only a strategic nuclear power but also a formidable global power with the means, like the United States, to project its influence far beyond its own borders. Soviet leaders interpreted their coming of age as evidence of a change in the 'correlation of forces'. With or without détente, they believed that irreversible trends, towards American decline and Soviet ascendancy, had been established. This was an exaggerated view but it did at least explain why Soviet aspirations during the decade of détente were so radically different from those of the United States. As Seweryn Bialer has observed:

In the 1970s, the United States and the Soviet Union were out of phase in their basic attitudes towards the international system, in their fears and ambitions, and in their ability to mobilize internal resources for international purposes. The Soviet Union was still in a rising phase as an international power. Having only recently acquired its global status, it was still flexing its muscles, eager to

crisis when he observed in March 1980: 'President Carter is asking for solidarity every morning, but solidarity is not taking orders every morning, and very frequently orders countermanding yesterday morning's orders'. The lack of consultation with the NATO allies over Afghanistan was, according to Sommer, a reflection of the 'untidy way' in which the Carter administration ran its foreign policy. All too often the impression was gained that the president was leading not a government but a 'revival meeting'.3

Whatever the later criticisms, the Carter administration began with a comprehensive foreign policy programme which, according to Brzezinski, was devised to achieve three broad objectives: to increase America's ideological impact on the world, to improve America's strategic position *vis-à-vis* the Soviet Union and to restore America's political appeal in the Third World. To this end, the administration set out its targets in a ten-point policy paper which was agreed in April 1977: (1) to promote closer political and economic cooperation with the advanced democracies of Western Europe and Japan; (2) to develop bilateral political and economic relations with the 'regional influentials' – Venezuela, Brazil, Nigeria, Saudi Arabia, Iran, India and Indonesia; (3) to promote more accommodating North-South relations through increased economic stability and decreased hostility towards the United States; (4) to negotiate a new SALT treaty by 1978 and a Strategic Arms Reduction Treaty (START) by 1980; (5) to normalise Sino-American relations with the restoration of full diplomatic relations by 1979; (6) to negotiate a comprehensive Middle East settlement; (7) to promote a peaceful transformation in South Africa and a majority-rule settlement in Rhodesia; (8) to restrict the level of global armaments; (9) to enhance global sensitivity about human rights; (10) to develop a defence posture capable of deterring the Soviet Union at both strategic and conventional levels.4

The emphasis which Nixon and Kissinger had placed on relations between the superpowers was deliberately downgraded in this ambitious programme. Both Carter and Brzezinski wanted to move away from what they regarded as an unhealthy American preoccupation with American-Soviet relations. This, according to Brzezinski, 'could only breed either excessively euphoric expectations of an American-Soviet partnership (which would inspire fears abroad of an American-Soviet condominium) or hysterical preoccupations with the United States-Soviet confrontation'.5 Brzezinski wanted the United States to concentrate more on Third World problems, either on its own or through trilateral cooperation with Western Europe and Japan. Given that the United States was now confronted by a polycentric communist world, he also wanted America to have a polycentric communist policy with more emphasis on relations with China and Eastern Europe. He argued that the United States should seek to engage the Soviet Union in a constructive response to global problems but not to the extent that it became the focal point of American interest to the detriment of the rest of the global agenda. On the question of détente, Brzezinski maintained that redefinition was called for: 'My view was that we should redefine détente into a more purposeful and activist policy for the West. The code words "reciprocal" and "comprehensive" meant to me that we should insist on equal treatment (retaliating in kind, if necessary) and that the Soviets could not have a free ride in some parts of the world while pursuing détente where it suited them'.[6] In particular, the United States should aim to put the Soviet Union 'ideologically on the defensive' by insisting on scrupulous fulfilment of the Helsinki accords and responsible global behaviour. One can see in Brzezinski's ideas why, during the Carter administration, the United States and the Soviet Union were set on a collision course. Faced with the almost inevitable Soviet non-compliance, the United States would be driven to use less carrot and more stick.

Brzezinski admitted in retrospect that there had been occasions when the Carter administration had given the impression of incoherence. This was particularly the case during the crises in the Horn of Africa and Iran. But he denied that the administration lacked direction or a central strategy. If anything, he argued that the strategy had been over-ambitious. The mistake, as he saw it, was that American policy was never sufficiently explained in public, nor modified to make it more realistic when it became clear that it would be impossible to accomplish all of the desired goals. But in this respect Brzezinski's analysis evaded the central issue. The problem which beset the Johnson and Nixon administrations in Vietnam ultimately destroyed the Carter administration in Iran. For all its military power and purpose, the United States had not the means to enforce its will when confronted by opposition determined to resist the imposition of a world order based on American values.

HUMAN RIGHTS

Human rights was the one issue upon which Carter was passionately committed. He described it in 1977 as the 'soul' of American foreign policy and set up a Bureau on Human Rights in the State Department. The crusade made a selective impact. In Latin and Central America the United States withdrew support from the military junta of Pinochet in Chile and stood by while the Sandinista insurgents forced Somoza, the Nicaraguan dictator, into exile. In Southern Africa, Andrew Young's support for the emergent nations and his insistence upon Black majority rule in Rhodesia won many friends for the United States. The Lancaster House conference, which opened in London in September 1979 and ended in December with agreement reached on a constitution for a newly-named independent republic of Zimbabwe, was as much a triumph for American diplomacy as it was for British. Elsewhere, however, American strategic interests took precedence over human rights. Vice-President Walter Mondale visited the Philippines in March 1977 and criticised the human rights record of the Marcos regime but the United States did not withdraw aid. It was a similar story in South Korea and Iran. Carter, on a visit to the Shah at the end of 1977, described Iran as 'an island of stability in one of the more troubled areas of the world'. In Central America, having previously suspended aid to the military junta in El Salvador following the revelation that three American nuns and a number of lay workers had been murdered by government forces, Carter resumed aid in January 1981 as one of his last acts as president. The inconsistency meant that Carter's policy lacked credibility abroad and provoked criticism at home. Carter's right-wing critics were quick to point out that while pressure had been brought to bear on some of America's allies, the Soviet Union had continued to receive American loans, credits, surplus grain and advanced technology.

However, Carter's human rights policy angered Moscow. In February 1977 the State Department described Andrei Sakharov, the dissident Soviet physicist, as an 'outstanding champion of human rights' and said that an attempt to 'intimidate' him would 'conflict with accepted international standards of human rights'. Carter wrote a personal letter to Sakharov and raised the question of his treatment in a letter to Brezhnev. He received a stinging reply in which the Soviet leader referred to Sakharov as a 'renegade' who had proclaimed himself 'an enemy of the Soviet state'.[7] Carter's correspondence with Sakharov was viewed as an unwarranted intrusion into the domestic affairs of the Soviet Union. Fearing that the Helsinki process would be turned into an anti-Soviet crusade on the issue of human rights, Moscow tightened the ideological reins in Eastern Europe still further.

enabled technology to develop new weapons systems which made the task of conducting negotiations still more difficult. The Soviet military build-up, in the form of a new generation of intercontinental missiles – the SS18s and SS19s – and a new generation of intermediate missiles – the SS20s – was condemned in the West as a yet further breach of the spirit of détente. 'We build, they build. We stop, they build', was how Harold Brown, Carter's Defence Secretary, put it. The Carter administration was later accused of having neglected America's defences to the extent that a new and more dangerous missile-gap had emerged. But the position was not so straightforward. In terms both of weapons systems and nuclear strategy, Carter made some significant decisions.[10] He pressed his NATO allies to introduce three per cent increases in defence expenditure and agreed to station cruise and Pershing 2 missiles in Europe. He cancelled the neutron bomb but pressed ahead with the development of the MX (Missile Experimental) missile which, once deployed in specially hardened underground silos, would constitute one rung in the American ladder of defence against the SS18s and SS19s. Carter also cancelled the B-1 bomber but not, as appeared at the time, as a conciliatory gesture. Instead he opted for cruise, arguing himself that cruise missiles launched from modified B-52 bombers would be both cheaper and less vulnerable than the B-1. He continued with the development of Trident nuclear submarines as a replacement for Polaris and began a programme to develop a new Stealth bomber. In all these areas the president laid the foundations for the subsequent defence policies adopted by Reagan's Defence Secretary, Caspar Weinberger. Carter did likewise by signing Presidential Directives 18 and 59 in 1977 and 1980 respectively. PD-18 provided for the creation of special military forces for use in wars in the Third World. It formed the basis for Reagan's Rapid Deployment Force, designed for use in the Persian Gulf. More significantly, PD-59 established 'counterforce' in place of 'countervalue' as America's nuclear doctrine. Under countervalue, the strategic arsenals of the United States had been concentrated on 'soft' civilian and economic targets in the Soviet Union. Under counterforce they were aimed exclusively at the military targets. Reagan's adaptation of this doctrine, and his refusal to commit himself to an agreement on the non-first use of nuclear weapons, led many Europeans to fear that the Americans considered it possible to wage limited nuclear war.

Strategic arms negotiations made an inauspicious beginning under Carter. In March 1977, Secretary Vance was sent to Moscow with instructions to negotiate from one of two different positions. The first, known as the 'deferral option', suggested proceeding upon the basis of the Vladivostok ceilings agreed by Ford and Brezhnev in 1974. The second, known as the 'comprehensive option', envisaged deep cuts in the strategic arsenals of both sides. Vance made it clear that the Americans favoured the second option. This was designed to reduce the numbers of launchers on both sides to between 1,800 and 2,000 and to reduce the numbers of launchers carrying MIRVed missiles to between 1,100 and 1,200. It was also designed to restrict the numbers of ICBMs on both sides carrying MIRVed missiles to 550 and to impose a sub-ceiling of 150 MIRVed missiles on the new Soviet SS18s. Vance's package met with an angry rejection from the Russians. His proposals were sprung upon them, amidst great publicity, with no advance preparation. Besides, any proposal to impose ICBM limits had to take account of the fact that while the Russians had 79 per cent of their strategic warheads in ICBM sites, the corresponding figure for the Americans was only 25 per cent. The bulk of the American warheads – 54 per cent – were submarine-based, a proportion which remains the same today. The Russians, with fewer naval bases around the world, had only 21 per cent of their warheads in submarines. Most impartial observers found it difficult therefore to disagree with the verdict of Andrei Gromyko, the Soviet Foreign Minister, that Vance's proposals were designed to 'obtain unilateral advantages for the United States to the detriment of the Soviet Union'.[11]

The SALT negotiations went back to the drawing board. They were concluded in June 1979 when Carter and Brezhnev signed a SALT 2 treaty at their summit meeting in Vienna.[12] The numbers of launchers stipulated in SALT 2 were more or less the same as those agreed at Vladivostok five years earlier. Strategic launchers of all kinds – ICBMs, SLBMs and bombers – were fixed for both sides at a maximum of 2,400. A further reduction to 2,250 was envisaged by the early 80s. In relation to MIRVed missiles, a number of sub-ceilings were fixed: an aggregate of 1,320 on ICBMs, SLBMs and bombers equipped to carry cruise missiles with a range in excess of 250 kilometres; an aggregate of 1,200 on ICBMs and SLBMs; and an aggregate of 820 on ICBMs alone. No more than 10 MIRVed missiles were to be placed on any one ICBM, and no more than fourteen on any one SLBM. By the same token, no more than one new ICBM was to be tested and deployed, and no more than one new SLBM. A protocol to the treaty, which expired at the end of 1982, prohibited the deployment, but not the testing, of ground and sea-launched cruise missiles with ranges in excess of 600 kilometres. On the Soviet side, Brezhnev assured Carter in an informal letter that the range and payload of the new backfire bomber would not be increased and that its rate of production would not rise above 30 a year. Intended to last until the end of 1985, SALT 2 was never ratified by the American Senate because of the Soviet invasion of Afghanistan. In the event, however, both sides continued, for the time being, to observe its provisions.

By the time Carter and Brezhnev put their signatures to the SALT 2 treaty at Vienna, a new dimension was being added to the nuclear debate in Europe. At their summit meeting at Guadeloupe in January 1979, the leaders of the United States, Britain, France and West Germany agreed in principle on the need to modernise NATO's theatre-based or intermediate nuclear forces in Europe. In December 1979 a full NATO meeting at Brussels made the famous 'dual-track' decision. NATO committed itself, on the one hand, to begin deploying 572 American ground-launched cruise missiles and Pershing 2 ballistic missiles in Western Europe by 1983. On the other, NATO also committed itself to explore the prospects of negotiating an agreement with the Soviet Union to establish permanent limitations on theatre nuclear forces in Europe as a possible alternative to deployment.[13]

West European governments defended the 1979 modernisation decision on the grounds of the threat posed by the SS20, a missile which, with three warheads and greater range and accuracy than its predecessors, represented a significant accretion of Soviet military power. But the deployment of the SS20s was not the sole reason for the dual-track decision. By the mid-70s, a serious deficiency had emerged in NATO's strategy of flexible response. NATO's existing intermediate forces, a range of artillery and aircraft such as the F111 and Vulcan bombers, were beginning to age. Doubts were expressed about the ability of the F111s and Vulcans to penetrate the recently-improved Soviet air defences. One rung of NATO's escalatory ladder was in danger of becoming obsolete. In the event of an attack by the numerically superior conventional forces of the Soviet Union, Western Europe would be dependent for its defence on the use by the United States of its intercontinental strategic forces. The NATO allies in Europe feared that an American president would be reluctant to contemplate such a drastic step and that the United States might abandon Western Europe to its fate. The implications of strategic parity between the superpowers, together with the concern which was being expressed in the United States about the vulnerability of America's own land-based missiles to a surprise Soviet attack, had raised fundamental doubts about the viability of the American nuclear guarantee to Western Europe. This was precisely the point made by Helmut Schmidt, the West German Chancellor, in his influential Alastair Buchan Memorial Lecture at the International Institute for Strategic Studies in London in October 1977. The indivisibility of Western defence, he argued, was in danger; Western Europe might be 'decoupled' from the United States. The need to maintain this psychological reassurance from the United States was the principal reason for the NATO modernisation decision. The SS20s were significant to the extent that they imparted a sense of urgency to the debate. West European leaders recognised that the decision to deploy cruise and Pershing would not be popular in their own countries. They placed considerable faith in a negotiated settlement as a means to avoid deployment. They bargained without the Soviet invasion of Afghanistan and the subsequent crisis in Poland.

THE COLLAPSE OF LINKAGE

The Carter presidency witnessed the complete collapse of linkage as regional disputes emerged in virtually all four corners of the globe: Central America, the Middle East, the Horn of Africa and Central Africa, South West Asia and Indo-China. The most serious, according to Brzezinski, covered what he described as an 'arc of crisis' stretching along the shores of the Indian Ocean, with the Horn of Africa at one end and Iran and Afghanistan at the other.[14] The problems began, however, in the Middle East.

At the outset Carter was committed, not only to a settlement in the Middle East, but also to one in which the United States would cooperate with the Soviet Union. Vance and Gromyko signed a memorandum to this effect in October 1977. But the powerful Israeli lobby in the United States, together with opposition from the governments in Egypt and Israel, reminded Carter of the risks he was taking in providing Moscow with the means to re-enter the arena of Middle Eastern diplomacy. Instead, he decided to back the peace initiative started by President Anwar Sadat of Egypt towards the end of 1977. Conscious of his own vulnerability since the inconclusive war of 1973, Sadat sought, in two contradictory ways, to reinforce his personal authority: to exploit Islamic symbolism at home and to promote a peace settlement with Israel abroad. In November 1977 Sadat made his historic visit to Israel, becoming the first Arab leader to step foot on Israeli soil since the creation of Israel in 1948. Addressing the Knesset (the Israeli parliament), he offered to recognise Israel in return for an Israeli withdrawal from occupied territory (including Jerusalem) and an acknowledgement of the right of the Palestinians to live within their own state. Menachem Begin, the Israeli prime minister, returned the compliment, visiting Ismailia in December 1977. However, subsequent bilateral attempts between Egypt and Israel to reach agreement soon ran into difficulties. At this point Carter intervened, inviting the two leaders for talks at his presidential retreat. The result was the Camp David Agreements of September 1978.[15]

The agreements fell in two parts. First, a Middle Eastern settlement involving the establishment of a 'self-governing authority' for the Palestinian inhabitants of the Gaza Strip and the West Bank. Secondly, a separate Egyptian-Israeli peace treaty based on a withdrawal by Israel from the Sinai Peninsula. The treaty was signed by Begin and Sadat at Washington in March 1979 and in February 1980 Israel and Egypt exchanged ambassadors. The second part of the Camp David Agreement ran its full course, Israel completing the withdrawal from Sinai on schedule in April 1982. But the first ran into immediate difficulties. The first part of the agreement envisaged that the powers of the self-governing authority for Gaza and the West Bank would be defined in negotiation between Egypt, Israel and Jordan, and such representatives of the Palestinians as could be agreed. But Israel refused to admit the Palestinian Liberation Organisation (PLO) to the negotiations and also rejected the Egyptian view that the self-governing authority would ultimately constitute the basis for an independent Palestinian state. Sadat's name was anathema to the other Arab states who regarded him as a traitor to the Arab cause. His peace initiative cost him his life when he was assassinated by Islamic fundamentalists in Egypt in October 1981. Israel, for its part, returned to an offensive strategy, continuing its settlement policy to annex the West Bank, annexing the Golan Heights in December 1981 and, a year later, invading southern Lebanon in the first of a series of manoeuvres designed to eliminate the PLO. Throughout, Moscow maintained a low profile but retained a foothold in the region by signing a new twenty-year Treaty of Peace and Friendship with Syria in October 1980.

Further south on the African continent, Washington was treated to a renewed bout of Soviet intervention by Cuban proxy. In 1977 Cuban forces supported Katangan guerrilla incursions from Angola into the Shaba province of neighbouring Zaire. In the Horn of Africa, the United States and Soviet Union found themselves on opposite sides of a simmering quarrel between Ethiopia and Somalia. Following the collapse of Haile Selassie's imperial regime in Adis Ababa in 1974, the United States supported Ethiopia, prompted no doubt by Moscow's conclusion in the same year of a Treaty of Friendship with Somalia which gave the Russians naval facilities at Berbera for their expanding Indian Ocean fleet. But in February 1977, after a military coup in Adis Ababa led by the Marxist-orientated Lieutenant-Colonel Mengistu, Washington used human rights violations as a pretext to suspend aid to Ethiopia. War broke out in 1977 when Somalia invaded the Ethiopian province of Ogaden which was inhabited by ethnic Somali nomads. Moscow's attempts to mediate angered President Barre of Somalia. He tore up the Friendship Treaty and expelled his East European advisers. Moscow then changed sides. With the assistance of Cuban forces, acting again with Soviet military advisers, the Ethiopians expelled the Somalis from the Ogaden and then suppressed a separatist movement in their own northern province of Eritrea. In 1978 the Russians signed a twenty-year Treaty of Friendship and Cooperation with Ethiopia. Events in the Horn of Africa produced a sharp divergence of opinion in Washington. Viewing the issue as a strategic one with linkage implications for the SALT negotiations, Brzezinski wanted to make a show of force by sending a carrier to the region.[16] He was defeated by a combination of Carter, Vance and Brown who maintained that the issue was a local one and thus unrelated to SALT. For Brzezinski, events in the Horn of Africa represented a repeat performance of Angola in 1975. SALT and, by implication, détente itself, he later claimed, 'lies buried in the sands of the Ogaden'.[17] However, whatever might be said of Moscow's action in supporting the suppression of the Eritrean separatist movement, it should not be forgotten that Russian support for Ethiopia postdated the revolution in Adis Ababa and also that the Russians used their influence to restrain the Ethiopians from carrying the fight into Somalia once the Somalis had been expelled from the Ogaden.

The Horn crisis persuaded the Carter administration to give greater priority to a measure outlined in its original programme – the normalisation of relations with China. In Beijing, a post-Mao leadership was beginning to take shape. Deng Xiaoping, victim of a purge during the brief radical interlude of the Gang of Four which followed the deaths of Mao and Zhou Enlai, was restored in January 1977 to his former positions within the party, state and military heirarchies.[18] Deng consolidated his position, securing the replacement of Hua Guofeng as prime minister and party chairman in 1980 and 1981 respectively. Internally, Deng began a major reform programme based on the four Modernisations of Industry, Agriculture, Science and Defence. Once the ideological conscience of the communist world, China now changed course and became a major revisionist power. Mao's legacy was discarded. Leninism, in the sense of the supremacy of the party, remained intact. But the new leadership recognised that the extreme fluctuations in government policy over the previous twenty years had retarded economic development. It also concluded that China had to relearn Marxism and go back to first principles. In so doing, Beijing was emphatic in its rejection of the Soviet model. As one senior Chinese Party official put it:

> [T]he tragedy of our Party was that it never knew and learned Marxism as it was thought by its founders. We got our Marxism from the Russians, in their own already corrupted version. Marx has determined that real socialism can be built only on the basis of the highest level of modernity attainable under capitalism. There are no shortcuts and alternatives to this precondition of successful socialism. What we are doing now is starting to create this precondition. To achieve this goal we need forty years of capitalism in China. We believe, however, that this goal will be achieved with the Communist Party in power.[19]

It was this reasoning which led China to look abroad, to the capitalist powers of the West and Japan, for the investment, expertise and technology required to promote the Four Modernisations.

Abroad, however, Mao's view of the Soviet Union as a hegemonist power continued to dominate China's foreign policy. Deng therefore extended Mao's strategy of building a Third World identity and establishing diplomatic relations with previously hostile countries. Improved relations with both Japan and the United States were central to this overall design. In August 1978, after six years of negotiation, China and Japan concluded a Treaty of Peace and Friendship. Without, as Beijing had wished, mentioning the Soviet Union by name, the treaty included an 'anti-hegemony' clause. In May of the same year Brzezinski visited Beijing and stressed the 'congruence of fundamental interests' between the United States and China, a clear statement that both countries had similar interests in resisting the expansion of Soviet influence.[20] Brzezinski's visit paved the way for the Sino-American normalisation communiqué of December 1978 and the establishment of formal diplomatic relations in January 1979. The communiqué represented a settlement, of sorts, of the Taiwan dispute. The United States agreed to end its Mutual Defence Agreement, and hence to terminate diplomatic relations, with Taiwan in 1980 but retained the right to continue supplying Taiwan with 'defensive' weapons. China, for its part, renounced the use of force to reincorporate Taiwan into the mainland.

In South East Asia, Vietnam stood firmly in the way of China's efforts to resist the growth of Soviet influence.[21] China welcomed the communist victory in 1975 but age-old differences soon began to surface. Border disputes over the land frontier and rival claims to the offshore islands in the Bac Bo Gulf (the Gulf of Tonkin) soured relations. So too did Hanoi's harassment of the ethnic Chinese population in Vietnam. In April and May 1978, an estimated 50,000 Chinese crossed the border from Vietnam into China. The breach deepened as Vietnam gravitated into the Soviet camp. In June 1978 Hanoi's economic dependence on the Soviet bloc became institutionalised when Vietnam became a member of Comecon, the East European Common Market. In November of the same year, as Moscow and Hanoi concluded a Treaty of Friendship and Cooperation, Beijing began to fear the emergence of a Cuban-style Soviet satellite on its southern frontier.

China had all the more cause for concern because of Vietnam's involvement in neighbouring Kampuchea (formerly Cambodia). The policy of mobilising Third World support against Moscow led Beijing to develop close ties with a number of quite repressive regimes – the Shah in Iran, Mobutu in Zaire and, in Kampuchea, Pol Pot, the leader of the Khmer Rouge. In January 1979 Vietnam invaded Kampuchea, a move precipitated by a border dispute along the ill-defined 750-mile frontier. The invasion also had regional implications. The timing of the Soviet-Vietnamese treaty was clearly intended to deter China from intervening in Kampuchea. But for this very reason,

Deng Xiaoping believed that China had to act. The Vietnamese invasion coincided with Deng's visit to the United States at the formal opening of Sino-American diplomatic relations. Throughout his visit, Deng urged the need for China and the United States to pursue collaborative measures against the Soviet Union. During private talks with Carter, he outlined the Chinese version of the Sino-Soviet dispute and indicated that China intended to 'teach Vietnam a lesson'.[22] Determined to prove that it would not be cowed by Moscow's alliance with Hanoi, seeking also to relieve the pressure on the beleaguered forces of Pol Pot and even, some have suggested, attempting to scupper the SALT 2 Treaty, China attacked Vietnam in February 1979. But if these were the objectives, China's war against Vietnam was a failure. The Americans were not persuaded, as yet, to abandon SALT 2. The war itself highlighted deficiencies in the People's Liberation Army which suffered 20,000 casualties at the hands of the battle-hardened Vietnamese before it was withdrawn in mid-March 1979. By the end of the year, when the Heng Samrin government was installed in Phnom Penh by Vietnamese troops, Vietnam dominated the whole of Indo-China.

Chinese fears that Vietnam would become a Cuban-style Soviet satellite were undoubtedly exaggerated. Having fought for centuries for its national independence, first against China and then more recently against France and the United States, it was inconceivable that Vietnam would accept satellite status. Vietnam continued to present problems to the Soviet Union. Seweryn Bialer has described Soviet-Vietnamese relations in the 80s in the following terms:

Already Vietnam's relationship with the Soviet Union is not precisely that of a subordinate and a superior. It is one of accommodation, mutual compromise, and some coordination of foreign policy issues of great importance to the Soviets. However, Vietnamese policies on Cambodia are not dictated by Moscow. Nor are they entirely pleasing to the Soviets because of the damage that the support of such Vietnamese policies causes Soviet relations with Third World countries, especially in Asia, and with China. The Vietnamese, on their side, are not satisfied with the extent and quality of Soviet economic aid: they are uneasy about the Soviet desire to make Ranh Bay into a permanent naval and air base, and they want to establish relations with the United States and the capitalist states of Europe and Asia, in order to lessen their dependence on the Soviet Union.[23]

The outcome of the 1979 Sino-Vietnamese War was thus a mixed blessing for the Soviet Union. Moreover, if Vietnam continued to pose problems for Moscow, so also did the emerging balance of forces in East Asia. The diplomatic triangle of the United States, China and Japan had been consolidated in a manner which aroused even greater Soviet fears about encirclement. The Russians attempted to intimidate Japan, describing the Sino-Japanese Treaty as a 'threat to stability in Asia'. Moscow responded to the treaty by fortifying the Northern Territories (the Kurile Islands) which had remained in dispute since the end of the Second World War and thus prevented the conclusion of a Soviet-Japanese peace treaty.[24] Against China, the Russians increased their armed strength on the Sino-Soviet border. The number of Soviet combat divisions rose to just under 50 and SS20s and backfire bombers were deployed against Chinese targets. A particular cause of Soviet anxiety was the development of military ties between China and the West. Deng Xiaoping had already been shopping for military hardware in Western Europe, purchasing for example the British Harrier jump-jet aircraft. Washington took the first tentative steps in the same direction. Carter offered to sell 'dual use' technology to China, such as radar and computers which were capable of serving a military as well as a civilian purpose. The degree of Soviet concern was demonstrated at the Vienna summit in June 1979. Facing each other across the negotiating table, both leaders read out statements prepared in advance. Carter's statement concentrated almost exclusively on human rights; Brezhnev's on the damage being done to Soviet-American relations by America's policy towards China.[25] A year earlier, speaking at Minsk, Brezhnev had already condemned the attempt to play the 'China card' as a 'short-sighted and dangerous policy, which its authors would bitterly regret'.[26] If, as suggested earlier, Moscow had embraced détente with the United States as a means to keep Beijing and Washington apart, the collective mind of the Kremlin leadership must by now have reached the conclusion that negotiations with the Carter administration had run their course. Conceivably, therefore, in the background, the Afghan scenario was already beginning to emerge.

America's Third World discomfiture was completed by the twin crises in South West Asia in 1979–80. In January 1979, after months of unprecedented demonstrations on the streets of his capital, Muhammad Riza Shah, the ruler of Iran, was forced into exile. In February, Ayatollah Khomeini, whom the Shah had sent into exile in 1963, returned to a tumultuous reception to begin the process of transforming Iran from an absolute monarchy into a fundamentalist Islamic republic.[27] The Shah's absolute powers dated from 1953 when British and American intelligence plotted the overthrow of Mohammad Mussadeq, the Iranian prime minister, as a means to overturn Mussadeq's nationalisation of the Anglo-Iranian Oil Company. Thereafter, although troubled occasionally by the repressive nature of the Shah's regime, the West, and the United States in particular, viewed Iran as an island of stability in one of the more troubled regions of the world. The Arab-Israeli war, and the oil crisis it generated in 1973, seemed to emphasise the Shah's pivotal role as the policeman of the Persian Gulf and the chief guarantor of the West's oil supplies. The West therefore pandered to the Shah's grandiose schemes to make Iran the world's fifth strongest industrial power by the 90s. He was supplied with the most up-to-date military hardware and over 150,000 foreigners flocked to Iran to run the oil and other high technology industries. At the same time, the West turned a blind eye to the excesses of SAVAK, the notorious Iranian secret police force which had been trained and equipped by the CIA. The secularisation of Iranian society and the subordination of Iran to foreign interests, particularly those of the United States and Israel, were the principal charges levelled against the Shah by Khomeini. Although neither the most learned nor the most senior of the *ulama* (scholars versed in the principles of Islamic law and science), Khomeini had emerged by mid-1978 as the strongest critic and most uncompromising opponent of the Shah's regime. From his exile in Paris he exhorted his followers in Iran to foment strikes, demonstrations and general chaos to force the Shah's abdication. The economic dislocation caused by the Shah's ill-considered schemes to promote rapid industrial growth provided combustible material for the *ulama* to exploit. In December 1979 an estimated five million people converged on the square in Tehran where the Shah had built the Shayyad monument to commemorate 2,500 years of Iranian monarchy and demanded the establishment of an Islamic republic.

Both immediately before and after the revolution, the West seemed incapable of comprehending what was happening in Iran. The reassertion of Islam, as a reaction against Westernisation and secularisation, was a phenomenon sweeping the Islamic world from Libya in the west to Pakistan in the east. The phenomenon acquired a dynamic of its own in Iran. The majority of Iran's Muslims are Shias whose faith is focused upon traditions of persecution and martyrdom. It was this aspect of the Iranian revolution, and the fear that it might be exported, which concerned the conservative Arab states of Saudi Arabia and the Persian Gulf. Here Islam is based on the more orthodox Sunni faith. In Iraq, Iran's neighbour, the Iranian revolution was viewed both as a threat and as an opportunity by the radical Ba'athist regime of Saddam Hussein. It was a threat because of Iran's support for the Shi'ite minority in Iraq. It was an opportunity because Hussein, facing mounting disaffection at home, believed that a short, victorious war against an allegedly weaker Iran, aimed ostensibly at the conquest of the disputed frontier territory on the Shatt-el-Arab River, would enable him to consolidate his domestic authority. Hence the outbreak of the Iran-Iraq war in October 1980. The complexities and subtleties of Gulf politics, however, eluded the Carter administration in Washington. Accustomed to viewing such manifestations of social and economic unrest in Cold War terms, the United States assumed that Moscow would be the chief beneficiary of the Iranian revolution. Washington therefore pinned its hopes on the moderate and secular elements of the Iranian revolution, little realising that although, in name, they constituted the new government in Tehran, in reality they existed only at the sufferance of Khomeini. Meanwhile Carter infuriated the Iranians by offering the Shah, who was dying of cancer, sanctuary in the United States. Not until the seizure of the American embassy in Tehran in November 1979 and the ensuing hostage crisis did Washington come to appreciate the meaning and significance of what was happening in Iran.

Experts differ in their assessment of precisely when détente finally collapsed and a new phase of Cold War began. For Kissinger, it was 1975 because of the Soviet-Cuban intervention in Angola. For Brzezinski, it was 1977–78 because of similar intervention by the same two countries in the Horn of Africa. Kissinger and Brzezinski, and others in the West, also emphasised what they regarded as persistent Soviet infringements of the code of détente – violations of human rights and the continued arms build-up. Viewed from Moscow, the collapse of détente was not linked to a single date or event but to a series of underlying trends – the menacing nature of the new Sino-American rapprochement, Russia's exclusion from the Middle East peace process and the human rights campaigns which were seen as a deliberate ploy to undermine the Soviet bloc. But if a date has to be fixed for the onset of a new Cold War it would be late 1979 when Soviet troops invaded Afghanistan.

The scale of the Afghan operation alarmed the West. Between 24 and 27 December, 50,000 Soviet troops were airlifted to Kabul, the Afghan capital. They were increased soon after to 85,000, the equivalent of 6 divisions. Yet the invasion was certainly a defensive move.[28] In part, it was Moscow's riposte to the threat of encirclement as posed by the Sino-Japanese peace treaty, the establishment of Sino-American diplomatic relations and China's attack on Vietnam. It might also have been dictated by Moscow's concern to ensure that the Muslim republics of Soviet Central Asia did not become infected by Islamic fundamentalism. But the primary motive for the invasion rested within Afghanistan itself. Dependent on Moscow for its economic and military aid since Khrushchev's visit in 1955, Afghanistan was a Soviet client in all but name. A new phase of political instability, which began in 1973 when the monarchy was overthrown, culminated in April 1978 with a military coup which brought the local communist party, the People's Democratic Party of Afghanistan (PDPA), to power. There was no evidence to suggest Soviet encouragement of the coup and the new regime was immediately recognised by governments of both East and West.

The situation was altered by the reckless and brutal reforming programme of the new regime. The rural opposition which it provoked threatened not only to undermine Afghanistan's socialist experiment, but also to destabilise the Soviet Union's southern frontier in a manner which hostile powers (China and Pakistan) might exploit. By invading, Moscow involved itself in the factional disputes of the PDPA, replacing the incumbent Hafizullah Amin with the more pliant Babrak Kamal. The Russians subsequently offered a totally spurious explanation of the timing and circumstances of the invasion. They said that they had been 'invited' to intervene but they could hardly claim that Amin issued the invitation because he was deposed and murdered during the airlift of Soviet troops. Instead, they claimed that Kamal had issued the invitation, but he was abroad in Eastern Europe at the time and it was not until the troops had intervened that he was installed in power.[29]

Western commentators were quick to point out that the invasion represented the first occasion upon which Soviet forces had been deployed in such a manner in a neighbouring country outside Europe since the end of the Second World War. By implication, the invasion was seen as a new and dangerous departure in Soviet foreign policy. But it could equally be argued that Afghanistan was very much in line with Soviet interventions, whether in Eastern Europe or elsewhere in the Third World. In the sense of preserving a communist regime, it was the equivalent of East Germany in 1953, Hungary in 1956 and Czechoslovakia in 1968. Within the context of Soviet policies in the Third World, Moscow's intervention over the previous twenty years had taken one of two forms: aid to movements resisting foreign rule or local dictatorships (Vietnam, the Portuguese colonies in Africa and the PLO); and defence of socialist states against the threat of counter-revolution or external aggression (Cuba, Angola and Ethiopia). Afghanistan fell within the second category. The Soviet Union was not, as Western governments claimed at the time, the cause of the instability, particularly in the 'Arc of Crisis' in South West Asia. The revolutions in these countries grew out of local conditions and Moscow could hardly be said to have benefited from its involvement.[30] The negative aspect of Soviet involvement, and one which certainly contributed to the deteriorating international climate, lay not so much in the act of intervention as in the consequences which followed. In Ethiopia and Afghanistan, the Russians were seen to export what the West regarded as the most anti-democratic features of the Soviet political system – the one-party state, a controlled media and a high profile for the security forces. Equally, in the case of Afghanistan, although the invasion was prompted by defensive considerations the consequences were clearly offensive. As Western statesmen pointed out, the invasion positioned Soviet forces for possible expansion further south towards the warm waters of the Indian Ocean and the Persian Gulf.

One can but speculate on how the Politburo viewed the likely international repercussions of the invasion before the troops were sent in. Presumably, in the case of the United States, the Kremlin believed either that there would be protests but no direct retaliation or, perhaps more likely, that the American reaction was immaterial because there was nothing further to be gained from negotiation with the Carter administration. In the event, however, the invasion proved to be a costly miscalculation. It was condemned by no less than 104 countries when the UN General Assembly voted in January 1980. Only eighteen countries sided with the Russians.[31] Given that these included the Soviet bloc countries of Eastern Europe, the voting figures testified to how few political returns Moscow had derived from its expensive Third World commitments and investments.

Carter responded to the invasion with a series of punitive measures which included the curtailment of grain shipments to the Soviet Union, the suspension of sales of high technology equipment, an indefinite postponement of the opening of new Soviet and American consular facilities and a deferral of new cultural and economic exchanges. The Senate complied with a presidential request to suspend consideration of the SALT 2 treaty and America's athletes did likewise in response to a call to boycott the 1980 Olympics in Moscow. Military aid was stepped up to the regime of General Zia in Pakistan and Harold Brown was sent to Beijing to conclude a new agreement to provide China with military equipment but as yet no offensive weapons. Finally, in his State of the Union address in January 1980, the president announced the Carter Doctrine: 'Let our position be absolutely clear. An attempt by any outside force to gain control of the Persian Gulf region will be regarded as an assault on the vital interests of the United States. It will be repelled by use of any means necessary, including military force'.[32]

The invasion of Afghanistan and the hastily conceived American response revealed a fundamental disunity in the Western alliance. At a time when Washington was also expecting European support over the issue of the hostages in Iran, the French and West German governments complained about the unpredictability of American foreign policy and the lack of consultation with the European allies. At one of the regular Franco-German summits at Paris in February 1980, Giscard d'Estaing, the French president, and Helmut Schmidt, the West German Chancellor, issued a statement in which they declared that the Soviet presence in Afghanistan was unacceptable and that détente 'could not withstand another shock' of the magnitude of Afghanistan. But Giscard and Schmidt were also concerned by what they saw as the increasing tendency of the United States to urge military solutions to problems which the Europeans regarded as political.[33] Schmidt in particular was worried about the delicate state of East-West relations in Europe and the implications of the Afghan crisis for the second part of NATO's dual-track decision of December 1979. Emphasising traditional French independence, Giscard d'Estaing infuriated Carter by travelling to Poland in May 1980 for damage-limitation talks of his own with Brezhnev.

At the beginning of 1980, as Soviet troops continued to pour into

Afghanistan, Carter bared his soul to the world when he declared that his opinion of the Russians had changed more in the last week than it had over the previous two and a half years. Carter's belated conversion to the harsh realities of international politics cut little ice with the American people. During his final year in office, American prestige and influence had sunk to a new low. Carter's problems abroad were by no means the sole reason for his domestic unpopularity. Interest rates were high, economic growth at zero level and inflation at 9 per cent. But the continuing saga of the hostage crisis and the disaster of the attempted rescue mission in April 1980 bit deep into the American consciousness as striking illustrations of America's impotence. In the election of November 1980 Carter went down to Ronald Reagan in the worst-ever defeat suffered by an incumbent president.

6 From Cold War to Constructive Confrontation 1981–87

Two schools of thought on Soviet-American relations were represented in the two Reagan administrations of the 80s. The first was anti-Soviet and, by preference, internationalist. Advocates of this school viewed Soviet expansionism as the major threat to world peace. To combat the growth of Soviet power, the anti-Soviets urged a strategy based on a strict application of the principle of linkage. They argued that American policy towards the Soviet Union should be made dependent on Soviet actions over specific issues, such as Afghanistan, Central America, Poland and Kampuchea. They were internationalist in the sense that they wanted the United States to coordinate its policies with those of its allies in Western Europe. The anti-Soviet school of thought represented the position of the State Department and Reagan's two Secretaries of State, Alexander Haig and George Shultz. The second school was anti-communist and, when necessary, isolationist. Advocates of this school viewed communist expansion as the main threat. The anti-communists maintained that the policies of the Soviet Union were either the direct cause of the regional conflicts and civil wars in the Third World or the main obstacle which prevented their resolution in accordance with American preferences. Their distrust of the Soviet Union led the anti-communists to conclude that permanent super-power accommodation was an illusion. However much the Russians might compromise on specific issues, they could not alter their behaviour because of the nature of the Soviet system. The anti-communists thus advocated a strategy of unrelenting opposition to the Soviet Union, Soviet clients and communism generally. They were isolationist in the sense that they argued that the United States should give greater priority to the defence of American interests, by unilateral action if necessary. The anti-communist school of thought represented the position of the Defence Department. Caspar Weinberger, the Defence Secretary, and Richard Perle, the Assistant Defence Secretary responsible for policy on international security, were its principal exponents. Of the two schools of thought, Ronald Reagan in the White House had a clear preference for the second.

To many observers, Ronald Reagan was the legatee of a nationalist or isolationist tradition on the far right of American politics. The president's defence outlays, projected at 1,600 billion dollars over the period 1981–86, and his defence programmes, particularly his Strategic Defence Initiative (SDI), evoked memories of 'Fortress America', the favourite military theme of the far right during the early years of the Cold War in the 50s. His anti-communist rhetoric, particularly his reference to the Soviet Union as an 'evil empire', and his campaigns to persuade Congress to provide military aid to resistance movements in Soviet client states as far afield as Afghanistan, Kampuchea and Nicaragua, invited comparisons with the theory of liberation or roll-back. His differences with his European allies over issues such as the imposition of sanctions against the Soviet Union after the declaration of martial law in Poland in 1981, the American invasion of Grenada in 1983 and, more generally, the means to combat international terrorism, invited comparisons with those on the far right who had, from the very beginning, questioned the merits of America's commitment to the NATO alliance. Parallels were drawn between Reagan and Senator Robert Taft,[1] a contender in 1952 for the Republican presidential nomination and the author in 1951 of *A Foreign Policy for Americans*. An opponent of NATO, Taft had argued that the Pacific and Asia, areas which, in his view, seemed in danger of passing by default into communist hands, should be given higher priority than Europe. Rejecting the concept of spheres of influence, Taft believed that America should develop its own military strength, eschew alliances which hampered its freedom of action and decide for itself when and where to intervene to check the growth of communist influence.

Demographic changes in the United States reinforced the significance of these analogies. By the 80s the outlook of the American right, labelled now the 'New Right', increasingly represented a national consensus. Between 1970 and 1980 the population of the United States grew by more than 23 million. Nearly 90 per cent of this growth was in the south and west. For the first time, the 'sunbelt' states were in a majority. California, Florida and Texas alone accounted for 40 per cent of the population growth. They also accounted for one-quarter of America's gross national product and for one-third of the votes required to win a presidential election. By contrast, the population of the old industrial centres of the north and east grew by only 1 per cent.[2]

In foreign affairs the states of the south and west are usually said to be isolationist, in contrast to the internationalist outlook of the traditional east coast establishment. But the south and west are not as inward-looking as is often assumed. They have different geopolitical perceptions of where America's real interests lie. The east coast looks to Europe but the south and west look to areas which for them are closer to home. Hence they place greater emphasis on Asia and the Pacific and on Latin and Central America. In economic as well as in political terms, these areas are of increasing importance to the United States. In 1984 East Asia and the Pacific accounted for 30 per cent of America's foreign trade.[3] The south and west also have their own distinct foreign policy concerns. They are the centres of the American arms and nuclear industry and hence they favour greater defence spending. They are the home of *laissez-faire* capitalism which is hostile to state intervention and trade unions. Hence they are more receptive to anti-communist rhetoric. They have always berated the liberals of the east coast establishment. They regard them as defeatist, supine in the face of communist aggression and too prone to compromise. In like manner, they have always indicated a willingness to ride rough-shod over the qualms of America's NATO allies. They bemoan what they interpret as pacifist or neutralist tendencies in Western Europe and urge American troop withdrawals as a means to force the Europeans to increase their own defence effort.

Reagan himself personified much of this outlook. During his first term, the president was as much concerned with image as he was with policy. He saw his main task as creating a new atmosphere for the conduct of East-West relations. Détente, he claimed at the outset, had been a 'one-way street'. Reagan's rhetoric, particularly his reference to the Soviet Union as the 'evil empire' which had outlawed itself from the international community of civilised nations, was designed first to influence the American public in favour of higher defence spending. Secondly, it was designed to influence America's allies in Western Europe. It signalled that détente was over and that the Europeans were expected to be more supportive of American interests if they wanted to maintain their ties with the United States. Third and last, the rhetoric was designed not so much to influence as to address the Soviet Union. With Soviet troops in Afghanistan, martial law in operation in Poland and an escalating series of civil wars in

Central America, notice was served on the Soviet Union that business as usual was no longer the order of the day.

Amidst the rhetoric, three broad policy objectives emerged during Reagan's first term. First, the rearming of America to a point at which, in the president's own words, 'no enemy will dare threaten the United States'. Reagan inherited from Carter military programmes which included the MX missile, the Trident submarine and the Rapid Deployment Force. The new administration added to these programmes, authorising a 70 per cent increase in the number of warheads in America's nuclear arsenal, resurrecting the neutron bomb and the B-1 bomber and expanding the development of space weapons through the SDI. But the greatest increases in the military budget were devoted to the expansion of America's conventional forces and the improvement of its command and communications structures. Spending in this respect was designed to enhance America's Third World deployment and intervention capability. Centcom, a new Central Command structure, was established in 1983 to oversee American deployments in nineteen countries of the Middle East and West Asia. The expansion of the navy was the key element in the conventional build-up. Weinberger approved the navy's plans to increase America's combat fleet from 455 ships to 600. The planned increase included 2 new nuclear-powered aircraft carriers and 58 new combat ships. The programme was well advanced when Weinberger resigned in November 1987. The navy had already acquired 21 new combat ships and 11 new submarines. Defence outlays for all services had increased by 89 billion dollars, or nearly 45 per cent, during Weinberger's tenure at the Pentagon.[4]

The second objective of the new administration was to exert economic pressure on the Russians by exploiting their dependence on Western imports. Weinberger put the case for this in his 1982 budget report to Congress: '[W]ithout access to advanced technology from the West, the Soviet leadership would be forced to choose between its military-industrial priorities and the preservation of a tightly-controlled political system. By allowing access to a wide range of advanced technologies, we enable the Soviet leadership to evade that dilemma'.[5] American policies in this respect were directed at the allies in Western Europe. Efforts were made to persuade then to limit their trade with Moscow, to withdraw from the gas pipeline project and to abolish their favourable credit arrangements with the Soviet bloc.

Finally, the Reagan administration endeavoured to check and

reverse the growth of Soviet and communist influence in the Third World, either by direct military intervention (as in the case of Grenada in October 1983) or by supplying economic and military aid on a vast scale to the resistance movements operating within those revolutionary states which had been nurtured by Soviet, East European and Cuban aid. American aid flowed to Pakistan and the Islamic resistance in Afghanistan and to the rebel forces of UNITA in Angola. In Central America, the scene of escalating guerrilla warfare since the overthrow of the Somoza dictatorship in Nicaragua in 1979, American aid was channelled in two directions. First, to those governments which were attempting to hold left-wing guerrillas at bay and secondly, to the Contra resistance in Nicaragua which was attempting to overthrow the Sandinista government. For the Reagan administration, vital issues of national security were at stake in Central America. The Sandinistas, with their army of 750,000 men and their Soviet, East European and Cuban advisers, were said to be exporting revolution to their neighbouring Central American states. Unless checked, the contagion might spread south, to the countries of Latin America, and north, to Mexico and the border with the United States. The Contras, originally a few hundred ex-members of Somoza's National Guard but now a guerrilla force of about 18,000, were the principal beneficiaries of American aid. The Reagan administration also aided the governments of El Salvador, Guatemala and Honduras. In these three countries, military dictatorships had been replaced by democratically elected presidents. Left-wing guerrillas continued to harass president José Napoleon Duarte of El Salvador and the Honduras of President José Azcona became a frontline state. Contra bases were established in Honduras and President Azcona permitted American military exercises on Honduran soil to keep the Sandinistas guessing about a possible invasion. By 1986, the Americans had sent about one billion dollars in military aid and four billion in economic aid to their various Central American clients. Nicaragua had received about 500 million dollars in military aid from the Soviet Union and 4 million from Cuba. The cost in human lives was enormous. Since 1979, there had been 70,000 political killings in Nicaragua, 65,000 in El Salvador and 15,000 in Guatemala.[6]

Throughout his first term, Reagan enjoyed considerable domestic popularity as the president who had restored America's pride, prestige and military strength. At home he established a reputation as a gifted political communicator, able almost at will to appeal direct to the

American people to win popular support for his policies. But in common with his predecessors, Reagan soon discovered that having enormous military power at his disposal was no guarantee that he would be able to enforce his will. His escalation of the arms race, and his inadvertent and often incoherent comments about the possibility of a limited nuclear exchange, created unease in Western Europe and rallied the European peace movements into still greater opposition against the deployment of cruise and Pershing. He was defeated on the issue of sanctions against Moscow during the Polish crisis. A greater setback awaited him in the Middle East where his 1982 peace initiative foundered on the twin rocks of Israeli intransigence and the internecine power struggle being waged between rival Christian and Muslim militias in the war-torn Lebanon.

Despite Camp David and the peace treaty with Egypt, Israel remained committed to a military solution to its problems and continued to encourage Israeli settlement on the West Bank of the Jordan. The conflict between Israel and the PLO shifted to southern Lebanon and both sides engaged in cross border raids and bombings. In June 1982 Israel invaded the Lebanon and besieged West Beirut which served as a base for the Palestinian army and a refugee camp home for tens of thousands of Palestinian civilians. The conflict escalated in July when Israel destroyed Syria's SAM-6 batteries in the Bekaa Valley. Philip Habib, Reagan's special envoy, was despatched to the Middle East in an endeavour to find a diplomatic solution to the crisis. A compromise was agreed in August. Israel lifted the siege and a multi-national force of American, French and Italian troops arrived to supervise the evacuation of the PLO army to Tunisia and Jordan, two countries which Habib had persuaded to accept Yassir Arafat's soldiers. Reagan chose this moment to announce his peace plan. While carefully avoiding recognition of the PLO and excluding the establishment of a separate Palestinian state, the president proposed in September 1982 that talks should be held to enable the Palestinians of the West Bank and Gaza to achieve self-government in association with Jordan. Israel denounced the plan and, following the assassination of Bashir Gemayel, the Lebanese president, Israeli troops yet again surrounded West Beirut. The Phalangist Christian militia of the Lebanon, Israel's close allies, then moved in to the Palestinian camps of Sabra and Chatila and slaughtered hundreds of civilians, including women and children. Amidst worldwide condemnation of this atrocity, the multinational force returned in an effort to restore peace and an

Israeli withdrawal but it came under fire from the Muslim Druze militia. Suicide bombings on the American embassy in Beirut in April 1983 and on American and French battalion headquarters in October 1983 claimed over 350 lives. Powerless to influence the tragic course of events which were unfolding, Reagan was left to make the futile gesture of ordering American warships to shell Druze positions in the Chouf Hills to the south of Beirut.[7]

Less was heard of the 'evil empire' during Reagan's second term which began in January 1985. The president's personal outlook had not changed but the realities of office, together with pressures from Congress, the European allies and the publicity-seeking Mikhail Gorbachev who came to power in the Soviet Union in March 1985, forced the president to modify his earlier Cold War stance. The Reagan administration now advocated a strategy which George Shultz described as 'constructive confrontation'.[8] The modified outlook was not intended to resurrect the 70s version of Soviet-American détente which had linked arms control with close cooperation in the fields of economic, scientific and technological exchange. It was constructive in the sense that it embraced negotiations to reduce certain categories of nuclear weapons and to eliminate others altogether. But it was confrontational on human rights and on regional issues. The administration engaged in military action to defend American interests in the Persian Gulf and exerted increased pressure on the Sandinista regime in Nicaragua. It also remained committed to a system of defence against nuclear weapons based on the SDI.

On the issue of arms control, the dialogue was resumed in March 1985 when the Russians returned to the negotiating table they had vacated at Geneva in November 1983 in protest against the first deployments of cruise and Pershing. The resumption of the Geneva arms talks paved the way for three summit meetings between Reagan and Gorbachev. The first, at Geneva in November 1985, provided an opportunity for a review of progress made at the arms talks and an exchange of views on regional issues. The second, at Reykjavik in October 1986, collapsed because of fundamental differences over the Strategic Defence Initiative. The third, at Washington in December 1987, delivered an INF Treaty signed by Reagan and Gorbachev. The first of its kind to eliminate rather than to limit the growth of nuclear weapons, the INF Treaty was hailed as retrospective justification for the zero option on intermediate-range nuclear weapons which Reagan had first proposed in 1981. Once again a conservative president with an impeccable record of anti-communism had turned somersault in his negotiations with the Soviet Union.

Although it had yet to be ratified by the American Senate and the Supreme Soviet, the INF Treaty represented the major foreign policy achievement of the Reagan presidency. It was seen as preparation for a more significant agreement to reduce by half the strategic arsenals of the superpowers. But events elsewhere cast a shadow over the president's achievement. His second term began on a note of high expectation, the president proclaiming in one of his more exuberant moments that America was back and that there were no limits to what the American people might achieve. But by the end of 1987 the expectations had turned sour. Reagan was in danger of becoming a lame-duck president, struggling to preserve his credibility during the final twelve months of his administration. The president's difficulties began a year into his second term when Ferdinand Marcos, one of America's closest allies, was swept from power in the Philippines by Corazon Aquino. At home, mounting opposition to Reagan's economic policies was a key factor which enabled the Democrats to increase their majority in the House of Representatives and to capture control of the Senate at the November 1986 mid-term elections. Several battles lay ahead between the White House and Capitol Hill. They included the issues of the budget deficit, defence spending, the president's ill-starred nominations to fill the vacant place on the Supreme Court and American policy in Central America and the Persian Gulf. In the case of the Gulf, Reagan vowed in June 1987 to keep the shipping lanes open and authorised American naval protection for Kuwaiti tankers which had been reflagged under the American flag. As American warships sparred with Iranian gunboats, Congress became nervous and threatened to invoke the 1973 War Powers Act. Above all, however, domestic confidence in the president, the key to so much of personal authority both at home and abroad, was undermined because of his handling of the Iran-Contra affair and the budget crisis.

The Iran-Contra affair began in July 1985. In an endeavour to secure the release of American hostages in the Lebanon, the president authorised secret arms sales to Iran through Israel. Ironically, just ten days earlier, Reagan had suggested that Iran was part of 'a new international version of Murder Incorporated' and vowed that the United States would 'never make concessions to terrorists'. Money from the arms sales was used, not only to finance the Contra war effort, but also to line pockets in the United States. The transactions generated profits of 16.1 million dollars but only 3.8 million went to the Contras. As the details became known, Reagan was forced to admit an error of judgement in authorising the sale of weapons to Iran but he denied all knowledge of the use to which the proceeds had been put. The president's version of events was accepted by the Tower Commission, which Reagan himself set up, and the Congressional Committee, both of which reported in 1987. But these reports, particularly that of the Congressional Committee, censored the president for his handling of the affair. The Congressional Committee blamed him for creating an environment in which 'those who did know of the diversion of [funds] believed with certainty that they were carrying out the president's policies'. The Committee concluded that 'a cabal of zealots' had been in charge, flouting laws (like the Arms Export Control Act which banned arms exports to terrorists) with impunity.[9] The affair confirmed a growing impression that the president exercised little direct control or supervision over his officials. Two of the officials most directly involved – Admiral John Poindexter, Reagan's former National Security Adviser, and Lieutenant Colonel Oliver North – were left facing criminal prosecutions.

The Iran-Contra affair cast serious doubts over Reagan's policy towards Central America. At the beginning of August 1987, the president unveiled a peace plan for Nicaragua. Largely the work of Jim Wright, the Democratic Speaker of the House of Representatives, the plan called for a ceasefire in Nicaragua, an end to Soviet bloc aid, the restoration of civil liberties, recognition of the Contras as a legitimate political group and a timetable for the holding of democratic elections. All this was to be in place by 30 September 1987, the date when the last officially approved American aid allocation of 100 million dollars to the Contras ran out. Reagan's critics argued that the plan was designed to be rejected by the Sandinistas so that the president could go back to Congress for more Contra aid. The critics also suggested that the plan was an attempt to undermine the regional peace initiative inspired by President Oscar Arias of Costa Rica. The Arias plan, signed in Guatemala City by the five presidents of Central America just three days after the announcement of the Reagan plan, established an extended timetable for the achievement of democratisation and national reconciliation throughout the region. 7 November 1987 was set as the first deadline for, on the one hand, the restoration of civil liberties and democratic rights and, on the other, cease-fire agreements to terminate the region's guerrilla wars and the outside aid which had financed and supported them. The Arias plan also established a Commission of Verification and Follow-Up – consisting of thirteen foreign ministers from Central and Latin America, together with the Latin General-Secretaries of the United Nations and the Organisation of American States – which was due to review progress one month later. The Commission's findings were to be discussed by the five Central American presidents at the beginning of January 1988 and direct elections to a Central American Parliament were to be held later in the year.[10]

From the outset, the Reagan administration was deeply sceptical about the Sandinistas' commitment to the Arias plan. But Daniel Ortega, the Nicaraguan president, readily complied with a number of the plan's preconditions. The war against the Contras had devastated the Nicaraguan economy. Inflation was said to be running at 700 per cent, oil imports had fallen 20 per cent below Nicaragua's requirements and large-scale Soviet aid could no longer be relied upon. Nicaragua's economic crisis persuaded Ortega to comply with the Arias plan by releasing political prisoners, allowing opposition groups to stage demonstrations and rallies, lifting the ban on *La Prensa*, the main opposition newspaper, and reopening Nicaragua's independent radio stations. On the crucial question of ending the Contra war, Ortega returned from Moscow (where he had attended the ceremonies commemorating the 70th anniversary of the Bolshevik Revolution) in time for the November 1987 deadline. He then proposed a negotiated ceasefire with Cardinal Miguel Obando y Bravo, Nicaragua's Roman Catholic Primate, acting as an intermediary.[11] Ortega also offered to lift the state of emergency and release all but the old Somozan political prisoners under a general amnesty on condition that the United States and Honduras agreed to withdraw their aid to the Contras. On this key point, Ortega's version of a negotiated settlement differed substantially from that of the Reagan administration. Reagan insisted that the Contras had to be kept in play, and armed, to ensure Sandinista compliance with the Arias plan. Ortega argued that full democratisation and an amnesty were not possible unless the armed conflict was brought to an end. The Reagan administration deferred a decision on renewed Contra aid until the beginning of 1988 but the president had become increasingly isolated. Wright, author of Reagan's peace initiative, switched allegiance to the Arias plan. In the light of the Iran-Contra affair, observers predicted that the president would be defeated if he sought renewed Contra funding from the Democratic majority in Congress.

The American budget crisis had more serious long-term implications.[12] Under the Reagan administration, the United States reverted once more to policies and strategies which suggested that American wealth and power were inexhaustible. By maintaining domestic and international commitments which the United States could no longer afford, the Reagan administration exacerbated the problem of the relative decline of the American economy. While pursuing a policy of expensive rearmament, the administration cut taxes to stimulate growth and prosperity at home. The result was a budget deficit which, in the space of five years, transformed the United States into the world's largest debtor nation. America became increasingly dependent on foreign (mainly Japanese) loans to maintain its domestic prosperity and its global position. To finance the deficit, the Reagan administration raised interest rates. This in turn attracted foreign capital into the American economy and increased the value of the dollar. With an overvalued dollar, American exports dropped and imports rose dramatically. By the mid-80s, the United States had acquired a trade deficit of some 170 billion dollars. The budget deficit and high interest rates had other unpleasant side effects, notably a decline in investment in American industry and a 13 per cent reduction in manufacturing employment. The president was at first loathe to increase taxes to tackle the deficit. America's trading partners, particularly Japan and West Germany, were reluctant to stimulate their own economies by adopting Reagan's economic methods in order to import more (American) goods. Congress began to see protection as the only solution. The prospect of a trade war loomed, with the United States having to impose high tariffs and import quotas. Failure to tackle the budget deficit undermined confidence in the American economy and precipitated a worldwide stock market collapse in the autumn of 1987. Under pressure from his Japanese and West European allies, Reagan negotiated a package with Congress to reduce the deficit by 75 billion dollars over the next 2 years with a further cut of 45 billion in 1989. The package included larger than expected tax increases, of 9 million dollars in 1987 and 14 billion in the following year.

The budget crisis demonstrated that America's longstanding commitment to a liberal, multilateral world economy was no longer practical. The regionalised world economy envisaged by Nixon and Kissinger had finally emerged as reality. The United States had slipped from a position of economic hegemony to one of first among equals. The trend could not be reversed. Western Europe (through the European Community) and Japan had developed as self-contained economic blocs, able to resist any American efforts to penetrate them. By living, during the Reagan years, on borrowed time and borrowed money, the United States had allowed its commitments to far exceed its resources. Experts predicted that Reagan's successor would be forced, as a matter of priority, to reduce expenditure in order to balance national objectives against national resources. This adjustment would require difficult decisions. As one American analyst explained in 1987:

> If the United States cannot continue to borrow abroad to finance its military and social programs, will not decrease domestic consumption, and can no longer afford to slight capital formation, then it will have no other choice than to reduce the costs of its overseas commitments in Western Europe, East Asia, and elsewhere. Unless major efficiencies are achieved in the Pentagon . . . the United States will be forced to cut back its commitments.[13]

In short, the United States would have to negotiate a new relationship with Western Europe and Japan which reflected contemporary political, economic and strategic realities. It would no longer be possible for the United States to behave as if the security of its allies was primarily an American responsibility. The West Europeans and the Japanese were left facing the long overdue prospect that they would have to assume a much greater responsibility for their own defence.

THE SOVIET UNION: FROM BREZHNEV TO GORBACHEV

Commenting in October 1986 on the manner in which the question of the SDI had collapsed the Reykjavik summit, Zbigniew Brzezinski observed: 'I think the Soviet Union realises that what they were predicting in the 70s, namely the general crisis of capitalism, is not coming to pass, and that we are witnessing instead the general crisis of communism. This means that the Soviet Union has to set its house in order, pull itself together, and in that context the wide-open, intense and largely scientific-technological competition with the United States is not in the Soviet interest'.[14] Brzezinski's crisis of communism began first in Poland in 1980 and 1981. It is discussed below (pp. 197–200).

At issue here is the crisis of Soviet communism which began right at the top, within the Soviet leadership.

With ageing or ailing leaders following each other in rapid succession, Moscow's leadership crisis at the beginning of the 80s destroyed the continuity of the Brezhnev era.[15] Brezhnev died in November 1982. He was succeeded by Yuri Andropov, Soviet Ambassador in Hungary during the 1956 uprising and then, successively, head of the Central Committee's department for handling relations with communist parties in other socialist countries and head of the KGB. Andropov did not survive two years in office and he spent the last few months of his life on a kidney dialysis machine before his death in February 1984. At home during his brief reign Andropov endeavoured to shake the party and bureaucracy from their complacency and lethargy. He criticised the received wisdom of the last decade of the Brezhnev years which maintained that the Soviet Union had entered the period of 'mature socialism', the penultimate stage before the attainment of full communism. Andropov challenged this line of thinking and contrasted the fiction of a Soviet system capable of generating growth and technological progress with the reality of an economy which was still relatively backward, of workers who lacked discipline, of bureaucrats who were corrupt and of party managers who were complacent. Andropov's reforms, if such they can be described during such a short period in office, concentrated on enforcing greater discipline among workers and greater accountability and responsibility among managers and bureaucrats. Abroad, Andropov presented a stern face. Reagan and his policies were seen as a test of Moscow's will and determination to maintain its international position. Andropov laboured unsuccessfully to forestall the deployment of cruise and Pershing missiles in Western Europe. He rejected Reagan's 'zero-option' and suggested as an alternative a reduction in Soviet intermediate-range missiles to the level of the combined totals of the British and French nuclear forces in exchange for the non-deployment of cruise and Pershing. His propaganda campaign against the new NATO missiles received a severe setback in September 1983 when a South Korean passenger aircraft was shot down over Soviet airspace. Bitter recriminations over the incident emanated from the White House and the Kremlin and relations deteriorated still further in November 1983 when, in response to the first deployments of cruise and Pershing, the Soviet delegation walked out of the Geneva arms talks.

After Andropov's death the choice of a successor seemed to lie between two of the more youthful members of the Politburo – Mikhail Gorbachev and Grigori Romanov. Similar in ambition, these two rival contenders for the top post were vastly different in outlook and personality. Gorbachev was liberal (by Soviet standards), methodical and hardworking. Romanov was a hardliner, impulsive and self-indulgent. In the event, however, the succession outcome was determined by the old guard on the Politburo, particularly Andrei Gromyko, the Foreign Minister, and Dimitrii Ustinov, the Defence Minister. At a time of international danger and unresolved problems at home, the old guard decided to play safe by supporting the nomination of the ageing Konstantin Chernenko. Clearly an interim leader, Chernenko would nonetheless be deferential towards his old Politburo comrades and their foreign and security policies would be safe in his hands. Gorbachev and Romanov, the 'Young Turks' in the leadership stakes, did not oppose Chernenko's nomination. Both recognised that time was on their side and that they could ill-afford, at this stage, to undermine their standing with the old guard. Foreign policy during Chernenko's brief tenure was controlled by the veteran Gromyko and it was at his initiative that the Geneva arms talks were reopened in March 1985. On the domestic scene, Gorbachev increasingly emerged as the most likely successor. He acquired a new range of responsibilities which included ideological pronouncements, meetings with foreign leaders, the handling of relations with Eastern Europe and the preparation of a new party programme. The post from which he operated was that of Secretary of the Central Committee. This gave him supervisory authority over his rivals. He prepared the agenda for the Secretariat, chaired meetings in Chernenko's absence and even, according to some sources, when Chernenko participated. Within hours of Chernenko's death in March 1985, Gorbachev was elected as General-Secretary.

Gorbachev immediately became the subject of intense media speculation in the Western world. At the age of 54 he presented, in contrast to his ageing or ailing predecessors, a youthful and energetic image. At first superficial comparisons were made between Gorbachev and Khrushchev. Both had specialised in Soviet agriculture but there the comparisons ceased. Khrushchev was not in the same mould as Gorbachev. A lawyer by training, although he never actually practised, Gorbachev had risen to the top as a professional party politician and as an organisation man. A protégé of Andropov, he represented a new generation of Soviet leaders who seemed to place less emphasis on ideology and more on efficiency in their approach to domestic policies. They wanted, above all, to modernise the Soviet Union after the years of inertia and stagnation under Brezhnev. Two key words – *glasnost* or openness and *perestroika* or reconstruction – set the tone for Gorbachev's reforming experiment. *Glasnost* involved modest proposals – plural candidacies for elections to the Soviets and secret ballots for the election of regional party secretaries – for the democratisation of some aspects of Soviet political life.[16] It also involved a more liberal and more relaxed attitude towards freedom of expression, relations with the non-Russian ethnic minorities and the treatment of dissidents. Representatives of the Crimean Tartars were allowed audiences with senior government officials to discuss resettlement in their former homeland and patriotic demonstrations passed without incident on the streets of the capitals of the Baltic republics. By the first half of 1987, over 200 dissidents had been released either from exile or labour camps. They included, most prominently, Anatoly Shcharansky who was released in February 1986, Dr Yuri Orlov and Dr Andrei Sakharov who were released in October and December 1986 respectively, and Josef Begun, the most celebrated of the *refuseniks* (people, usually Jews, who had been refused permission to emigrate), who was released in February 1987. On a still more sensitive note, wide publicity was given to the reassessment of Stalinism by a number of prominent Soviet historians. Gorbachev himself addressed the legacy of Stalin in November 1987 in his speech marking the 70th anniversary of the Bolshevik Revolution. The speech was so worded as to avoid undermining Stalin's achievements. The struggle against the kulaks (wealthy peasants) over collectivisation was described as 'basically correct' and 'of fundamental importance' in 'consolidating socialism in the countryside'. But picking up where Khrushchev had left off in 1956, Gorbachev attacked Stalin's methods. He referred to the 'bitter truth' about the 'many thousands of people inside and outside the party' who had been subjected to 'wholesale repressive measures'. Promising a commission to rehabilitate some of Stalin's victims, Gorbachev described as 'enormous and unforgivable' the acts of lawlessness and the repressive measures for which Stalin and his entourage had been responsible.[17]

But if *glasnost* created the climate for Gorbachev's reforms, success or failure depended much more on *perestroika*. Here, as Henry Kissinger observed, the Soviet Union found itself in the unenviable position of being threatened simultaneously by two crises – an economic crisis if it did nothing to change its system, and a political crisis if it did anything. For Seweryn Bialer, the paradox inherent in the Soviet system found expression in two dilemmas:

> First, military growth is one of the chief sources of the internal problems besetting the Soviet Union and makes more difficult their resolution; at the same time, military growth is regarded by the leadership as a supreme value to which the economy and society must be subordinated. Second, economic revitalization of the system would require a devolution of political power; yet the paramount goal of the leadership, from the regime's inception, has been the centralization and concentration of political power.[18]

In opting for *perestroika*, Gorbachev demonstrated that he was prepared to take the political risks of economic reforms. The economic problems which Gorbachev faced were far more acute than those which confronted Brezhnev in the late 60s and early 70s. The rate of growth had fallen to under 3 per cent and the value of food imports had risen from 5 billion dollars in 1974 to over 15 billion dollars in 1980. To achieve the pace of economic and technological growth essential to sustained military and economic competition with the West, Gorbachev insisted on a minimum annual growth rate of 4 per cent. But whereas Brezhnev sought to compensate for the Soviet Union's economic shortcomings by promoting an enormous expansion of foreign economic relations, Gorbachev advocated a strategy based on socialist self-reliance. 'Socialism must achieve this advance in its own way', he declared of the 4 per cent growth rate in May 1985, 'or, to put it concretely, by Soviet methods.'[19] *Perestroika* implied that more efficient use be made of the productive resources of the socialist bloc. It also urged greater accountability on the part of industrial managers and, given the chronic level of worker absenteeism, improved discipline on the factory floor. It demanded that the system of planning be overhauled and streamlined. Individual work units would no longer be judged, and rewarded, by their ability to meet their plan targets. Account would now be taken of the quality of their products and of their labour productivity. *Perestroika* also suggested that new incentives were necessary to reward individual initiative. In November 1986, Gorbachev evoked memories of the New Economic Policy introduced by Lenin at the end of the Russian Civil War by legalising privately owned cottage industries and small family firms and allowing them to operate outside the state system. Equally, *perestroika* called for more realistic methods of economic management. In June 1987, at a meeting of the Central Committee, Gorbachev spoke of 'switching from fundamentally administrative methods to fundamentally economic methods' of managing the economy. The enormous state subsidies on housing rents (which had remained fixed since 1928) and on certain items of food, were to be replaced by a pricing system which reflected costs and the worth of goods in the marketplace. In the immediate future, Soviet citizens faced the prospect of rising prices, the closure of inefficient enterprises and job losses.[20]

Above all, *perestroika* called upon the Soviet scientific establishment to devise, on its own, revolutionary solutions to technological problems. Gorbachev did not rule out economic relations with the West but he made it clear that there would be no political trade-offs for increased trade, whether in the form of Jewish emigration, treatment of dissidents, loosening of the Soviet bloc in Eastern Europe or limitations on Soviet behaviour in other areas of the world. The release of dissidents and an increase in Jewish emigration no doubt improved the image of the Soviet Union in the West, making it possible, for instance, for the Soviet leaders to organise a 'peace forum' at Moscow in February 1987. Addressing the forum, Gorbachev himself denied that the 'new approach to humanitarian problems' had been the result of 'pressure on us from the West'. He described it instead as the result of 'the new way of thinking', by which he meant that a more open society would be better placed to meet the challenge of an increasingly technological age.[21] That the Soviet union would not bow to external pressure was demonstrated by the circumstances under which both Anatoly Shcharansky and Dr Yuri Orlov were released. Shcharansky was released in February 1986, not as a Jewish dissident, but as part of a spy exchange. The same applied when Orlov was released and allowed to leave the Soviet Union in October 1986. Orlov was part of a spy-swap in which the Soviet Union released Nicholas Daniloff, an American journalist arrested in Moscow as a suspected spy, in exchange for Gennady Zakharov, a Soviet official at the United Nations in New York whom the Americans had arrested on similar suspicion.

The success or otherwise of *glasnost* and *perestroika* remained an imponderable at the end of 1987. Gorbachev spent the late summer of 1987 outlining his views on disarmament and the economic problems confronting the Soviet Union in his new book, *Perestroika and New*

Thinking for Our Country and the Whole World. He emerged from his seclusion in September to warn that the next eighteen months would be critical. 'It is a revolution – without shots, but a deep and serious one,' he told workers at Murmansk. 'You have to keep yourselves in check comrades, and you must not panic.'[22] Murmurings of discontent could be heard within the establishments of both the security forces, who feared the consequences of releasing dissidents and of allowing the ethnic minorities to stage nationalist demonstrations, and the bureaucracy which resented and feared the economic reforms because they threatened positions of power and privileged lifestyles. The strains and tensions generated by Gorbachev's reforms had also reached the upper echelons of the party. At a meeting of the Central Committee in October, Boris Yeltsin, a reform enthusiast who headed the Moscow City Communist Party, clashed with Yegor Ligachev, the Kremlin's chief ideologue, over Yeltsin's accusation that the reforms were being blocked. Viktor Chebrikov, the head of the KGB, sided with Ligachev and Yeltsin offered to resign both from his Moscow job and his post as a candidate (non-voting) member of the Politburo. Ligachev was not an opponent of *perestroika* but he warned of possible excesses. The party, he argued, should be on its guard against the enemies of socialism who posed as reformers and those who took advantage of *glasnost* to pour out 'filth and froth'.[23] In his speech marking the 70th anniversary of the revolution, Gorbachev trod a delicate path, attacking the conservative forces who were resisting his reforms but also the headstrong elements within the party who wanted to quicken the pace.[24] The strength of conservatism within the party was demonstrated shortly after when Yeltsin was dismissed from his Moscow post. At the end of 1987 it was still too early to judge whether Gorbachev would be able to eclipse or convert the opposition and chart the Soviet Union on a course of domestic reform which would extend, under his leadership, into the 90s. But an equally significant question begged a more immediate answer: to what extent would the reform experiments at home influence the conduct of foreign policy abroad?

Philip Stewart, an American analyst, has identified three different foreign policy orientations within the Soviet leadership of the past twenty years. He describes the first as 'accommodationist', the second as 'Leninist-internationalist' and the third as 'nationalist-isolationist'. The first, which Stewart identifies with Brezhnev, is focused primarily on Soviet-American relations. It is symbolic of the Soviet Union's coming of age as a great power. It assumes a superpower partnership to manage crisis situations, to negotiate agreements about arms control and to promote economic, scientific and technological exchange. To all intents and purposes, it represents détente. The second pays more heed to doctrine and ideology in the making of Soviet foreign policy. It places more emphasis on the unyielding nature of the competition between capitalism and socialism, particularly in the Third World. Stewart identifies this position with Mikhail Suslov, the chief Soviet ideologue of the Brezhnev years who died in 1982. He suggests that the influence of Suslov might have been decisive when the decisions were taken to intervene in Angola and the Horn of Africa in the 70s. The third orientation maintains that the primary concern of Soviet foreign policy is the security of the homeland and of communist rule within it. A secondary concern, which is so closely related to the first that at times it becomes indistinguishable, is the security of the 'empire' in Eastern Europe. Soviet leaders of all persuasions have long been accustomed to viewing the question of communist rule and dominance in Eastern Europe as an 'internal' Soviet problem. Stewart identifies this position with the new leader, Mikhail Gorbachev.[25]

Stewart appreciates that Soviet leaders do not fit neatly into single categories. The three positions he describes collectively represent a cross-section of each of the major Soviet foreign policy concerns. They combine, at one and the same time, elements of ideology, international status and power, state security and Russian nationalism. A leader in one category frequently exhibits tendencies from the other two. But his distinctions remain valid in the sense that priorities and points of emphasis do vary according to the leader's personal outlook. And, with clear reservations about the 'isolationist' component, the evidence to date suggests that Stewart is right in placing Gorbachev in the third, nationalist, category.

Gorbachev's own assessment of the economic problems facing the Soviet Union, together with his analysis of the balance of international forces, suggested the emergence of a regime which would be less expansionist abroad and which would give greater priority to domestic economic reconstruction. This was made clear in Gorbachev's address to the Moscow peace forum in February 1987: 'Our foreign policy is more than ever determined by domestic policy, by our interest in concentrating our constructive endeavours to improve our country. This is why we need lasting peace, predictability and constructiveness in international relations.'[26] In the wider context of relations with the

West, Gorbachev believed that many of the perceptions which had underpinned Brezhnev's détente strategy were no longer valid. Brezhnev had engaged in détente at a time when, as seen from Moscow, the balance of international forces was moving in favour of the Soviet Union. The American involvement and defeat in Vietnam suggested that an era of American global dominance had come to an end. This, together with strategic parity, suggested that the United States was now ready to accept the Soviet Union as an equal superpower. Gorbachev, however, was faced by a resurgent America. During Reagan's first term, the increase in American defence expenditure and the administration's attitude towards arms control were viewed in Moscow as evidence that the United States no longer accepted the concept of strategic parity. Equally, the renewed American assertiveness in Grenada, the Lebanon and Nicaragua, together with the lifting of the congressional ban on aid to the rebels in Angola and the reactivation of what the Russians regarded as West German revanchism, all suggested to Moscow the opening of a new imperialist offensive. As Gorbachev put it in April 1985, a month after his appointment as General-Secretary: 'One does not need special political vision in order to see how imperialism has intensified its subversive work and coordinated its activities against socialist states in the course of the last few years. This applies to all areas: political, economic, ideological, and military.'[27]

Over the next two years, Reagan toned down his anti-Soviet rhetoric and embarked on serious negotiations to either eliminate or reduce certain categories of nuclear weapons. But the president maintained the pressure on the Sandinista regime in Managua, confronted Iran in the waters of the Persian Gulf and clung tenaciously to the SDI. Gorbachev had little reason to modify his initial outlook. The American challenge continued to impart a sense of urgency to his domestic reform programme and to shape his attitude towards American-Soviet relations. To buy time for the Soviet Union to rebuild its economy, Gorbachev articulated a foreign policy which was defensive in the sense that it emphasised security and domestic reconstruction as the priorities. But at the same time Gorbachev recognised the need for the Soviet Union to explore new options as a means of consolidating and enhancing its international influence. In a manner quite unlike that of any of his predecessors, Gorbachev argued that Soviet foreign policy should be based on a view of the world as it was, not on how the Russians imagined it or wanted it to be. In this context, he

acknowledged that the outcome of the historic contest between capitalism and socialism remained open and undecided. Specifically, therefore, Gorbachev's foreign policy had two main objectives. First, to
obtain an agreement on nuclear weapons which would enable the
Soviet Union to concentrate on more pressing economic and social
problems and which would also halt the American military build-up.
Secondly, to probe where possible in order to improve the Soviet
Union's international standing and restrict any further extension of
America's political and military influence. Both objectives explained
the reasoning and justification behind his early 'peace campaigns',
which were designed to mobilise anti-American sentiment in Europe
and anti-Western pressures in the Third World. They also explained
the radical nature of his subsequent proposals to reduce the nuclear
arsenals of the superpowers. In May 1985, in his Victory Day speech
commemorating the 40th anniversary of the end of the Great Patriotic
War, Gorbachev declared:

> Of course, special responsibility for the destiny of the world today
> rests with the nuclear powers and primarily with the USSR and
> the US. However, the Soviet Union has never looked at the world
> in the context of USSR-US relations alone. We are deeply convinced
> that all states can and must be involved in a search for realistic
> solutions to urgent problems and in efforts to ease international
> tensions. The voices of millions of people in various countries, raised
> in favour of effective measures to end the arms race and to reduce
> arms stockpiles, against attempts to use negotiations as cover for
> the continuation of this race, is of tremendous importance.[28]

Two years later, at the peace forum in Moscow, Gorbachev advanced
the argument a significant stage further by declaring that no political
objectives were worth the risk of nuclear war:

> We came to conclusions that made us review something which once
> seemed axiomatic. Since Hiroshima and Nagasaki, war has ceased
> to be a continuation of politics by other means. The human race
> has lost its immortality. It can only be regained by destroying
> nuclear weapons .... This is no one-off adjustment of position, but
> a new methodology for international affairs ... military doctrines
> must be of a purely defensive nature.[29]

Gorbachev's outlook also explained a series of new Soviet political initiatives on China, the Middle East and Afghanistan. With regard to China, Deng Xiaoping's modernisation programme added a fresh competitive edge to the Sino-Soviet conflict. Designed to create centres of high technology on the level of the most advanced world standards around such existing industrial centres as Shanghai and Canton, China's modernisation programme embraced only 10 per cent of the country's 1 billion plus population. But this 10 per cent constituted 120–130 million people. Western and Soviet observers began to speculate on the prospect that if China succeeded, another Japan would emerge upon the global economy and world market within the next 30 or 40 years. The principles of China's modernisation programme were confirmed and extended at the Thirteenth Congress of the Chinese Communist Party in Beijing in October-November 1987. Deng Xiaoping successfully engineered a smooth transition to a new and more youthful leadership committed to his reform programme. Nine senior party leaders, all in their seventies or eighties, stood down. They included Deng himself, although he remained a powerful figure by retaining his chairmanship of the Central Military Commission which controlled the People's Liberation Army. The mantle of political leadership descended on Deng's protégé, Zhao Ziyang. China's new pragmatic course posed far greater problems for the Soviet Union than the ideological fanaticism of Mao Zedong. As Seweryn Bialer has written: 'Few countries in the world have a great past and a great future. China is foremost among them, and it is its future that the Soviets fear more than its present'.[30] Soviet concern in this respect, particularly at a time of growing economic ties between China and the West, gave added impetus to Gorbachev's own reform programme. It might also explain why Gorbachev signalled a new willingness to consider China's conditions for a thaw in Sino-Soviet relations. Since 1979 Beijing had insisted on the fulfilment of three conditions: a Soviet withdrawal from Afghanistan, reductions in Soviet troop deployments along the Sino-Soviet frontier, and an end to Soviet support for Vietnam in Kampuchea. In an important speech at Vladivostok in July 1986, Gorbachev extended an olive branch on the first two of these conditions. He offered to withdraw six battalions from Afghanistan and also revealed that he had asked Mongolia (a Soviet satellite on the Chinese border with a large Soviet military presence) to agree to the removal of a 'considerable number' of Soviet troops.[31]

Within the context of the Middle East, Gorbachev declared in April 1987 that the absence of diplomatic relations between the Soviet Union and Israel 'cannot be considered normal'. His statement was followed in July 1987 by the arrival of an official Soviet consular delegation in Jerusalem. Both moves marked the culmination of two years' behind the scenes diplomatic activity which had begun in July 1985 with an informal meeting in Paris between the Soviet and Israeli ambassadors to France and which had been continued through a series of contacts between Israeli and East European (chiefly Polish and Bulgarian) diplomats. Having severed relations with Israel after the Six-Day War of 1967, Moscow had eliminated itself as a potential mediator between the Arabs and the Israelis. That role had fallen, more or less exclusively, to the United States. After the expulsion of Soviet diplomats and technicians from Egypt in 1972 and the subsequent Arab-Israeli conflict in 1973, Moscow could not afford to risk alienating the radical Arabs still further by renewing relations with Israel. Soviet leaders therefore insisted that the resumption of relations depended upon Israel withdrawing from the occupied territories, abandoning its 'strategic understanding' with the United States and accepting PLO representation in peace negotiations at a reconvened Geneva conference. Israeli rejection of these conditions left the Soviet Union with a peripheral role in the Middle East. Soviet diplomacy between 1985 and 1987 demonstrated that Gorbachev had moderated the Soviet position. Soviet demands were now presented as Moscow's view of what was required for a Middle East settlement, not as preconditions for the resumption of diplomatic relations with Israel. By expanding Soviet options in the Middle East, Gorbachev wanted to break the American monopoly on the peace process, to limit American political and military influence in the region and to gain support for the resumption of an international Middle Eastern conference at which the Soviet Union would play a leading role. The same motives led Gorbachev to place less emphasis on forging a bloc of radical Arab allies in the Middle East and rather more on establishing relations with the more conservative and moderate states. His first two years in power witnessed a flurry of Soviet diplomatic activity in the Gulf states, an attempt to improve relations with Saudi Arabia, the return of a Soviet ambassador to Cairo and a statement from King Hussein of Jordan to the effect that an international conference should be convened with Soviet participation.

Gorbachev's efforts to improve relations with Israel and to forge new links with the conservative and moderate Arab states, complicated relations with Syria, Moscow's principal radical ally in the Middle East. President Assad of Syria, Israel's most implacable adversary, visited Moscow in April 1987 and was told by Gorbachev that a military solution to the Middle East conflict was no longer credible. Gorbachev therefore opposed Syrian ambitions to establish political control over the PLO, territorial control in the strife-torn Lebanon and 'strategic parity' with Israel. The Gulf conflict added a further complication, not least because up until the Arab summit at Amman in November 1987, Syria supported Iran in the war of attrition against Iraq, Moscow's other radical ally in the Middle East.[32] The Soviet Union had every reason to want a negotiated end to the Gulf conflict. The UN Security Council resolution of July 1987, which called for a cease-fire and troop withdrawals from occupied territory, was passed unanimously. From Moscow's viewpoint, the effectiveness of Soviet military assistance would again become suspect in Arab eyes if Iraq were defeated. Worse still, an Iranian victory would allow Khomeinism to spread along the Soviet frontier. An escalation of the conflict, with the United States intervening against Iran, might persuade Baghdad to turn to Washington for the aid needed to maintain its war effort. Above all, with the war in its seventh year in 1987, the United States had established a significant military presence in the Persian Gulf – the very circumstance which Gorbachev's Middle Eastern diplomacy had been designed to avoid. But however much he wanted the war to end, Gorbachev was reluctant to enforce compliance with the UN resolution by supporting the call for sanctions and an arms embargo against Iran. In 1987, Yuli Vorontsov, the Deputy Soviet Foreign Minister, paid a number of visits to Tehran to negotiate what Moscow described as 'large-scale projects of mutually beneficial economic cooperation'. These included a Soviet-Iranian gas pipeline and the construction of a new Iranian steelworks at Isfahan. The negotiations made slow progress but Moscow was clearly manoeuvring to improve its position with all parties involved in the Gulf conflict.[33]

Soviet initiatives on Afghanistan suggested that Gorbachev viewed the invasion of 1979 and the more extreme policies pursued since by the PDPA as mistakes. They also suggested that he had more in mind than the appeasement of China. In May 1986 Dr Najibullah replaced Babrak Kamal as the leader of the PDPA. Under its new leadership, the PDPA launched a policy of 'national reconciliation'. Political prisoners were released and, to appease the mullahs, Islam was restored as the central tenet of Afghan society. The land reforms which had so alienated the traditional landowners were abolished and the PDPA announced proposals for a coalition government within a multi-party system. With the United Nations mediating, negotiations continued between Afghanistan and Pakistan on the composition of a new Afghan government and the timing of the withdrawal of Soviet troops. Moscow itself approached the exiled King Zahir Shah in Italy, asking him to return to Afghanistan in a leadership capacity, possibly as head of state. The United States, which provided the various factions of the Afghan resistance with arms and money, was sceptical about the policy of national reconciliation. Besides, Washington derived enormous propaganda value from a war which had entered its seventh year in 1987 and which had engaged 115, 000 Soviet troops. Concern to improve Moscow's image abroad in a manner which would deny the Americans any further advantage ranked equally with the unpopularity of the war in the Soviet Union and the ever present China factor in explaining Gorbachev's new initiatives on Afghanistan.[34]

Regarding Soviet commitments elsewhere in the Third World, Gorbachev began to weigh more carefully the costs incurred against the benefits received. The costs, in the form of military expenditures in Africa and heavy subsidies to the likes of Cuba and Vietnam, had brought few tangible rewards. Communist movements in the Third World had proved difficult to control and Third World instability, while providing opportunities for Soviet aggrandisement, had also acted as a barrier to the maintenance of Soviet influence. Above all, the rulers of many Third World countries had come to realise that their own economic ambitions could not be fulfilled through ties with a socialist bloc which had only Soviet and Cuban military forces to offer. Soviet military expenditures were no match for Western economic aid and trade. Moreover, the concept of the national liberation struggle in the Third World had taken a new and ironic twist. Regimes spawned by Soviet and Cuban military aid had themselves become the targets of national liberation struggles. What was true of Afghanistan and Nicaragua in this respect was also true of Angola and Mozambique in Africa.

At the beginning of 1984, a combination of economic crisis and continuing guerrilla war obliged Angola and Mozambique to seek respite outside the boundaries of their friendship treaties with the Soviet Union. Swallowing their distaste for apartheid, both countries were persuaded to sign regional security agreements on terms broadly dictated by South Africa. In the Lusaka Agreement of February 1984, a deal brokered by the United States, South Africa agreed to remove its raiding forces from Angola in return for the closure by Angola of the bases from which guerrillas of the South West Africa People's Organisation (SWAPO) operated in Namibia. A month later, in the Nkomati Accord, President Machel of Mozambique agreed to curb the use made by the African National Congress (ANC) of Mozambique as a base from which to infiltrate guerrillas into Northern Natal and Eastern Transvaal. In return, South Africa agreed that it would end its covert aid to the insurgents of the Mozambique National Resistance (RENAMO) who had plagued the Frelimo government since independence in 1975. Under the accord, Mozambique also agreed to open its borders to South African tourists, to allow South African goods to flow through its ports and to accept economic aid and investment from Pretoria. Within a year, the Lusaka Agreement had all but broken down. South African troops were still 25 miles inside Angola and in June 1985 Pretoria made clear its determination to resist international pressure on Namibia by introducing a 'transitional government of national unity' designed to keep Namibia under South African control. The Nkomati Accord was still in play but under considerable strain. Although it was renewed in March 1985 when Pik Botha, the South African Foreign Minister, visited Maputo, the capital of Mozambique, Pretoria admitted that there had been an increase in RENAMO activities.[35] The accord finally collapsed in October 1986 when Machel was killed in a plane crash in circumstances which left many outside observers pointing accusing fingers at the Pretoria regime. Mozambique had also become heavily dependent on Western economic aid which was channelled through the South African Development Coordination Conference (SADEC), a body founded in 1980 to reduce the economic dependence on South Africa of the Black states in the region. Particularly close ties were established with Britain. President Machel's cooperation over the Lancaster House settlement for majority rule in Zimbabwe persuaded the right-wing Thatcher government to pledge £819 million in aid. These ties were further extended in October 1987 when Mozambique was invited to send a delegation with 'observer status' to the conference of Commonwealth leaders at Vancouver in Canada.

Given the limits on Soviet resources and the pressing need to reverse the domestic decline, expansion in the Third World was less important to Gorbachev than it had been to Brezhnev. But Soviet restraint in the Third World did not, in itself, suggest the possibility of a better relationship with the United States. Gorbachev had not been appointed in 1985 to preside over the dissolution of the Soviet Union's empire in Eastern Europe or the abandonment of its international position. He criticised the old Brezhnev regime for its failure to recognise that to be successful in the long run, Soviet foreign policy had to be conducted from a position of domestic strength. Hence Gorbachev viewed his domestic reforms as the necessary preconditions to maintain Moscow's international status and to make the Soviet Union a dominant world power. His foreign policy was not isolationist and he showed no signs of retreating from positions already achieved. Soviet credibility and prestige were at stake. A settlement in Afghanistan would in no sense diminish that country's dependence on Moscow and in Africa Gorbachev remained committed to the maintenance of socialist bloc military forces as the only means of achieving lasting power and influence. Competition with the West in the Third World had not been abandoned but postponed. Continuing regional conflicts – in the Middle East, the Persian Gulf, Central America, the Philippines and the Korean Peninsula – afforded several long-term opportunities for the expansion of Soviet influence. In short, the Kremlin no less than Washington viewed the future of Soviet-American relations in terms of constructive confrontation.

ARMS CONTROL

Arms talks made little progress during Reagan's first term. The president himself showed little enthusiasm. He regarded SALT 2 as fundamentally flawed because it had done nothing to close the alleged window of vulnerability. He was also influenced by a widespread suspicion in the United States that the Russians were violating earlier agreements. By building a large early warning radar screen at Krasnoyarsk deep in Siberia, the Russians were said to be violating the 1972 ABM Treaty. By deploying two new strategic missiles – the railmobile SS24 and the roadmobile SS25 – they were said to be violating SALT 2 which permitted the deployment of one new missile only.

Nonetheless, two sets of arms talks got under way during Reagan's first term. In November 1981, INF talks on intermediate nuclear forces in Europe opened in Geneva. In June 1982, amidst considerably less publicity, a new round of talks on the reduction of strategic weapons (START) began. The INF talks were more newsworthy, largely because of the opposition of the peace movements in Western Europe to the proposed deployment of cruise and Pershing missiles. At the end of 1981, in an effort to counter the opposition, Reagan proposed the complete elimination of American and Soviet long-range intermediate weapons under a formula which became known as the 'zero option'. The Russians rejected this, arguing that the SS20s created a balance of intermediate forces in Europe which the NATO modernisation programme threatened to overturn. Reagan's subsequent offers to reduce the numbers of INF weapons – in September 1983 he specifically suggested an equal global warhead ceiling of 420 – met with an equally firm Russian refusal. Both sets of talks, on START as well as INF, eventually broke down in November 1983 when, in response to the first deployments of cruise and Pershing in Western Europe, the Russian delegations walked out. The Soviet tactic of launching a massive propaganda drive against cruise and Pershing in the hope that this would drive a wedge between America and its European allies had been thwarted by an unusually firm display of alliance unity.

Preliminary moves to resume negotiations began a year later. The initiative came from the Soviet side. Andrei Gromyko, the veteran Soviet Foreign Minister, met Reagan in the White House in October 1984. The Russians were clearly anxious to stem the tide of the American military build-up, to which Reagan had added an entirely new dimension in March 1983 when he unveiled the Strategic Defence Initiative, popularly known as 'Star Wars'. The SDI was conceived as a six-year research programme, with an expected cost of 26 billion dollars, aimed at devising a system of destroying incoming missiles with non-nuclear chemical X-ray lasers and space-based and ground-based particle beam weapons. Enthusiasts hailed SDI as a defensive system which would reduce reliance on nuclear weapons and thus effect a reduction in the numbers of strategic weapons. They also argued that the Russians were engaged in a similar research programme of their own. The critics maintained that SDI would violate the 1972 ABM Treaty and that it would therefore end the theory of deterrence based upon the concept of Mutual Assured Destruction. They suggested that it would lead to an escalation of the arms race, with the Russians being encouraged to build still more heavy intercontinental missiles with a view to penetrating any future system of space defence. In this respect, doubts were also expressed as to whether any such system could ever be regarded as completely impregnable. With the prospect of America retreating behind its own defensive shield in space, SDI raised yet more questions and doubts for the NATO allies about the reliability of the American nuclear guarantee. Reagan assuaged some of these fears by offering to share the results of SDI research and to defer a decision about deployment. His proposals, however, cut little ice with Moscow which saw SDI as a dangerous escalation of the arms race.

THE NUCLEAR BALANCE IN 1987[41]

STRATEGIC WEAPONS

		USA	USSR
ICBMs			
	Launchers	1010	1398
	Warheads	2110	6420
SLBMSs			
	Launchers	640	944
	Warheads	6656	3216
BOMBERS			
	Launchers	260	160
	Warheads	4080	1080
TOTAL			
	Launchers	1910	2502
	Warheads	12846	10716

SDI was one reason why Reagan's enthusiasm for arms talks increased towards the end of his first term. Together with new nuclear-armed B-1 bombers, new Trident submarine missiles and thousands of air, land and sea-based cruise missiles, SDI encouraged the president to believe that he would be in a position to negotiate from strength. Reagan was also anxious to avoid being branded a warmonger in the November 1984 presidential election. His meeting with Gromyko led to another between Gromyko and Shultz in January 1985 which prepared the way for the resumption of the Geneva talks in March 1985. The talks represented an umbrella approach with two sets of negotiators discussing INF missiles, strategic weapons and space weapons within a single forum.

Reagan and Gorbachev discussed all three components of these talks when they met for their own summit at Geneva in November 1985. Their joint statement called for a 50 per cent reduction, 'appropriately applied', in their strategic arsenals, an interim INF agreement and appropriate measures 'to prevent an arms race in space'. In ensuing months, a veritable barrage of proposals emanated from Moscow on the means to translate these principles into practice. These centred chiefly on Gorbachev's test ban proposals. In August 1985, before the Geneva summit, he announced a unilateral moratorium on Soviet nuclear testing. The moratorium was extended on three separate occasions, the last being scheduled to run until the end of 1986. The United States rejected the idea of a test ban but countered with Reagan's offer to defer deployment of Star Wars until 1993. Thereafter, events moved swiftly. At the end of September 1986, a last-minute agreement was reached at the Stockholm Conference on Confidence and Security Building Measures and Disarmament in Europe. Both sides agreed that they would give one year's warning of military movements involving up to 40,000 troops, and two years' warning of movements involving between 40,000 and 72,000 troops. Armies above 72,000 could not be moved at all. Agreement was also reached on verification and inspection, both from the ground and in the air.[36] Upon the simultaneous resolution of the Daniloff affair, Gorbachev invited Reagan to meet him at Reykjavik in Iceland. A major breakthrough on INF weapons was said to be imminent.

INTERMEDIATE AND SHORTER-RANGE WEAPONS WITH RANGES BETWEEN 300 AND 3000 MILES

	USA			USSR			
Missile	Pershing 1A	Pershing 2	Cruise	SS23	SS12	SS20	SS4
Number Deployed	72	108	240	20	110	441	112
Warheads	1	1	1	1	1	3	1
Range in miles	450	1,120	1,500	310	560	3000	1,240

In the event the discussions which took place at Reykjavik in October 1986 extended far beyond the question of an agreement on INF weapons. Closeted together in the small Hofdi Guest House, the two leaders sketched the outline of the most comprehensive disarmament package since the end of the Second World War. They agreed to cut strategic weapons by 50 per cent over the next five years and to eliminate them altogether over ten years. On intermediate forces, they agreed to a zero option for land-based European weapons.

Each side would have been left with 100 INF missiles to be deployed
at locations in Soviet Asia and the United States. Gorbachev for his
part set aside all previous demands that Britain and France should
limit their own independent deterrents. Agreement was also reached
to freeze shorter-range ballistic missiles in Europe at their current
levels and to begin negotiations on their reduction once an INF
agreement had been signed. With a range of between 300 and 600
miles, 72 such missiles had been deployed by the United States and
somewhere between 595 and 740 by the Soviet Union. Finally, on the
testing of nuclear weapons, Gorbachev accepted the Reagan position
that instead of an immediate and total ban on tests, the two sides should
first reach agreement about verification procedures. The number of
tests would then be reduced and finally ended after both sides had
eliminated their nuclear weapons.

But of course there was a catch. Gorbachev insisted that the
fulfilment of each of these agreements was conditional upon an
American undertaking that the United States would not test, let alone
deploy, weapons in space for at least ten years. The Soviet leader
refused to accept Reagan's offer that the United States would abide
by the 1972 ABM Treaty for ten years. He insisted that the United
States should accept the 'narrow' interpretation of the treaty which
maintained that any testing of space weapons outside the laboratory
was illegal. Reagan for his part was equally insistent on the 'wide'
interpretation of the treaty which argued that full-scale testing and
development of space weapons outside the laboratory was legally
permissible. After two days of exhaustive discussions the two leaders
abandoned their efforts to reach agreement. The SDI had scuppered
the Reykjavik summit.[37]

The scope of what might have been at Reykjavik drew a sceptical
response from seasoned observers. Zbigniew Brzezinski commented:
'I really do not think that either power – the United States or the
Soviet Union – wishes to create a situation in which all of a sudden
the real nuclear superpowers by the end of this century are China
and France'.[38] In the immediate aftermath of Reykjavik, Gorbachev
made it clear that the agreements were still on offer but that the
condition about space weapons remained unchanged. The Soviet
leader was clearly attempting to mobilise public opinion, particularly
in Western Europe, against the SDI. Reagan was on the defensive.
The president had not been prepared for such far-reaching discussions
at Reykjavik and his critics argued that he had lost the propaganda

battle. Secretary Shultz met with Eduard Shevardnadze, who had replaced Gromyko as Soviet Foreign Minister in July 1985, at Vienna in November 1986. But the deadlock over SDI persisted and the meeting dispersed with no agreement. Simultaneously, the United States finally breached SALT 2 by introducing a B-52 bomber adapted to carry cruise missiles.

The dialogue was resumed in the spring of 1987. Gorbachev assumed the initiative in a manner which suggested that he now acknowledged the failure of his Reykjavik strategy. Gorbachev's economic reforms required reductions in military expenditure. A disarmament agreement was therefore essential and time was of the essence. Gorbachev concentrated on the INF issue because common ground had already been established. In the process, he diluted his hardline stance on the SDI. In March 1987 Gorbachev made an offer which repeated the Reykjavik formula on INF missiles. But in urging 'substantial' reductions in strategic weapons, the Soviet leader modified his previous insistence that such reductions be linked to a ban on the testing and development of space weapons. Instead, he argued that a strategic agreement 'should be conditioned by a decision on the prevention of deployment of weapons in outer space'. Deployment was the key word here because it gave the United States much greater latitude in relation to both the testing and development of the SDI programme.[39] Gorbachev followed this up in April 1987 with a new offer to begin immediate talks on the elimination of shorter-range nuclear weapons and he also announced that the Soviet Union had stopped making chemical weapons.

The new Soviet initiative was favourably received in the United States. With the Tower Commission into the Iran-Contra arms scandal indicting the president for lack of control over his subordinates, Reagan was also under pressure. An INF agreement with the Soviet Union suggested itself as the most obvious means of restoring his domestic credibility. But doubts still persisted, particularly in Western Europe. Ironically, the prospect of a separate INF agreement revived the old fear that the United States might be decoupled from the defence of its European allies. In recent years, the INF issue had become the focus of sharp political controversy in West Germany. At the beginning of the 80s, Chancellor Schmidt had been unable to muster support within his own Social Democratic Party for the proposed deployments of both cruise and Pershing on West German soil. His government was brought down in October 1982 when the

Free Democrats left the coalition and formed a new government with the Christian Democrats. Helmut Kohl, the leader of the CDU who became the new Chancellor, promised elections in March 1983. The CDU-FDP coalition, which was committed to the deployment of the new missiles, was returned after the most fiercely fought campaign in West Germany's post-war electoral history. The coalition was re-elected again in January 1987 but this time on a tripartite basis. Representatives of the CSU, the Bavarian sister party of the CDU, entered the cabinet with a distinct position of their own. The election also enhanced the position of the FDP. The INF issue continued to dominate West German politics. Chancellor Kohl was torn between his FDP coalition partners, who now welcomed the prospect of an agreement to eliminate INF weapons, and his CSU partners, who argued that such an agreement would jeopardise West Germany's security and leave the country defenceless against Soviet short-range battlefield nuclear weapons which were stationed in East Germany. Reverses for the CDU and CSU at regional elections during the early months of 1987 suggested popular support for the INF position adopted by Hans Dietrich Genscher, the Foreign Minister and leader of the FDP. In June 1987, after months of wrangling, the coalition agreed to support a separate INF deal on condition that West Germany be allowed to retain 72 old-fashioned Pershing 1A rockets. Twenty-five years old and with a range of 450 miles, the Pershing 1As were maintained by the *Bundeswehr* (the West Germany army) but their warheads were controlled by the United States.

Sceptical American voices were also raised in opposition to a separate INF deal. They included General Bernard Rogers, NATO's Supreme Allied Commander in Europe, and Richard Nixon and Henry Kissinger, the architects of the first SALT agreement. All three argued that the proposed INF deal would weaken NATO's defences. In a joint article published in April 1987, Nixon and Kissinger suggested that an INF agreement should be made subject to two conditions. First, that INF weapons should be eliminated completely. Without literal adherence to a zero option, they argued that there was no guarantee that the Russians might not at some future date transfer their 100 missiles in Asia back to Europe. Secondly, that the Russians should be required to make substantial cuts in their conventional forces.[40]

But a hard-pressed Reagan was not to be dissuaded. In June 1987 he appointed General John Galvin as Supreme Commander in Europe in place of Rogers. Gorbachev had already eased the president's passage by making one of the concessions demanded by the American critics, namely the elimination of the 100 INF missiles on either side in Asia and the United States. The West Europeans helped too by agreeing, with some misgivings, to support an INF deal. The West Germans, the last to be converted, removed the remaining obstacle by agreeing in September 1987 to relinquish their ageing Pershing 1A rockets. Bonn's only conditions were that there should be a tight timetable, with adequate verification procedures, for the elimination of all INF missiles and that their Pershings would be the last to go after the Soviet and American missiles had been dismantled.

The stage was thus set for a series of meetings between Shevardnadze and Shultz and their respective disarmament experts which paved the way for the Reagan-Gorbachev summit at Washington in December 1987. The signing of an INF Treaty was the principal achievement of the summit. The treaty incorporated what had become known as the 'double zero' option. It provided for the elimination of medium-range missiles and short-range missiles which collectively could hit targets at distances between 300 and 3,000 miles. In terms of the missiles to be eliminated, the treaty went further than expected. It included missile systems already listed – cruise and Pershing 1A and 2 on the American side; and the medium-range SS4s and SS20s and the shorter-range SS12s and SS23s on the Soviet side. But it also included systems the details of which had not hitherto been revealed. On the American side, these included the Pershing 1B, a system originally intended to replace the ageing Pershing 1A. Production of the Pershing 1B had been suspended but the missiles remained as part of the American stockpile. On the Soviet side, they included two new systems – the SS5, which was similar to the SS4 but with a longer range (2,300 miles as opposed to 1,200) and greater accuracy, and the SS-CX-4, a Soviet version of a ground-launched cruise missile with a range between 1,500 and 1,900 miles. Collectively, the INF Treaty provided for the elimination of 2,800 missiles (2,000 Soviet, 800 American) and 3,800 warheads, a cut of about 5 per cent in the combined nuclear stockpiles of the two sides. Intended to last for thirteen years, the treaty also included strict verification procedures. Teams of American and Soviet inspectors were to be stationed at chosen sites in the Soviet Union and the United States for the full thirteen years. American inspectors were to be based at a plant at Votkinsk in European Russia which assembled long-range missiles as missiles to be destroyed under the treaty. Soviet inspectors were to be based at a similar facility at Magna in Utah which also made Trident and MX rocket motors. Each side would be able to demand twenty annual short-notice inspection visits to an agreed list of other facilities, including those in Europe, during the first three years of the treaty, the time set aside for the destruction of the medium-range missiles. Thereafter, ten snap inspections would be allowed during each year of the next five years, and five annual inspections during the final five years.

The INF Treaty was the only substantive agreement reached at Washington. In a joint statement issued at the end of the three-day summit, the two leaders instructed their negotiators at Geneva to work towards an agreement to limit and reduce strategic weapons. They anticipated signing a START Treaty at their next meeting during the first half of 1988. Moscow was not specifically mentioned in the statement but the Soviet capital was expected to be the venue of the next Reagan-Gorbachev meeting. The Washington summit endorsed the Reykjavik formula of a 50 per cent reduction in strategic weapons but no agreement was reached on the crucial question of how the number of missiles to be reduced would be divided between those deployed on land and those deployed at sea. The summit also failed to resolve the vexed question of the SDI. Indeed, the issue was sidestepped. In their joint statement, Reagan and Gorbachev instructed their negotiators at Geneva to work out an agreement which would commit both sides to observe the ABM Treaty as signed in 1972 but which would also permit research, development and testing as required within the limits prescribed by the treaty. In other words, it was still not clear how far the development and testing of space weapons could be taken. Agreement was reached that space defences should not be deployed for a specific period but not on whether that period should be seven years (the American position) or ten years (the Soviet position). Concerned to make a positive impression with public opinion in the United States, Gorbachev did not make an issue of the SDI at Washington. Speculation suggested that the Russians were no longer worried about SDI. The reasons given included the belief that Congress would trim the SDI budget and also the confidence, as Gorbachev had written in his recent book, that the Russians would be able to 'puncture SDI' by shooting down space weapons at a 'hundredth' of the cost of SDI. Frank Carlucci, who succeeded Weinberger as Defence Secretary in November 1987, had a different view which suggested that nothing had changed. The day after Gorbachev's departure from Washington, Carlucci stated that 'the Soviet Union continues to link a Strategic Arms Agreement to the strengthening of the ABM treaty'. On other issues, the joint statement at the end of the summit indicated that the two sides were still far apart. It acknowledged the existence of 'serious differences' on regional issues which ranged from Afghanistan, to the Gulf War, the Middle East, Kampuchea, Southern Africa and Central America. On human rights, the statement said only that the two leaders had engaged in a 'thorough and candid discussion'. Throughout his meetings with Reagan, Congressional leaders and the press, Gorbachev insisted that the United States had no 'moral right' to preach to the Soviet Union about human rights.[42]

THE EUROPEAN DIMENSION

With the United States and the Soviet Union retreating into entrenched Cold War positions after the invasion of Afghanistan, it was left to the Europeans, both East and West, to preserve détente on their own continent as best they could. West European concern over the attitude of the Reagan administration was expressed by Lord Carrington, the former British Foreign Secretary who became Secretary General of NATO in 1984. In a famous speech in 1983 Carrington criticised what he described as a policy of 'facing [the] Russians down in a silent war of nerves, broken only by bursts of megaphone diplomacy ... crude, one-dimensional moralism'.[43] The Polish crisis of 1980–81, and the subsequent crisis over the deployment of the new NATO missiles, imposed severe strains on the network of détente agreements which had been so painstakingly constructed in Europe in the 70s. Both crises demonstrated that these agreements, although vulnerable to external pressures, had acquired a substantial degree of durability and permanence. Europeans on both sides of the East-West divide recognised that it was in their interests to sustain the process of dialogue and exchange.

The crisis in Poland must first be set in its East European context. For the Soviet Union, the countries of Eastern Europe had become important in a number of ways. They acted as a buffer zone and as a counterbalance to NATO. They were also useful as intermediaries, moderating Western policies towards the Soviet Union and acting as bridgeheads through which the Soviet Union could pursue its objectives in the Third World. But none of these considerations explained the reasoning behind Soviet determination to maintain such a high level of political control in Eastern Europe and to insist that the communist parties retained a monopoly of power. The explanation, according to Seweryn Bialer, lay beyond considerations of 'security and utility':

> Soviet rule [in Eastern Europe] provides one of the ideological foundations of Great Russian and Communist Party control within the Soviet Union itself. It also contributes decisively to the credibility of Soviet foreign policy. Victory in World War II was the central legitimizing experience of Soviet rule at home and is associated with, even focused on, control over Eastern Europe. As the major spoil of war, the empire serves to legitimize the Kremlin's rule in Russia . . . . The continuing domination of Eastern Europe confirms the basic ideological proposition that the establishment of communist rule is irreversible . . . . If this trend can be reversed in Eastern Europe then the question will inevitably arise why it cannot be reversed in the homeland itself.[44]

Viewed from this perspective, the Polish crisis of 1980–81 was of much greater significance than the Hungarian Revolution of 1956 or the Prague Spring in Czechoslovakia in 1968. By most criteria, Poland had become the key country in the Soviet bloc. Strategically, it provided the main route from the West to the Soviet Union. With a standing army of 300,000 it contributed about one-third of the combined forces of the Warsaw Pact. It represented one-third of the entire territory of the Soviet bloc and its population of 36 million was more than double the size of the next largest East European country. Instability in Poland threatened the cohesion of the Soviet bloc. The instability generated by the emergence of the Solidarity movement in Poland in 1980 had the most profound political implications. Unlike the crises in Hungary and Czechoslovakia, both of which originated from struggles between different factions of the ruling communist party, the upheaval in Poland represented a crisis between party and people. The communist system itself was brought to the verge of collapse.[45]

In August 1980, Polish workers won the right to form free trades unions after a series of major strikes centered on the Baltic port of Gdansk. As in 1970 and 1976, the strikes were triggered by increases in the price of food, particularly meat. But the increases were less than they had been in 1970 and 1976. The unrest of 1980 went far beyond the issue of wages and prices and developed into a crisis of legitimacy. Denied popular support through the traditional expression of nationalism or the legal mechanism of free elections, all East European regimes had become dependent on economic performance to win public approval. The regimes in East Germany and Hungary had been relatively successful in this respect but Poland had not. Indeed, economic mismanagement and foreign indebtedness were identified as the principal failures of the old regime. The debt crisis was particularly serious. Edward Gierek, leader of the Polish United Workers Party (PZPR), embarked at the beginning of the 70s on an ambitious programme of economic growth. Imports of Western technology, financed by Western credits, were designed to facilitate rapid increases in exports from a modernised Polish industry. But by the mid-70s, Gierek's programme had come to grief. World economic conditions were in part responsible. The energy crisis pushed up the cost of oil and the recession in the West meant that Poland was unable to sell its goods in Western markets and obtain the foreign currency needed to repay its debts. But the government was equally responsible, failing to implement the structural reforms of the planning system and the methods of management which were needed to accommodate the new technology. By the end of 1980, the Polish debt was estimated at 25 billion dollars. Western banks compounded the problem by loaning still more money, long after it had become apparent that the Polish government had not the means to service the original loans. Western governments were also to blame, providing credits at concessionary rates of interest for the purchase of equipment to be used in industrial projects which had no hope of generating sufficient income to meet the repayments. In the meantime, the Polish economy plunged deeper into crisis. The Polish GNP fell by 2.3 per cent in 1979, by 4 per cent in 1980 and by 15 per cent in 1981.

With the country approaching bankruptcy, Lech Walesa was elected Chairman of Solidarity. Membership soared to over eight million and Solidarity began to present itself as an alternative government. It was supported by Polish intellectuals and the Roman Catholic Church, long regarded as the symbol of Polish nationalism. The PZPR virtually collapsed. Stanislaw Kania replaced Gierek in September 1980 but he too was unable to stem the tide. Voting by free and secret ballot, delegates at the Ninth Congress of the PZPR in July 1981 attacked the party leaders and set about dismantling the party apparatus. In

the elections to the Central Committee, seven of the eleven members
of the existing Politburo lost their seats. 750,000 party members were
also said to be members of Solidarity. After a year as General-Secretary
of the PZPR, Kania gave way to General Wojciech Jaruzelski, the
Defence Minister and prime minister. The new leadership began to
retreat from the concessions granted when Solidarity was first established in September 1980. Jaruzelski appealed in vain to Solidarity to
moderate its demands for wage increases and a shorter working week.
But Solidarity, egged on by the militants in its ranks, would only
exercise economic restraint in return for major political concessions
which included the establishment of a pluralist political system in
Poland. This demand, together with the messages of support being
sent by Solidarity to workers in other East European countries who
wanted free trades unions, was the final straw for Moscow. Unlike
Hungary and Czechoslovakia, however, Poland was not invaded by
Warsaw Pact forces. The Brezhnev Politburo undoubtedly considered
this option but eventually settled for an 'internal invasion' through
the introduction of martial law under Jaruzelski in December 1981.
Solidarity was outlawed and its leaders arrested. A number of factors
explained why Moscow decided to stay its hand. They included the
probability of armed resistance within Poland, uncertainty about how
the West might react, reluctance to shoulder responsibility for Poland's
debts and the unsettling impact on the military balance in Europe of
an invasion force estimated to need as many as 300,000 troops.

The expedient of an internal invasion took Solidarity by surprise,
not least because the leadership of the movement had dismissed it as
an unworkable solution. But in the event, martial law succeeded
beyond Jaruzelski's and Moscow's most optimistic expectations. Solidarity was not equipped to mount an underground resistance movement. Having relied from the outset on its ability to organise mass
movements of civil disobedience, it proved no match for the ruthless
efficiency and professionalism of the Polish intelligence and security
forces. Yet Jaruzelski and Moscow had won a pyrrhic victory. The
Russians had already acquired one unenviable reputation in their
dealings with their communist allies. Since the end of the Second
World War, the only shots fired in anger by Russian troops had been
against other communist countries – Hungary, Czechoslovakia, China
and even Afghanistan. Now, the imposition of martial law in Poland
added fresh poignancy to the opening words of the *Communist Manifesto*
written by Marx and Engels and published in 1848: 'A Spectre is

haunting Europe'. Then, as now, the spectre was one of workers' revolution.

The imposition of martial law provoked an open split in the Atlantic Alliance. Reagan responded with a series of punitive measures against Poland which included the suspension of Polish civil aviation rights in the United States and the curtailment of sales of high technology equipment. He wanted to extend sanctions to the Soviet Union and argued that the crisis was comparable to that in Afghanistan because martial law was tantamount to an invasion. The Americans threatened to pull out of the Madrid Security Conference and to postpone the disarmament negotiations. The West Europeans, particularly the French and the West Germans, distanced themselves from the White House. Emphasising the divisibility of détente, they maintained that arms negotiations were too important to be used as pawns in any East-West ideological game. With some three million ethnic Germans still held hostage in Poland and the Soviet Union, and dependent on the East for most of its energy supplies, West Germany was anxious to play down the Polish crisis as a domestic political affair. West Germany received 16 per cent of its natural gas, 6 per cent of its oil and 50 per cent of its enriched uranium from the Soviet Union.[46] The figure for gas was projected to rise to 30 per cent by 1990. The West Germans, along with the French, Italians, Dutch, Swedes, Austrians and Belgians, had agreed to finance the construction of a 3,500-mile pipeline to carry an extra 40 billion cubic metres of natural gas a year from the Yamal peninsula in north-west Siberia to Western Europe. The Reagan administration attacked these agreements. Weinberger voiced his concern about the military implications: 'The policy of the United States has not been to engage in any kind of economic warfare. But I draw the line at deliberately giving them [the Russians] things that can and will be of enormous military benefit to them and the pipeline is in that category'.[47] The Americans also argued that the West Europeans were holding themselves hostage and providing Moscow with foreign currency. The Europeans replied that Moscow was unlikely to kill the goose that laid the golden egg and that the Soviet Union was hardly a less reliable source of energy than the Middle East. They also pointed out that Reagan had not seen fit to reimpose the embargo on sales of grain to the Soviet Union which had been lifted when he came into office to appease the farmers of the American mid-west. Reagan, however, seemed determined to force the issue. In June 1982 he extended his existing embargo on the export to the

Soviet Union of oil and gas equipment to the subsidiaries and licensees of American companies abroad, many of whom were involved in the European pipeline project. The Europeans were livid at this attempt to force them to renege on their agreements with the Russians and Reagan eventually gave way by lifting the embargo in November 1982.

Concern to preserve that part of the *Ostpolitik* which had improved relations with East Germany also underpinned West Germany's attitude throughout the Polish crisis. East German fears that the Polish infection might spread to other East European countries prompted the Honecker regime to shut the door in the face of its Western neighbour. In October 1980, a month after the initial Solidarity victory at Gdansk, East Germany announced a sudden and dramatic increase in the amount of currency West Germany visitors had to exchange daily. Honecker also imposed four conditions for any further improvement in relations between the two Germanies: the permanent missions established by the Basic Treaty of 1972 had to be raised to embassy level; East German citizenship had to be recognised, the frontier between the Federal and Democratic Republics had to run through the middle of the River Elbe; and the Federal Republic had to close the centre at Salzgitter which monitored human rights violations in East Germany. Aware that East Germans would learn still more about the Polish situation from their West German visitors (they were already receiving West German television), Honecker and his colleagues were going as far as they could to insulate East Germany.[48]

The declaration of martial law in Poland in December 1981 assuaged East German fears. Chancellor Schmidt was visiting East Germany at the time and a potentially embarrassing situation was overcome when both German leaders agreed that the Poles had every right to solve their domestic problems in their own way. Thereafter, the Honecker regime moderated its position, entering into negotiations with the government of Helmut Kohl, the Christian Democratic Chancellor of the Federal Republic who succeeded Schmidt in 1982. Two reasons explained Honecker's more accommodating attitude. First, in common with most other East European leaders, Honecker realised that the key to personal survival no longer lay in loyalty to Moscow but in the economic well-being of his country. With the Russians unable to provide either the finance or the technology to maintain the viability of East German industry, Honecker increasingly turned to his West German neighbour. Secondly, the East German leader recognised that even in a conventional war in Europe, both Germanies would be reduced to rubble. Hence, like Kohl, Honecker believed that the Federal and Democratic Republics had a special responsibility to ensure that war never occurred again on German soil.

This recognition of mutual interests enabled the two Germanies to extend the essential ingredients of the *Ostpolitik*. The Federal Republic had become East Germany's largest Western trading partner, accounting for 40 per cent of the communist state's external trade. West German companies such as Volkswagen and Siemens negotiated multimillion dollar contracts with the East Germans to build several jointly owned factories. West Germany benefited by the easing of travel and emigration facilities. Not only were West Germans permitted to visit their relatives in the East in increasing numbers; by 1984 an unprecedented 30,000 East Germans were allowed to emigrate to the West. In July 1984 Bonn and East Berlin negotiated an agreement whereby the Federal Republic provided the Democratic Republic with a loan worth 950 million Deutschemark in return for an East German promise to ease still further travel restrictions between the two Germanies. Bonn was prepared to shoulder the financial burden while East Berlin paid the ideological price. The agreement was intended to set the seal on a long-awaited visit, which had been postponed once already, by Honecker to West Germany in September 1984. In the event, however, the visit was sabotaged as a result of the acrimony caused by the issue of the new NATO missiles in Europe.

Moscow was angered by the decision of the *Bundgstag* in West Germany in February 1984 to go ahead with the deployment of cruise and Pershing missiles. The Russians were also fearful that if East Germany became too dependent economically on Bonn, it might drift towards neutralism and seriously weaken the Warsaw Pact. They therefore put pressure on Honecker to cancel his visit, using West German revanchism as a pretext. Much was made of Chancellor Kohl's presence at a rally of expellees from the East at Braunschweig not far from the East German border. Honecker eventually gave way but not before he had demonstrated, in public, his differences with Moscow. He responded to the *Bundestag's* decision by urging the need to limit the damage, to resume the arms talks and to revive the process of détente. A furious debate ensued in the editorials of *Pravda* and *Neues Deutschland*, its East German equivalent. The *Pravda* editorials concentrated on West German revanchism, but they were clearly aimed at Honecker. The East German leader argued that it would be a 'tragic miscalculation to seek to solve world problems by military means, including the historic contest between capitalism and socialism. Such a course can only lead to disaster'. In response to the charge that fundamental socialist interests could not be sacrificed to momentary national interests, Honecker defended himself by asserting East German independence. The international communist movement, he argued, was nothing more than a 'voluntary community of equal and independent parties'.[49] Honecker's position was supported by the Hungarians. Matyas Szuros, the Hungarian Party Secretary responsible for international affairs, declared the priority of domestic needs over international factors in shaping the foreign policy of smaller socialist states.[50]

Honecker was eventually able to make his long-delayed visit to West Germany, which included a sentimental journey to his birthplace in the Saarland, in September 1987. Opinion polls indicated that most West Germans were indifferent about the visit. But when he arrived, Honecker was accorded an official reception which would have been unthinkable twenty or even ten years earlier. The flags of the two countries were hoisted and a military band played the two national anthems. Honecker was thus received as the ruler of a foreign country, a significant step forward in the evolution of West German thinking about relations with East Germany. The visit itself demonstrated that significant differences still separated the two sides. The precise location of the border on the River Elbe remained unresolved. Kohl raised the question of the Berlin Wall, the building of which Honecker had supervised in 1961. The East German shoot-to-kill policy at would-be escapees, which was relaxed during the visit, was also raised. Honecker responded with a renewed call for the closure of the West German human rights monitoring post at Salzgitter. On a more constructive note, agreements were signed on scientific cooperation, environmental protection and the safety of nuclear reactors. Fresh impetus was also given to a long-discussed scheme to link East Germany to the West German electric power grid. Of still greater significance, Honecker was able to announce that in the six months up to August 1987 a record 3.2 million East Germans, including 860,000 who were below the retirement age, had been allowed to visit West Germany.[51] For Honecker, the visit represented a landmark in East Germany's quest for international recognition and legitimacy. For Kohl and the

West Germans, the visit was a yet further exercise in pragmatism. Without abandoning their constitutional objective of reunification, the West Germans acknowledged that they had to accept existing realities if they wanted to improve and change them.

The saga of Honecker's visit to West Germany demonstrated the continuing extent to which efforts to improve contacts between the two Germanies were still subject to the fluctuations in Soviet-American relations. It also demonstrated the continuing extent to which Moscow could impose its will on a recalcitrant East European ally when vital Soviet interests were said to be at stake. But this second observation requires an important qualification. Honecker's open expression of defiance and dissent in 1984 was a clear indication that the days of absolute Soviet domination in Eastern Europe had long-since passed. On fundamental issues – the monopoly of political power by the communist parties and military security within the framework of the Warsaw Pact – Moscow could still crack the whip. But in other respects, Eastern Europe exhibited considerable diversity. National interests and priorities had become increasingly important. In economic policy, the traditional centralised control in Czechoslovakia contrasted with the emergence of market forces in Hungary and the continuation of private farming in Poland. In foreign policy, Romania's independence, manifest in its maintenance of relations with China and Israel and in its refusal to allow Warsaw Pact troops or manoeuvres on its soil, contrasted with the predictable conformism of Bulgaria. On the question of nuclear weapons, Czechoslovakia, like East Germany, expressed concern when obliged to accept Soviet missiles in response to the West's deployment of cruise and Pershing. For most East European countries, which pride themselves on sporting excellence, Moscow's decision to enforce a boycott of the 1984 Los Angeles Olympics came as a bitter blow. Romania defied the boycott and sent its athletes. Equally, the nuclear accident at Chernobyl in the Soviet Union in April 1986 heightened the perception of the East Europeans that they should resist Soviet attempts to sacrifice their interests for the sake of Soviet priorities in periods of Soviet-American tension. On the need for dialogue, negotiation and restraint, there was thus much in common between Western and Eastern Europe.

Nowhere was this more apparent than in the field of socialist bloc economic relations. Moscow found it increasingly difficult to obtain what it wanted from its East European allies. The majority of East European states successfully resisted Soviet attempts to convert Comecon, the Council for Mutual Economic Assistance, into a supranational mechanism of control. At a long-delayed meeting of Comecon in June 1984, the Soviet Union announced its intention to end its subsidised deliveries of energy (gas and oil) and of raw materials to Eastern Europe. Henceforth, the prices for energy and raw materials would reflect prices on the world market.[52] The Russians also pressed their allies to improve the quality of the manufactured goods which they exported to the Soviet Union. Moscow's demands were borne of frustration at a situation which effectively meant that the Soviet Union had been subsidising higher standards of living for the working populations of Eastern Europe than those enjoyed by the working population of its own people. During the 70s, it was estimated that the Soviet Union had spent as much as 3.5 per cent of its GNP on subsidies to its East European allies and its Third World clients. This was clearly a proportion which the Soviet Union could no longer afford. Moscow wanted to distribute the burden still further. Arguing the case for greater integration of the Soviet and East European economies through Comecon, the Russians wanted investments to be coordinated, technology to be exchanged and the East Europeans to become partners in the development of Soviet resources in Siberia. But little progress was made in these areas. The increased prices for energy and raw materials were hardly calculated to endear themselves to the East Europeans. They served only to exacerbate the serious economic problems confronting the already debt-laden governments of Eastern Europe. They made it still more difficult for the East Europeans to earn foreign currency, to compete with Western goods in Third World markets and to gain access to markets in the West. They also emphasised, in the manner of the oil crisis and the Western recession of the 70s, the continuing extent to which East European leaders were at the mercy of world economic conditions over which they had no control in planning their economic strategies. Strongest resistance to tighter economic integration came from Hungary and East Germany. By virtue of modest concessions to market forces in Hungary and managerial reforms within the traditional mechanism of central planning in East Germany, these two countries enjoyed, when judged by East European conditions, relatively high standards of living. Neither Kádár nor Honecker, the two party leaders, wanted Hungary and East Germany to become permanently tied to a technologically backward Soviet Union. In the words of Seweryn Bialer, they had no wish to become part of 'The Greater Eastern European

Co-Stagnation Sphere'.[53] In common with many Third World leaders, Kádár and Honecker realised that their plans for economic growth, the necessary precondition of social stability and political tranquility, could not be satisfied through dependence on the Soviet Union. Both wanted to improve and expand their economic relations with the West.

The situation in Eastern Europe which confronted Gorbachev when he came to power in 1985 was thus a test and a challenge. At first, with the INF issue still unresolved, Gorbachev demanded a show of East European solidarity against the West. The Soviet propaganda machine condemned what it described as nationalist 'deviations' and the efforts being made to isolate Eastern Europe from the 'class struggle' inherent in the Soviet-American confrontation. The propaganda became less intense as Moscow and Washington moved towards an INF agreement. However, Soviet objectives towards Eastern Europe remained the same. *Glasnost* and *perestroika* became exportable commodities and were seen by Moscow as the means of strengthening the Soviet bloc and weaning Eastern Europe away from too great an economic dependence on the West. But *glasnost* and *perestroika* posed awkward questions for the regimes of Eastern Europe. Their last experience of a thaw in the Soviet Union had led to riots in Poland and an uprising in Hungary. Besides, the East European experience of reform experiments was significantly different from that of the Soviet Union. Reform in the Soviet Union had always been a controlled process, dictated and implemented by the men at the top. Gorbachev's version of democratisation was one which allowed a little more choice within the ruling party, not between competing ones. In Eastern Europe, pressure for reform had usually emanated from below in a manner which combined an economic demand for greater prosperity with a political demand for greater freedom within a pluralist system. The issues of *glasnost* and *perestroika* were particularly sensitive in Czechoslovakia. Since the Prague Spring and the Warsaw Pact's invasion in 1968, Czechoslovakia had been governed as an orthodox communist state, combining centralised economic planning with a firm line against political and cultural dissent. *Glasnost*, which implied a rehabilitation of the Dubček experiment of 'socialism with a human face', produced an open split within Czech ranks. Lubomir Strougal, the moderate prime minister, and Vasil Bilak, the hardliner in the Czech Party, clashed in public over their different interpretations of Gorbachev's reforms. In April 1987 Gorbachev visited Prague and chose the occasion to announce his proposals for cutting shorter-range nuclear weapons. But his visit was delayed by a week, an indication to most observers of continuing tension within the Czech Party. The timing of Gorbachev's visit was awkward for the Czechs in other ways. A month earlier Prague had witnessed another human rights trial. Two committee members of the Jazz Section received prison sentences of sixteen and ten months. Three others were given suspended sentences. Formerly part of the Czechoslovak Musicians Union which had been outlawed in 1980, the Jazz Section had continued to operate in a manner which made it the focus of intellectual and cultural dissent. It published a large number of non-political paperbacks and pamphlets which fell foul of the authorities. The accused were charged with the 'economic crime' of having used their organisation to make personal profits. The trial was closely monitored by Western representatives at the Helsinki review conference in Vienna, a fact which perhaps explained the relatively lenient sentences. The state prosecutor had asked for four years.[54]

Whatever their individual reservations, most East European countries, including Czechoslovakia, followed the Soviet lead and announced plans of their own to improve productivity in their state-run factories and to allow greater latitude to small private businesses. In Poland, General Jaruzelski announced that a referendum would be held on the party's economic plans to end the enormous subsidies on food and rents, to allow small businesses to operate and to devolve decision-making in state factories to the local level. The referendum was also designed to test public opinion on a number of political options which the party had devised to establish the legal limits within which opposition groups might be allowed to operate. Under Polish law, a majority of 51 per cent of eligible voters is needed for the results of a referendum to be binding. The referendum, which was held at the end of November 1987, represented a defeat for Jaruzelski. Only 44 per cent of eligible voters supported the proposed economic changes and only 46 per cent supported the party's ideas on political liberalisation. Observers predicted that price increases would still be implemented but that they would be more modest than those originally planned.[55] Only two East European countries– East Germany and Romania – resisted the pressure for change of any nature. East German officials argued that they had done enough already to modernise and rationalise their economy. They feared that self-criticism would undermine their success. Morover, *glasnost* and talk of democratisation sat uncomfortably with the authorities in East Berlin as innovations which might prove difficult to control. This view was reinforced in the summer of 1987 when police had to disperse demonstrations by hundreds of young East Berliners gathered at the Berlin Wall to listen to a rock concert on the Western side. President Ceausescu's Romania was the maverick in the East European pack. Governed on personality-cult and police-state lines by assorted members of the president's family, Romania remained stubbornly independent.

In November 1987, the ageing leaders of Eastern Europe gathered at Moscow and sat in obedient silence as they listened to Gorbachev's speech commemorating the 70th anniversary of the Bolshevik Revolu-tion. They were told that they were on their own and that it was not Soviet policy to insist on socialist uniformity in Eastern Europe. *Glasnost* and *perestroika* posed risks for the individual leaders of Eastern Europe but the collective risk for Gorbachev was much greater. To be successful from a Soviet viewpoint, reforms in Eastern Europe had to overcome two seemingly irreconcilable contradictions.[56] First, the Soviet Union wanted to lessen Eastern Europe's economic dependence on the West. But at the same time Soviet policymakers realised that Western economic support for East European economic development eased the pressure on scarce Soviet resources. Secondly, the Soviet Union realised that social peace and a limited degree of cultural freedom in Eastern Europe improved relations with the West. But the policymakers were equally aware that greater freedom had a tendency to encourage the emergence of anti-Soviet liberal forces in Eastern Europe in a manner which made it difficult to contain then. As in the case of his own domestic reforms, time alone would tell whether Gorbachev would succeed in presiding over a peaceful transformation in Eastern Europe.

As the countries of Eastern Europe moved towards greater inde-pendence of the Soviet Union, an equally significant reappraisal of roles was emerging within the Western alliance. The West Europeans began taking the first tentative steps towards a common defence identity. In a major speech at Brussels in March 1987, Sir Geoffrey Howe, the British Foreign Secretary, warned his European partners that they needed to be 'alert to trends in American thinking' which might diminish their security – 'perhaps not today or tomorrow, but possibly in the longer run'. The trends to which Howe referred included the shift in American interests from Europe to East Asia and the Pacific, trade disputes and the undercurrent of protectionism and the manner in which the United States had begun to re-examine the basis of its own strategic defence. To prepare, in the long term, for a world in which there might be fewer nuclear weapons, Howe argued that the West Europeans would have to assume much greater responsibility for their own defence. He did not suggest that the American commitment to NATO had been undermined. Nor did he suggest that the Europeans should pose as military competitors to the United States. Instead, he argued that Western Europe should become a 'more truly equal second pillar of the alliance'.[57]

The American budget crisis and the INF Treaty of 1987 reinforced the strength of Howe's arguments. The budget crisis and the prospect of defence cuts in the United States raised fresh doubts about the ability of the United States to maintain American forces in Europe at their existing levels. Some 354,000 American military personnel were stationed in Europe, a total which many American observers regarded as excessive and unnecessary. Zbigniew Brzezinski complained: 'Surely, 374 million Europeans with an aggregate economy of $3.5 trillion should not need to depend for their defence as heavily as they do on 241 million Americans with an economy of $4 trillion – against an opponent with 275 million people and a GNP of only $1.9 trillion'.[58] American defence policy in Europe was said to have robbed the West Europeans of any incentive to defend themselves. In like manner, the INF Treaty raised fundamental questions about the future of West European security. West European governments welcomed the treaty but they also sounded several notes of caution. In his capacity as Secretary General of NATO, Lord Carrington had already warned that the world was not about to enter 'some mythical non-nuclear nirvana'. Many West Europeans were suspicious that Gorbachev's long-term objective was a denuclearised Europe which would stop at the Soviet Union and leave the Western half vulnerable to Soviet blackmail. They therefore argued that a 'triple zero' proposal, for the elimination of shorter-range missiles which could hit targets up to a distance of 300 miles, should be linked, not only to cuts in strategic weapons, but also to substantial cuts in the Warsaw Pact's conventional forces and a ban on chemical weapons. To ensure that European interests were heard and taken into account in any subsequent disarmament agreement between the United States and the Soviet Union, the West Europeans recognised that a common defence view was both essential and urgent.

The forum within which the debate about West European defence and security took place was the West European Union (WEU) which had been established in 1955 and which consisted of Britain, France, West Germany, Italy and the Benelux countries. For many years WEU remained a moribund institution. West European defence policies were developed within the framework of an integrated NATO command and the American nuclear guarantee, from both of which the French withdrew in the 60s. WEU was revived in 1979. Thereafter, France and West Germany assumed the initiative. Franco-West German cooperation in the field of military strategy was strengthened considerably when François Mitterand became the first socialist president of France in 1981. Experts on both sides examined a plan first suggested by Helmut Schmidt according to which West Germany would increase its conventional forces in return for the extension of France's nuclear umbrella to the Federal Republic. France and West Germany also staged a number of joint military exercises which involved the French Rapid Deployment Force (RDF). Consisting of some 47,000 troops, the RDF was specifically designed to demonstrate France's willingness to join in anti-tank operations alongside or in support of the NATO allies if hostilities broke out in Europe. In July 1987 Helmut Kohl, Schmidt's successor, suggested much closer cooperation through the establishment of an 'integrated brigade level unit' which would exchange officers and other ranks. The details were both ambitious and vague. According to André Giraud, the French Defence Minister, the proposal meant either the formation of an 'airborne brigade, with squadrons' or a 'mechanised unit, with its artillery'. The size of the unit, the nature of its equipment and the question of whether there should be a common uniform remained undecided. But the most significant problem concerned the command structure of an integrated unit. West Germany's forces were part of NATO's operational command structure but French forces were under their own national command. Sceptical voices were raised in France. Socialists as well as Gaullists took exception to what they saw as the cavalier manner in which such ideas were being floated. They were also suspicious that an indirect attempt might be made to place French troops under American command.[59]

But despite these considerable difficulties, a WEU meeting at the Hague in October 1987 signalled the beginning of a common West European defence policy. The meeting issued a declaration entitled 'Platform on European Security Interests'. In part, the declaration was designed to allay any American suspicions that the Europeans were breaking ranks with NATO. Emphasising that American conventional and nuclear forces played an 'irreplaceable' part in the defence of Europe, the declaration argued that alliance security was indivisible: 'Just as the commitment of the North American democracies is vital to Europe's security, a free, independent Europe is vital to the security of North America'. But the declaration also stressed that the overall credibility of Western defence and security strategy could not be maintained without a major European contribution. It therefore called for the integration of military resources, the expansion of bilateral and regional military cooperation and closer cooperation on crises outside Europe which affected West European security interests. The declaration also emphasised that nuclear weapons were an essential component of Western Europe's defence. The need for a balance of conventional and nuclear weapons was recognised but only the latter were said to be capable of confronting a potential aggressor with an 'unacceptable risk'. The declaration therefore endorsed the maintenance of the British and French nuclear deterrents and also the continuation of nuclear cooperation between any WEU member and the United States. Finally, the declaration insisted that European security interests should not be ignored in any general policy of arms control. This was seen as a coded message of West European irritation at having been left out of an INF agreement between the United States and the Soviet Union which affected Europe directly.[60]

Translating these principles into practical policies would not be easy. West European attempts to coordinate economic policies (the EEC budget and the farm subsidies under the Common Agricultural Policy) and political policies (terrorism and the means to combat it) had frequently encountered difficulties. Equally, it was by no means certain that public opinion would welcome increases in defence spending. Above all, the main opposition parties in both Britain and West Germany were committed to non-nuclear defence policies which had cost them dear in electoral terms throughout the 80s. Yet now, with the INF Treaty and the impending removal of cruise and Pershing, it was not inconceivable that the balance of argument might shift in favour of the British and West German socialists. In a similar vein, any attempt to extend the membership of WEU would encounter difficulties in the shape of the non-nuclear policies of such countries as Greece and Spain. But the practical problems were perhaps less important than the principle which had been established. In anticipation, not of the break-up of NATO, but a of gradual process of

American disengagement and withdrawal from Europe, the West
Europeans had at least acknowledged their own responsibility for
their own defence.

This book began with the emergence of the First Cold War in Europe
and identified 1947 as the crucial year. Forty years on, the INF Treaty
of December 1987 seems an appropriate place to end. When Reagan
and Gorbachev signed the treaty in Washington, not a single European
leader was present. In a sense, there was nothing exceptional about
this. The weapons were not owned by the Europeans, the United
States and the Soviet Union were still recognised as the leaders of
their respective alliances and the treaty itself had the unanimous
backing of European governments from both East and West. But the
image which this picture creates of stable and fixed alliance relationships is highly misleading. Within each alliance, the relationships
between the leaders and their allies had changed significantly. Interests
were no longer identical and they had begun to diverge. The relative
decline in the economic power of the United States and the Soviet
Union had enabled the Europeans of both East and West to become
more independent on the one hand and interdependent on the other.
In time, the INF Treaty might be seen as symbolic of the American
and Soviet decline. A number of arguments were put forward to
explain why the United States and the Soviet Union wanted fewer
offensive missiles. First, there was the moral argument that the two
sides were responding to the pressure of world opinion which had
become justifiably alarmed about the escalation of the arms race
during Reagan's first years in office. Secondly, there was the military
argument that space technology made it possible to switch from a
strategy of offence to one of defence. Gorbachev admitted that the
Russians were indeed working on their own version of SDI. Finally,
there was the economic argument that with diminishing resources,
both sides wanted to escape the generational modernisation programmes which were required to update their offensive weapons
systems. History will place these arguments in their order of significance. For now, beyond the INF Treaty and a possible halving of the
American and Soviet strategic arsenals, the constructive elements of
a relationship based on constructive confrontation had little to offer.
A wide ideological and geopolitical gulf still separated Washington
and Moscow. Perhaps, in the nature of things, no more could be
expected. The alternatives – Cold War and détente – had been tried

and found wanting. The first was too dangerous and too expensive. The second required a degree of confidence, trust and tolerance which simply did not exist. But for the Europeans it was different. They had much more in common, much more to lose and therefore much more which was worth preserving. Détente had served the Europeans well. Although far from perfect, the principal achievements had proved positive, lasting and beneficial. Now, more than ever, the Europeans had a special and a joint responsibility to preserve the peace and well-being of their own continent.

Chronological Table

1943	April	Discovery of mass grave at Katyn Forest in Poland
	May	Dissolution of Comintern
	November–December	Tehran Conference
1944	July	Soviet Union sets up Lublin Committee in Poland
		American Dixie Mission to China
	October	Churchill visits Moscow
	December	Beginning of Civil War in Greece
1945	February	Yalta Conference
	April	Death of Roosevelt; Truman becomes president
	May	German Act of surrender
	June	United Nations Charter signed
	July–August	Potsdam Conference
	August	Atomic bomb dropped on Hiroshima (6 Aug.)
		Atomic bomb dropped on Nagasaki (9 Aug.)
		Japanese surrender (15 Aug.)
	September	Democratic Republic of Vietnam proclaimed by Ho Chi Minh
	November	General Marshall appointed Special Envoy to China
1946	February	Kennan's Long Telegram
	March	Churchill's Iron Curtain speech
		Soviet Union agrees to withdraw from Azerbaijan (withdrawal complete 6 May)
	July	Beginning of Civil War in China
	July–October	21-nation Peace Conference in Paris
	September	Byrnes' Stuttgart speech on Germans having responsibility for running their own affairs and American troops remaining in Germany
	November	War in Indo-China begins
1947	January	United States and Britain establish Bizonia in Germany
		Communist-controlled elections in Poland
	February	Peace Treaties signed with Italy, Romania, Bulgaria, Finland and Hungary

	March	Anglo-French Dunkirk Treaty
		Truman Doctrine
	May	Communists expelled from governments in France and Italy
	June	Marshall's speech at Harvard opens prospect of Marshall Aid
	June–July	Meeting in Paris of British, French and Soviet Foreign Ministers to consider Marshall Plan; Molotov walks out (2 July)
	July	Conference of 16 European States in Paris to plan Marshall Aid; Committee on European Economic Cooperation set up
		Kennan's 'Mr X' article published in *Foreign Affairs*
	August	Defeat for Smallholders Party in Hungarian elections
	September	Petkov executed in Bulgaria
		Cominform established
	October	Peasant Party dissolved in Romania
		Mikolaczyk flees Poland
	December	King Michael of Romania abdicates
1948	February	Communist takeover in Czechoslovakia
		Conference of South East Asian Communists held in Calcutta
	February–March	London Conference of three Western powers and Benelux countries on future of Germany
	March	Death of Jan Masaryk
		Brussels Treaty on military cooperation signed by Britain, France and Benelux countries
		Soviet withdrawal from Allied Control Council on refusal of Western powers to account for London Conference
	April	Organisation of European Economic Cooperation set up in Paris
	June	American Senate approves Vandenberg Resolution on US association with defence pacts
		Western powers announce currency reform for West Germany
		Berlin blockade begins (24 June)
		Berlin airlift begins (25 June)
		Yugoslavia expelled from Cominform
1949	January	Comecon established
	April	North Atlantic Treaty signed in Washington
	May	Berlin blockade lifted (May 12)
	July	Soviet atom bomb exploded
	September	Federal Republic (West Germany) comes into being
	October	Proclamation of People's Republic of China by

		Mao Zedong
		German Democratic Republic (East Germany) comes into being
1950	January	Acheson's speech excludes Korea from American defence perimeter in Pacific
	February	Sino-Soviet Treaty of Friendship signed in Moscow
	May	Idea of European Coal and Steel Community put forward by Robert Schuman, French Foreign Minister
	June	Outbreak of Korean War
	October	UN forces cross 38th parallel in Korea; China intervenes
	December	Eisenhower appointed Supreme Allied Commander, Europe
1951	July	Three Western powers issue declaration formally terminating state of war with Germany
		Korean Armistice talks begin
	September	Japan Peace Treaty signed in San Francisco; China and the Soviet Union denounce its terms
		Western powers announce readiness to replace Occupation Statute by new relationship to enable West Germany to join European Defence Community (EDC)
1952	March	First of Soviet notes proposing German Peace Treaty upon basis of a withdrawal of foreign troops and a ban on entering military alliances
	May	Bonn Agreement revoking Occupation Statute
		EDC Treaty signed in Paris
	July	European Coal and Steel Community established
	November	United States detonates H-bomb
		Eisenhower elected president
1953	March	Death of Stalin
	June	East Berlin uprising
	July	Korean Armistice signed
	August	Soviet Union detonates H-bomb
	September	Khrushchev becomes First Secretary of Soviet Communist Party
1954	February	Colonel Nasser becomes prime minister and Military Governor of Egypt
	April	Opening of Geneva Conference on Korea and Indo-China
		Panch Sheel emerges in commercial agreement between India and China
	May	Fall of Dien Bien Phu
	June	Zhou Enlai visits India
	July	Geneva Agreement on Indo-China
	August	French Assembly refuses to ratify EDC Treaty

	September	Beijing begins bombardment of Quemoy and Matsu
		SEATO Treaty signed in Manila
		Khrushchev and Bulganin visit Beijing
	October	Occupation of West Germany ended; West Germany and Italy accede to Brussels Treaty in West European Union
	December	United States and Taiwan sign Mutual Defence Treaty
1955	February	Baghdad Pact agreed
	April	Bandung Conference of Asian and African nations
	May	West Germany joins NATO
		Warsaw Pact signed and joint command established
		Austrian State Treaty establishes Austria as a neutral state
		Khrushchev and Bulganin visit Yugoslavia
	July	Summit Conference at Geneva
	September	Adenauer visits Moscow; West Germany and the Soviet Union establish diplomatic relations
		Czech arms deal with Egypt
	December	Khrushchev and Bulganin visit India, Burma and Afghanistan
1956	February	Khrushchev attacks Stalin and unveils peaceful coexistence at 20th Congress of the Soviet Communist Party
	April	Cominform dissolved
	June	Riots in Poland; Gomulka returns to public life
	July	Nationalisation of the Suez Canal
	October	Demonstrations in Budapest; Imre Nagy reappointed prime minister of Hungary
		Israel attacks Egypt
	November	Nagy renounces Warsaw Pact, declares neutrality (1 Nov.)
		Soviet troops enter Budapest (4 Nov.)
		British and French forces land in Egypt; forced to withdraw
1957	January	Eisenhower Doctrine on Middle East
	February	Mao Zedong's first 'Hundred Flowers' speech
	March	Rome Treaty on European Economic Community signed
	August	First Soviet ICBM launched
	October	Sputnik launched; Sino-Soviet secret atomic agreement
	November	Conference of Communist Parties in Moscow; debates on revisionism and dogmatism; Mao Zedong speaks on prevailing wind and nuclear war

1958	March	Khrushchev replaces Bulganin as prime minister
	May	Great Leap Forward begins in China
	July	Revolution in Iraq
		United States intervenes in Lebanon, Britain in Jordan
		Khrushchev visits Beijing
	August	Beijing resumes bombing of Quemoy and Matsu
	November	Soviet Note on future status of Berlin
	December	De Gaulle elected president of France
1959	January	Victory of Fidel Castro in Cuba
	February–March	Macmillan visits Moscow
	May	Death of Dulles
	June	Khrushchev renounces atomic agreement with China
	September	Camp David meeting between Eisenhower and Khrushchev
1960	April	China attacks Khrushchev and Soviet Union in article entitled 'Long Live Leninism'
	May	U-2 shot down
		Paris summit breaks up
		Khrushchev issues new ultimatum over Berlin
	June	Heated exchanges between Soviet and Chinese delegates at Congress of Romanian Communist Party in Bucharest
	August	Soviet and East European technicians withdrawn from China
	November	John F. Kennedy elected president
		Summit meeting in Moscow of 81 Communist Parties; peaceful coexistence approved in face of strong Chinese opposition
	December	National Front for the Liberation of South Vietnam (NFLSV) established
1961	April	Bay of Pigs landing
	May	Geneva Conference on Laos
	June	Kennedy meets Khrushchev at Vienna summit
	August	Berlin Wall put up
	December	Albania severs relations with Soviet Union
		Kennedy increases American 'advisers' in Vietnam to 15,000
1962	October–November	Cuban Missile Crisis
	December	Cancellation of Skybolt
		Nassau agreement between Kennedy and Macmillan on Polaris missiles
1963	January	Discussion of American plans for a Multilateral Force (MLF)
		De Gaulle vetoes British entry to EEC and refuses

		American offer of Polaris
		Adenauer visits Paris; Franco-West German Treaty of Friendship and Cooperation signed
	June	China publishes 25-point indictment of Soviet Communist Party
		Hot Line agreement signed between United States and Soviet Union
	August	Nuclear Test Ban Treaty signed by United States, Soviet Union and Britain
	September	West Germany opens trade mission in Poland
	October	Adenauer resigns; succeeded by Erhard
		Romania and West Germany sign protocol establishing trade mission in Bucharest
	November	Kennedy assassinated; Johnson becomes president
1964	January	France recognises People's Republic of China
	April	Central Committee of Romanian Communist party issues Declaration asserting equality of Communist Parties
	July	West Germany opens trade mission in Hungary
	October	Khrushchev relieved of all posts; replaced by Brezhnev and Kosygin
		West Germany opens trade mission in Bulgaria
		China detonates first A-bomb
1965	February	Kosygin visits Beijing and Hanoi
		American bombing of North Vietnam begins
1966	March	De Gaulle announces French withdrawal from NATO
		Brezhnev becomes General-Secretary of Soviet Communist Party
	April	Cultural Revolution begins in China
	June	De Gaulle visits Moscow
	December	Resignation of Erhard in West Germany; formation of Grand Coalition between CDU and SPD; Kiesinger Chancellor, Brandt Foreign Minister
1967	January	West Germany establishes diplomatic relations with Romania
	April	Conference of European Communist Parties at Karlovy Vary in Czechoslovakia; agreement that no Eastern bloc country should open diplomatic relations with West Germany without prior agreement of East Germany
	June	Six-Day War in Middle East
		Johnson meets Kosygin at Glassboro, New Jersey
	December	Harmel Report defines purposes of NATO as military security and détente
1968	January	Dubček elected First Secretary of Czechoslovak Communist party

	January–February	Tet offensive in South Vietnam
	March	Johnson orders partial halt to bombing of North Vietnam
	May	Vietnamese peace talks open in Paris; Johnson announces he will not stand in presidential election
	July	United States, Soviet Union and Britain sign Non-Proliferation Treaty
	August	Warsaw Pact invasion of Czechoslovakia
	November	Nixon elected president
		Brezhnev Doctrine of Limited Sovereignty
1969	February	Nixon allows American command in South Vietnam to bomb Cambodia
	March	Clashes on Sino-Soviet border at Damanski Island on Ussuri River
	April	Dubček resigns as First Secretary of Czech Party; replaced by Gustav Husak
	July	Nixon Doctrine on American commitments in Asia
	September	West German elections; Brandt becomes Chancellor of SPD-FDP Coalition
	October	Brandt announces readiness to negotiate with Soviet Union and Poland and declares need to establish dialogue with East Germany
	November	West Germany signs Non-Proliferation Treaty
1970	March	Prince Sihanouk of Cambodia overthrown in military coup organised by Marshal Lon Nol
		Brandt meets Stoph, East German prime minister, at Erfurt in East Germany
	April	SALT talks begin in Vienna
	May	Second meeting between Brandt and Stoph at Kassel in West Germany
	August	Soviet-West German Treaty of Non-Aggression signed in Moscow
	November	First meeting between Michael Kohl and Egon Bahr, East and West German Ministers of State; talks continue over 2 years in 70 meetings
		Brandt visits Warsaw for signing of Polish-West German Treaty on renunciation of force and inviolability of frontiers
	December	Riots at Gdansk in Poland against food price increases; Edward Gierek replaces Gomulka as First Secretary of Polish Party
1971	April	American table-tennis team invited to China
	May	Erich Honecker replaces Ulbricht as First Secretary of East German Party

		Soviet Union signs Treaty of Friendship and Cooperation with Egypt
	July	Kissinger visits China
	September	Quadripartite Agreement on Berlin (in force June 1972)
		Brandt visits Brezhnev in Soviet Union; agreement to work for Security Conference
		Lin Biao's abortive coup in China
	October	People's Republic of China admitted to UN
	December	Transit and Visitors' Traffic Agreements between East and West Germany (in force June 1972)
1972	February	Nixon visits China; Shanghai Communiqué on Taiwan
	May	West German *Bundestag* ratifies treaties with Soviet Union and Poland
		Nixon visits Moscow; SALT 1 Agreement and Declaration on Basic Principles of Soviet-American Relations
	July	First round of European Security and Cooperation Talks in Helsinki
	September	Japanese prime minister, Mr Tanaka, visits China
	December	Basic Treaty signed between East and West Germany
1973	January	US–Vietnamese Armistice Agreement signed in Paris
	June	Brezhnev visits Washington; agreement calling for prevention of nuclear war signed
	July	President Sadat of Egypt expels Soviet advisers
	August	American Senate passes War Powers Act
	September	East and West Germany admitted to UN
	October	Arab-Israeli (Yom Kippur) War; American forces on nuclear alert
		Mutual Balanced Force Reduction (MBFR) Talks open in Vienna
	December	Treaty between West Germany and Czechoslovakia annuls 1938 Munich agreement
		West Germany establishes diplomatic relations with Hungary and Bulgaria
1974	February	Alexander Solzhenitsyn expelled from Soviet Union
	April	Military coup in Portugal overthrows regime of Dr Caetano
	May	Brandt forced to resign over East German spy scandal; Helmut Schmidt becomes West German Chancellor
	June	Nixon visits Moscow
	July	Soviet Union signs Treaty of Friendship and Cooperation with Somalia

	August	Culmination of Watergate scandal; Nixon resigns, replaced by Vice-President Gerald Ford
	September	Deposition of Haile Selassie of Ethiopia
	November	SALT 2 outline agreed by Brezhnev and Ford at Vladivostok
	December	Trade Reform Bill approved in United States with Jackson-Vanik amendment (originally tabled December 1973) on Jewish emigration
1975	January	Soviet Union cancels 1972 Soviet-American trade agreement because of publicity given to emigration issue
	April	Saigon capitulates and South Vietnam is taken over by North Vietnam
		Lon Nol's regime capitulates to Khmer Rouge in Cambodia
	June	Mozambique achieves independence from Portugal
	August	Final Act signed at Helsinki Conference on Security and Cooperation in Europe
		South African forces intervene in Angola
	November	Angola achieves independence from Portugal; Cuban troops arrive in Angola in support of Agostino Neto's MPLA
	December	Ford visits China
		Communist Pathet Lao takes over in Laos
1976	January	Death of Zhou Enlai
	April	Deng Xiaoping removed from posts in China as a result of opposition conducted by Gang of Four
	September	Death of Mao Zedong
	October	Gang of Four arrested in China; Hua Guofeng becomes Party Chairman
		Soviet Union signs Treaty of Friendship and Cooperation with Angola
	November	Carter elected president
1977	February	Carter pledges support for promotion of human rights in Soviet Union in open letter to Andrei Sakharov; Brezhnev writes to Carter describing Sakharov as a 'renegade who proclaimed himself an enemy of the Soviet State'
		Marxist coup in Ethiopia led by Lt-Col. Mengistu
	March	Vance visits Moscow and proposes deep cuts in strategic weapons beyond levels agreed at Vladivostok in 1974; Russians reject
		Soviet Union signs Treaty of Friendship and Cooperation with Mozambique
	March–June	Cuban troops support Katangan incursions into Shaba province of Zaire
	May	Cuban advisers arrive in Ethiopia

	July	Rehabilitation of Deng Xiaoping in China
		Ogaden War between Ethiopia and Somalia; Cuban troops under Soviet command and Soviet arms tilt balance in favour of Ethiopia and are used to help Ethiopia suppress Eritrean separatist movement; Carter administration divided over appropriate response
	October	Belgrade Security Conference to review Helsinki agreements opens; ends six months later with little practical result
	November	President Barre of Somalia tears up 1974 Treaty with Soviet Union and expels Soviet advisers
		Sadat visits Israel and addresses Knesset on terms for Middle Eastern peace settlement
	December	Israeli prime minister, Menachem Begin, visits Egypt
1978	April	People's Democratic Party of Afghanistan seize power in military coup
	May	Brzezinski visits China; stresses 'congruence of fundamental interests' in resisting Soviet expansion
	June	Vietnam becomes member of Comecon
	August	Sino-Japanese Peace Treaty signed with 'anti-hegemony clause'; Moscow denounces Treaty as a 'threat to stability in Asia'
	September	Camp David Agreement on peace treaty between Egypt and Israel and Palestinian autonomy
	November	Soviet Union signs Treaties of Friendship and Cooperation with Ethiopia and Vietnam
	December	Sino-American communiqué on normalisation of relations
		Soviet Union signs Treaty of Friendship, Good Neighbourliness and Cooperation with Afghanistan
		Vietnam launches offensive into Cambodia
1979	January	Sino-American diplomatic relations established
		Deng Xiaoping visits United States and informs Carter of China's plans to teach Vietnam a lesson
		Shah of Iran forced into exile
		Guadeloupe Summit (Carter, Giscard, Schmidt, Callaghan) on modernisation of NATO's IMF nuclear weapons
	February	Culmination of Iranian Revolution; Ayatollah Khomeini returns to Tehran
		China launches attack on Vietnam
	March	Revolution (New Jewel Movement) in Grenada
		Egyptian-Israeli Peace Treaty signed by Sadat

		and Begin in Washington
		China withdraws troops from Vietnam
	April	Sino-Soviet Treaty of 1950 abrogated
	May	Dr Yuri Orlov sentenced to seven years' hard labour in Soviet Union
		Arrest of members of Charter 77 in Czechoslovakia
	June	Summit between Brezhnev and Carter in Vienna; SALT 2 signed
	July	Sandinistas overthrow Somoza in Nicaragua
	September	Lancaster House Conference on Rhodesia opens in London
	November	Seizure of American embassy in Tehran; hostage crisis begins
	December	NATO dual-track decision on deployment of cruise and Pershing by 1983 and negotiations as an alternative to deployment
		Lancaster House Conference concludes with agreement on constitution for independent Republic of Zimbabwe
		Soviet Union invades Afghanistan; Hafizullah Amin murdered in coup and replaced by Babrak Kamal
1980	January	Carter announces sanctions against Soviet Union and Carter Doctrine on Persian Gulf
		Secretary of Defence Harold Brown visits China
		Sakharov exiled to Gorky in Soviet Union
	February	Franco-German Summit in Paris on Afghan situation
	April	Failure of mission to rescue hostages in Tehran; Vance resigns
	May	Brown announces sale of military equipment to China
		Giscard d'Estaing meets Brezhnev in Warsaw
	June	President Tito of Yugoslavia dies
		EEC summit at Venice proposes Middle East peace plan based on recognition of Israel's right to exist and negotiations on Palestinian self-determination with PLO representatives included; Israel rejects
	July	American boycott of Moscow Olympics
	August	Gdansk Agreements on free trades unions in Poland; birth of Solidarity under Lech Walesa
	September	Stanislaw Kania replaces Edward Gierek as leader of Polish Party
		Outbreak of Gulf War between Iran and Iraq
	October	East Germany increases amount of currency to be exchanged by West German visitors and

	imposes four conditions for improvement of relations with Bonn
	Hua Guofeng resigns as premier in China; victory for Deng Xiaoping and further move away from Mao's legacy
November	Reagan elected president
	Security Conference opens in Madrid
December	Former Soviet premier Alexei Kosygin dies
	Brezhnev proposes Zone of Peace in Persian Gulf and Indian Ocean during visit to New Delhi
1981 January	Release of American hostages in Tehran
	Reagan, at his first press conference, claims détente has been a 'one-way street' and accuses Russians of being cheats and liars
February	Wojiech Jaruzelski becomes prime minister of Poland
	Reagan administration claims to have evidence of 'international communist conspiracy' in El Salvador
May	François Mitterand becomes first post-war socialist president of France
June	Secretary Haig visits China; Reagan's emphasis on right to supply military equipment to Taiwan impedes Sino-American relations
	Hua Guofeng resigns Chairmanship of Chinese Communist Party
July	Attack on party leadership at 9th Congress of Polish Party in Warsaw
October	Jaruzelski replaces Kania as party leader in Poland
	Sadat assassinated, succeeded by Hosni Mubarak
November	INF talks begin in Geneva
	Reagan proposes 'zero option' on INF weapons
	Soviet Union and West Germany sign gas pipeline contract
December	Martial Law declared in Poland; Walesa and other Solidarity leaders arrested
	Schmidt and Honecker say Poles have right to solve problems in their own way
	Reagan announces sanctions against Poland and Soviet Union; sanctions against Moscow include gas pipeline equipment but not grain
1982 April	Israeli jets bomb PLO positions south of Beirut in Lebanon
June	Israel invades Lebanon by land, air and sea and surrounds Beirut
	START talks begin in Geneva
	Reagan extends existing embargo on export of oil

		and gas equipment to Soviet Union to subsidiaries and licensees of American companies abroad
	July	Israel destroys Syrian SAM-6 missiles in Bekaa Valley
		George Shultz replaces Haig as Secretary of State
	August	Multinational force arrives to supervise PLO evacuation from West Beirut; PLO Chairman, Yassir Arafat, leaves Beirut
	September	Multinational force leaves Beirut but then returns after massacre at Sabra and Chatila refugee camps by Christian Phalangist militia
		Reagan proposes self-governing Palestinian state linked with Jordan; Israel rejects
	October	In West Germany, Schmidt forced from office as FDP defects and forms new coalition with CDU under Helmut Kohl
	November	Death of Brezhnev; succeeded by Yuri Andropov
		Reagan lifts gas pipeline embargo
	December	Martial law ended in Poland
1983	March	Elections in West Germany; CDU-FDP coalition continues (fierce-fought campaign over new NATO missiles)
		Reagan announces SDI
	April	Suicide bomber destroys American embassy in Beirut; 46 killed, including 16 Americans
	September	Soviet Union shoots down South Korean airliner
		Madrid Security Conference ends
		American Defence Secretary Caspar Weinberger visits China
	October	American invasion of Grenada
	November	NATO begins deploying new missiles; Soviet delegations walk out of IMF and START talks; Honecker emphasises need to limit damage
1984	January	Conference on Confidence and Security Building Measures and Disarmament in Europe opens in Stockholm
		Reagan visits China
	February	Death of Andropov; succeeded by Konstantin Chernenko
		Lusaka Agreement between Angola and South Africa
	March	Nkomati Pact between Mozambique and South Africa
	July	Soviet and Eastern bloc boycott of Los Angeles Olympics (Romania takes part)
		West Germany loans DM 950 million to East Germany in return for further lifting of travel

		restrictions
	August	Culmination of open split between East Berlin and Moscow on détente and East Germany's relations with West Germany; Honecker forced to cancel visit to birthplace in Federal Republic
	October	Soviet Foreign Minister Gromyko meets Reagan in White House
	November	Reagan elected for second term
1985	January	Meeting on arms control between Gromyko and Shultz in Geneva
	March	Geneva arms talks resumed; umbrella approach on strategic weapons, INF weapons and space weapons
	August	Death of Chernenko; replaced by Mikhail Gorbachev
	August	Gorbachev announces moratorium on Soviet nuclear testing; extended on three occasions to end of 1986
	November	Reagan-Gorbachev summit at Geneva
1986	February	Duvalier dynasty overthrown in Haiti
		Corazon Aquino defeats Ferdinand Marcos in Philippines elections
		Anatoly Shcharansky released as part of a spy exchange
	April	American bombing raids in Libya
		Nuclear reactor explodes at Chernobyl in Soviet Union
	May	South African commando raids in Zimbabwe, Botswana and Zambia
	June	Gorbachev proposes 30 per cent reductions in strategic weapons
		Reagan announces that by the end of the year, the United States will not be bound by terms of SALT 2
		State of Emergency declared in South Africa
	July	Gorbachev's Vladivostok speech aimed at improving Sino-Soviet relations
	August	American Senate approves Reagan's 100 million dollar Contra aid request
	September	Stockholm Security Conference ends with agreement on advance notice of military movements, presence of observers and verification
		Reagan offers not to deploy SDI weapons in space for seven years
	October	Yuri Orlov released as part of spy exchange to resolve Daniloff affair
		Senate overrules Reagan on South African

		sanctions
		Reagan-Gorbachev summit at Reykjavik collapses over SDI
		President Samora Machel of Mozambique killed in plane crash
	December	Andrei Sakharov released from internal exile at Gorky
1987	February	Josef Begun released
		At Moscow Peace forum Gorbachev declares that no political objectives are worth the risk of nuclear war
	March	Report of Tower Commission on Iran-Contra affair
		Gorbachev makes new proposals for INF agreement
		British prime minister, Margaret Thatcher, visits Moscow
	June	Reagan vows to keep Gulf open to prevent economic dislocation and authorises US naval protection for Kuwaiti tankers reflagged under the American flag
	August	Reagan and Arias Peace Plans for Central America
	September	Honecker visits West Germany
		Shevardnadze in Washington: agreement to dismantle INF weapons
	October	13th Congress of Chinese Communist Party at Beijing: Deng Xiaoping and old guard stand down
	November	Gorbachev's speech marking the 70th anniversary of the Bolshevik Revolution
		Daniel Ortega proposes negotiated ceasefire with Contras
		Arab summit at Amman pledges Arab support for Iraq in Gulf War and sanctions restoration of diplomatic relations with Egypt
		Boris Yeltsin dismissed as head of Moscow City Communist Party
		Report of Congressional Committee on Iran-Contra affair
		Reagan and Congress agree terms for reduction of budget deficit
		General Jaruzelski fails to win majority support for his economic and political reforms in Polish referendum
	December	INF Treaty signed at Reagan-Gorbachev summit in Washington

Bibliography

THE number of books on this subject is formidable and growing. Only those which have proved most useful in writing this study are listed here. Details of newspaper articles and periodical literature will be found in the References.

HANNES ADOMEIT, *Soviet Risk-Taking and Crisis Behavior: A theoretical and empirical analysis* (London: George Allen and Unwin, 1982).

G. ALPEROWITZ *Atomic Diplomacy: Hiroshima and Potsdam* (New York: Vintage Books, 1967).

NEAL ASCHERSON, *The Polish August: The Self-Limiting Revolution* (Harmondsworth: Penguin, 1981).

SEWERYN BIALER, *The Soviet Paradox: External Expansion, Internal Decline* (London: I.B. Tauris and Co. Ltd., 1985).

MICHAEL BALFOUR, *The Adversaries: America, Russia and The Open World 1941–1962* (London: Routledge and Kegan Paul, 1981).

DOROTHY BORG AND WALDO HEINRICHS (eds), *Uncertain Years: Chinese-American Relations 1947–1950* (New York: Columbia University Press, 1980).

WILLY BRANDT, *People and Politics* (London: Collins, 1978).

BILL BRUGGER, *China: Liberation and Transformation 1942–1962* (London: Croom Helm, 1981).

——, *China: Radicalism to Revisionism 1962–1979* (London: Croom Helm, 1981).

ZBIGNIEW BRZEZINSKI *The Soviet Bloc: Unity and Conflict* (Cambridge, Mass.: Harvard University Press, 1971).

——, *Power and Principle: Memoirs of the National Security Adviser 1977–1981* (London: Weidenfeld and Nicolson, 1983).

JIMMY CARTER, *Keeping Faith* (London: Collins, 1982).

KENNETH C. CHERN, *Dilemma in China: America's Policy Debate 1945* (Hamden, Conn.: Archon Books, 1980).

NOAM CHOMSKY, JONATHAN STEELE AND JOHN GITTINGS, *Superpowers in Collision: The New Cold War of the 1980s* (Harmondsworth: Penguin, 1984).

D. S. CLEMENS, *Yalta* (New York: Oxford University Press, 1970).

HUGH DE SANTIS, *The Diplomacy of Silence: The American Foreign Service, the Soviet Union and the Cold War 1933–1947* (Chicago: Chicago University Press, 1980).

ISAAC DEUTSCHER, *Russia, China and the West* (Harmondsworth: Penguin, 1970).

MILOVAN DJILAS, *Conversations with Stalin* (New York: Harcourt, Brace and World, 1962).

KENNETH DYSON (ed.), *European Détente: Case Studies of the Politics of East-West Relations* (London: Frances Pinter, 1986).

Robin Edmonds, *Soviet Foreign Policy 1962–1973* (London: Oxford University Press, 1975).

——, *Soviet Foreign Policy: The Brezhnev Years* (Oxford: Oxford University Press, 1983).

Thomas H. Etzold and John Lewis Gaddis (eds), *Containment: Documents on American Policy and Strategy 1945–1950* (New York: Columbia University Press, 1978).

Herbert Feiss, *Churchill, Roosevelt, Stalin* (Princeton, New Jersey: Princeton University Press, 1957).

——, *Between War and Peace: The Potsdam Conference* (Princeton, New Jersey: Princeton University Press, 1960).

——, *The Atomic Bomb and The End of World War II* (Princeton, New Jersey: Princeton University Press, 1966).

——, *From Trust to Terror* (New York: Norton, 1970).

John Lewis Gaddis, *The United States and The Origins of the Cold War* (New York: Columbia University Press, 1972).

John Gittings, *The World and China 1922–1972* (London: Eyre Metheun, 1974).

——, *Survey of the Sino-Soviet Dispute: A Commentary and Extracts from the Recent Polemics 1963–1967* (London: Oxford University Press, 1968).

Norman A. Graebener, *Cold War Diplomacy: American Foreign Policy 1945–1975* (New York: D. Van Nostrand, 1977).

William E. Griffith, *The Sino-Soviet Rift* (London: Allen and Unwin, 1964).

Alfred Grosser, *The Western Alliance: European-American Relations since 1945* (London: Macmillan, 1980).

Wang Gungwu, *China and the World since 1949: The Impact of Independence, Modernity and Revolution* (London: Macmillan, 1977).

Fred Halliday, *Threat From the East?: Soviet Policy from Afghanistan and Iran to the Horn of Africa* (Harmondsworth: Penguin, 1982).

——, *The Making of The Second Cold War* (London: Verso, 1984).

G. F. Hudson, R. Lowenthal and R. MacFarquhar (eds), *The Sino-Soviet Dispute* (New York: reprint from *The China Quarterly*, 1961).

C. G. Jacobsen, *Sino-Soviet Relations since Mao: The Chairman's Legacy* (New York: Praeger, 1981).

Keesing's Research Report, *The Sino-Soviet Dispute* (Keesing's Publications Ltd, 1970).

George F. Kennan, *Memoirs 1925–1950* (Boston: Little, Brown, 1967).

Henry Kissinger, *The White House Years* (London: Weidenfeld and Nicolson, 1979).

——, *Years of Upheaval* (London: Weidenfeld and Nicolson, 1982).

Gabriel Kolko, *The Politics of War* (London: Weidenfeld and Nicolson, 1968).

Joyce and Gabriel Kolko, *The Limits of Power: The World and United States Foreign Policy 1945–1954* (New York: Harper and Row, 1972).

Josef Korbel, *Détente in Europe: Real or Imaginery?* (Princeton, New Jersey: Princeton University Press, 1972).

B. Kuklick, *American Policy and the Division of Germany* (Ithaca: Cornell University Press, 1972).

JEAN LACOUTRE, *Ho Chi Minh* (Harmondsworth: Penguin, 1969).

WALTER LAFEBER, *America, Russia and The Cold War 1945–1980* (New York: John Wiley, 4th ed., 1980).

PETER LYON, *Eisenhower: Portrait of a Hero* (Boston: Little, Brown, 1974).

RODERICK MACFARQUHAR, *Sino-American Relations 1949–1971* (Newton Abbot: David and Charles, 1972).

ROBERT JAMES MADDOX, *The New Left and The Origins of The Cold War* (Princeton, New Jersey: Princeton University Press, 1973).

WILLIAM MANCHESTER, *Remembering Kennedy: One Brief Shining Moment* (London: Michael Joseph, 1983).

MARTIN MCCAULEY, *Communist Power in Europe 1944–1949* (London: Macmillan, 1977).

——, *The Origins of the Cold War* (London: Longman Seminar Studies in History, 1983).

ROY AND ZHORES MEDVEDEV, *Khrushchev: The Years in Power* (London: Oxford University Press, 1977).

ROGER MORGAN, *The Unsettled Peace: A Study of the Cold War in Europe* (London: British Broadcasting Corporation, 1974).

——, *The United States and West Germany 1945–1973: A Study in Alliance Politics* (Oxford: Oxford University Press, 1977).

JOSEPH L. NOGEE AND ROBERT H. DONALDSON, *Soviet Foreign Policy since World War II* (New York: Pergamon, 2nd ed., 1986).

GARETH PORTER (ed.), *Vietnam: The Definitive Documentation of Human Decisions 1941–1975*, 2 Vols (London: Heyden, 1979).

TERENCE PRITTIE, *Konrad Adenauer 1876–1967* (London: Tom Stacey, 1972).

JAMES REARDON-ANDERSON, *Yenan and the Great Powers: The Origins of Chinese Communist Foreign Policy 1944–1946* (New York: Columbia University Press, 1980).

DAVID REES, *The Age of Containment: The Cold War 1945–1965* (London: Macmillan, 1967).

ARKADY N. SCHEVCHENKO, *Breaking with Moscow* (London: Jonathan Cape, 1985).

ARTHUR M. SCHLESINGER, *A Thousand Days: John F. Kennedy in The White House* (London: André Deutsch, 1975).

WILLIAM SHAWCROSS, *Sideshow: Kissinger, Nixon and the Destruction of Cambodia* (London: André Deutsch, 1979).

RALPH B. SMITH, *An International History of the Vietnam War, Vol. 1, Revolution versus Containment 1955–61* (London: Macmillan, 1983).

——, *An International History of the Vietnam War, Vol. 2, The Struggle for South East Asia 1961–65* (London: Macmillan, 1985).

I. F. STONE, *The Hidden History of the Korean War* (New York: Monthly Review Press, 1970).

STROBE TALBOTT (ed. and trs.), *Khrushchev Remembers* (Boston: Little, Brown, 1970).

ADAM B. ULAM, *Titoism and The Cominform* (Cambridge, Mass.: Harvard University Press, 1952).

——, *Expansion and Coexistence: Soviet Foreign Policy 1917–1973* (New York: Praeger, 1974).

——, *Dangerous Relations: The Soviet Union in World Politics 1970–1982* (Oxford: Oxford University Press, 1983).

ALLEN S. WHITING, *China Crosses the Yalu: The Decision to Enter the Korean War* (New York: Macmillan, 1960).

PHIL WILLIAMS (ed.), *The Nuclear Debate: Issues and Politics*, Chatham House Special Paper published on behalf of the Royal Institute of International Affairs (London: Routledge & Kegan Paul, 1984).

W.A. WILLIAMS, *The Tragedy of American Diplomacy* (New York: Delta Books, 1962).

DANIEL YERGIN, *Shattered Peace: The Origins of the Cold War and the National Security State* (Harmondsworth: Penguin, 1980).

DONALD S. ZAGORIA, *The Sino-Soviet Conflict 1956–1961* (London: Oxford University Press, 1962).

References

1. IN THE SHADOW OF STALIN: THE COLD WAR IN EUROPE 1945-53

1. In April 1943 the Germans discovered the graves of 4,000 Polish officers at Katyn Forest near Smolensk in Poland. The Russians have always denied the accusation that they were responsible. They have also denied the charge that they could have done more to assist the Polish resistance during the Warsaw Uprising between August and October 1944.

2. At the meeting in Moscow in October 1944, Churchill handed Stalin a piece of paper upon which he had scribbled the following terms for the division of Eastern Europe into spheres of influence: Romania (Russia 90 per cent, the West 10 per cent); Greece (the West 90 per cent, Russia 10 per cent); Hungary and Yugoslavia (50 per cent each); Bulgaria (Russia 75 per cent, the West 25 per cent). Stalin, according to Churchill's account, put a big tick on the paper and passed it back.

3. The full exchange between Roosevelt and Churchill is recounted in Robert James Maddox, *The New Left and The Origins of the Cold War* (Princeton, New Jersey: Princeton University Press, 1973), pp. 82–86.

4. The orthodox interpretation is stated in four books by Herbert Feiss: *Churchill, Roosevelt, Stalin* (Princeton, New Jersey: Princeton University Press, 1957); *Between War and Peace: The Potsdam Conference* (Princeton, New Jersey: Princeton University Press, 1960); *The Atomic Bomb and the End of World War II* (Princeton, New Jersey: Princeton University Press, 1966); *From Trust to Terror* (New York: Norton, 1970). For a more concise orthodox interpretation, see David Rees, *The Age of Containment: The Cold War 1945–1965* (London: Macmillan, 1967). For a current restatement of the orthodox case, see Zbigniew Brzezinski, 'The Future of Yalta', *Foreign Affairs* (December 1984), pp. 279–302.

The principal revisionist interpretations are: W.A. Williams, *The Tragedy of American Diplomacy* (New York: Delta Books, 1962), G. Alperowitz, *Atomic Diplomacy: Hiroshima and Potsdam* (New York: Vintage Books, 1967); Gabriel Kolko, *The Politics of War* (London: Weidenfeld and Nicolson, 1968); D.S. Clemens, *Yalta* (New York: Oxford University Press, 1970); B. Kuklick, *American Policy and the Division of Germany* (Ithaca: Cornell University Press, 1972).

A critique of revisionist interpretations may be read in Maddox, *The New Left and The Origins of the Cold War*.

The centrist view is represented in J.L. Gaddis, *The United States and The Origins of the Cold War* (New York: Columbia University Press, 1972) and

Daniel Yergin, *Shattered Peace: The Origins of the Cold War and the National Security State* (Harmondsworth: Penguin, 1980).

5. Cited in Martin McCauley, *The Soviet Union since 1917* (London: Longman, 1981), p. 133.

6. For an interpretation of Stalin's post-war outlook, see Adam B. Ulam, *Expansion and Coexistence: Soviet Foreign Policy 1917–1973* (New York: Praeger, 1974), esp. ch. 8.

7. At the end of the war the Red Army had reached its maximum size of 11,365,000. The figure for the United States was 12,300,000. By 1948, as a result of demobilisation on both sides, the Red Army stood at 2,874,000 and the American armed forces (a combined total for the Army, Navy and the Marines) at 2,736,000. Yergin, *Shattered Peace*, p. 270, and Ulam, *Expansion and Coexistence*, p. 414.

8. Cited in Yergin, *Shattered Peace*, p. 85.

9. Maddox, *The New Left and The Origins of the Cold War*, p. 46.

10. For a detailed discussion of the issues surrounding the atomic bomb, see Barton J. Bernstein, 'Roosevelt, Truman and The Atomic Bomb 1941–1945: A Reinterpretation', *Political Science Quarterly* (Spring 1975), pp. 23–69.

11. Ibid., p. 66.

12. Yergin, *Shattered Peace*, p. 161.

13. Excerpts from the Long Telegram are reprinted in George F. Kennan, *Memoirs 1925–1950* (Boston: Little, Brown, 1967), pp. 547–59.

14. In his Memoirs, Kennan commented thus on the Long Telegram: 'I read it over today with a horrified amusement. Much of it reads exactly like one of those primers put out by alarmed congressional committees or by the Daughters of the American Revolution, designed to arouse the citizenry to the dangers of the Communist conspiracy.' Ibid., p. 294.

15. For the reaction in Washington to the Long Telegram, see Yergin, *Shattered Peace*, pp. 170–71, and Hugh De Santis, *The Diplomacy of Silence: The American Foreign Service, the Soviet Union and the Cold War, 1933–1947* (Chicago: Chicago University Press, 1980), pp. 174–75.

16. Wallace Murray, divisional head of Near Eastern Affairs in the State Department. Cited in Yergin, *Shattered Peace*, p. 181.

17. Ibid., p, 176.

18. Ibid., p. 243.

19. For a discussion of the Greek situation, see the paper on Greece by Richard Clogg in Martin McCauley (ed.), *Communist Power in Europe 1944–1949* (London: Macmillan, 1977), pp. 184–98.

20. Yergin, *Shattered Peace*, pp. 281–82.

21. Excerpts from Truman's speech to Congress on 12 March 1947 are reprinted in Norman A. Graebener, *Cold War Diplomacy: American Foreign Policy 1945–1975* (New York: D. Van Nostrand, 1977), pp. 186–89.

22. Kennan, *Memoirs*, p. 342.

23. Yergin, *Shattered Peace*, pp. 314–17.

24. Ulam, *Expansion and Coexistence*, p. 448.

25. See the paper on Poland by Norman Davies in McCauley (ed.), *Communist Power in Europe*, pp. 39–57.

26. Quoted by Bela Vago in a paper on Romania, ibid., p. 120.

27. See the paper on Finland by Anthony Upton in ibid., pp. 133–50.

28. See the paper on Czechoslovakia by Vladimir V. Kusin in ibid, pp. 73–94.

29. Yergin, *Shattered Peace*, p. 324.

30. Quoted by Vladimir V. Kusin in paper on Czechoslovakia in McCauley, *Communist Power in Europe*, p. 81.

31. Yergin, *Shattered Peace*, pp. 343–50.

32. On the split with Yugoslavia, see Adam B. Ulam, *Titoism and the Cominform* (Cambridge, Mass.: Harvard University Press, 1952).

33. The discussion which follows is largely based on the extensive references to the German question in Yergin, *Shattered Peace*, and Ulam, *Expansion and Coexistence*. Reference should also be made to that section which deals with the Berlin crisis of 1948 in Hannes Adomeit, *Soviet Risk-Taking and Crisis Behavior: A theoretical and empirical analysis* (London: George Allen and Unwin, 1982).

34. Milovan Djilas, *Conversations with Stalin* (New York: Harcourt, Brace and World, 1962), p. 153.

35. Ibid.

36. Hannes Adomeit, *Soviet Risk-Taking and Crisis Behavior*, p. 123.

37. Ibid., p. 79.

38. Ibid., p. 69.

39. Ibid., p. 72.

40. Ibid.

41. Ibid., pp. 141–44.

42. See the paper on East Germany by Martin McCauley in McCauley (ed.), *Communist Power in Europe*, pp. 58–72.

43. David Childs, *East Germany* (London: Ernest Benn Ltd, 1969), pp. 23–24.

44. Ibid.

45. McCauley, *Communist Power in Europe*, p. 70.

46. Ibid., pp. 68–69,

47. John Hilldring, Assistant Secretary of State for Occupied Territories. Cited in Yergin, *Shattered Peace*, p. 318.

48. Ulam, *Expansion and Coexistence*, pp. 536–37.

2. REVOLUTION AND CONTAINMENT IN ASIA 1945–53

1. For Stalin's policies towards China, see Ulam, *Expansion and Coexistence*, esp. ch. 9, and John Gittings, *The World and China 1922–1972* (London: Eyre Metheun, 1974).

2. Milovan Djilas, *Conversations with Stalin* (New York: Harcourt, Brace and World, 1962), p. 182.

3. For American policies towards China, see Gittings, *The World and China*; Roderick MacFarquhar, *Sino-American Relations 1949–1971* (Newton Abbott: David and Charles, 1972); Dorothy Borg and Waldo Heinrichs (eds), *Uncertain Years: Chinese-American Relations 1947–1950* (New York: Columbia University Press, 1980): and Kenneth C. Chern, *Dilemma in China: America's Policy Debate 1945* (Hamden, Conn.: Archon Books, 1980). For documents on the years 1944–48, see United States, State Department, *United States' Relations with China*

(Washington, 1949; reissued in two volumes by Stanford University Press, 1967).

4. Gittings, *The World and China*, p. 102.

5. See, besides Gittings, James Reardon-Anderson, *Yenan and The Great Powers: The Origins of Chinese Communist Foreign Policy 1944–1946* (New York: Columbia University Press, 1980). Also, papers by Michael H. Hunt and Steven M. Goldstein in Borg and Heinrichs (eds), *Uncertain Years*.

6. Gittings, *The World and China*, p. 132.

7. For extracts from Acheson's Letter of Transmittal, see MacFarquhar, *Sino-American Relations*, pp. 67–69.

8. Gittings, *The World and China*, pp. 142–48.

9. For extracts from Truman's statement on the status of Formosa (Taiwan) and Acheson's speech to the National Press Club, see MacFarquhar, *Sino-American Relations*, pp. 70–75.

10. NSC-68 is reprinted in Thomas H. Etzold and John Lewis Gaddis (eds), *Containment: Documents on American Policy and Strategy 1945–1950* (New York: Columbia University Press, 1978), pp. 385–442. The author of NSC-68 was Paul Nitze, Kennan's successor as head of the Policy Planning Staff in the State Department. In the mid-70s, Nitze was an influential member of the Committee on The Present Danger, a new conservative pressure group which attacked détente with the Soviet Union and called for a reassertion of American power. He was Reagan's negotiator at the IMF talks in 1981–83 and 1985–86.

11. For a discussion of the view that Stalin precipitated the Korean War, see Ulam, *Expansion and Coexistence*, pp. 516–34. For the conspiracy theory, see I. F. Stone, *The Hidden History of the Korean War* (New York: Monthly Review Press, 1970).

12. For China's entry into the war, see Allen S. Whiting, *China Crosses the Yalu: The Decision to Enter the Korean War* (New York: Macmillan, 1960). Also, Gittings, *The World and China*, ch. 9, and MacFarquhar, *Sino-American Relations*, pp. 78–100.

13. Kennan, *Memoirs*, p. 359.

14. Cited in Jean Lacoutre, *Ho Chi Minh* (Harmondsworth: Penguin, 1969), p. 104.

15. Gareth Porter (ed.), *Vietnam: The Definitive Documentation of Human Decisions 1941–1975*, in 2 volumes (London: Heyden, 1979), vol. 1, p. 11.

16. Ibid., p. 140.

17. Ibid., p. 180.

18. Ibid., pp. 353–57.

19. Ibid., p. 393.

3. FALSE START: KHRUSHCHEV, PEACEFUL COEXISTENCE AND THE SINO-SOVIET CONFLICT 1954–65

1. Strobe Talbott (ed. and trs.), *Khrushchev Remembers*, with an introduction, commentary and notes by Edward Crankshaw (Boston: Little, Brown, 1970), p. 392.

2. Porter (ed.), *Vietnam*, vol. 1, pp. 498–501.

3. Ralph B. Smith, *An International History of the Vietnam War*, vol. 1, *Revolution versus Containment 1955–1961* (London: Macmillan, 1983), pp. 59–60.

4. Ibid., p. 60.

5. Porter (ed.), *Vietnam*, vol. 1, pp. 666–68.

6. Ibid., pp. 697–702.

7. On China's role at the Bandung Conference, see Wang Gungwu, *China and the World since 1949: The Impact of Independence, Modernity and Revolution* (London: Macmillan, 1977), pp. 50–53.

8. Paul Zinner (ed.), *National Communism and Popular Revolt in Eastern Europe: A Selection of Documents on Events in Poland and Hungary, February–November 1956* (New York: Colombia University Press, 1956), p. 6.

9. Talbott (ed.), *Khrushchev Remembers*, pp. 393–95.

10. Khrushchev's remarks on peaceful coexistence and different roads to socialism at the Twentieth Congress may be read in G. F. Hudson, R. Lowenthal and R. MacFarquhar (eds), *The Sino-Soviet Dispute* (New York, reprinted from the *China Quarterly*, 1961), pp. 42–46.

11. Deutscher's assessment of the Twentieth Congress written on 29 February 1956 has stood the test of time remarkably well. See Isaac Deutscher, *Russia, China and the West 1953–1966* (Harmondsworth: Penguin, 1970), pp. 64–69.

12. On the Eisenhower administration, see Peter Lyon, *Eisenhower: Portrait of a Hero* (Boston: Little, Brown, 1974).

13. On the development of the Sino-Soviet rift during the Khrushchev era, see William E. Griffith, *The Sino-Soviet Rift* (London: Allen and Unwin, 1964); Donald S. Zagoria, *The Sino-Soviet Conflict 1956–1961* (London: Oxford University Press, 1962); Hudson (*et al*), *The Sino-Soviet Dispute*; John Gittings, *Survey of the Sino-Soviet Dispute: A Commentary and Extracts from the Recent Polemics 1963–1967* (London: Oxford University Press, 1968) and Keesing's Research Report, *The Sino-Soviet Dispute*, covering the years 1949–69 (Keesing's Publications Ltd, 1970). One of the best short accounts of the conflict, which brings developments up to the beginning of the Gorbachev era in the Soviet Union, is in Seweryn Bialer, *The Soviet Paradox: External Expansion, Internal Decline* (London: I. B. Tauris & Co Ltd, 1986).

14. Sidney Moras, in his postscript to the essay by the Soviet dissident Andrei Amalrik, 'Will the Soviet Union Survive until 1984?', quoted in Bialer, *The Soviet Paradox*, p. 241.

15. Quoted in ibid.

16. For the development of this argument, see Ulam, *Expansion and Coexistence*, p. 623.

17. Khrushchev's speech to the Romanian Party Congress at Bucharest in June 1960, in Hudson (*et al*), *The Sino-Soviet Dispute*, p. 136.

18. On Adenauer and West German foreign policy, see Terence Prittie, *Konrad Adenauer 1876–1967* (London: Tom Stacey, 1972); Roger Morgan, *The United States and West Germany 1945–73: A Study in Alliance Politics* (Oxford: Oxford University Press, 1977), and Alfred Grosser, *The Western Alliance: European-American Relations since 1945* (London: Macmillan, 1980).

19. On Khrushchev's domestic programmes and problems, see Roy and

Zhores Medvedev, *Khrushchev: The Years in Power* (London: Oxford University Press, 1977).

20. Between 1952 and 1966 the Politburo of the Soviet Communist Party was known as the Presidium.

21. Mao's remarks on nuclear war and the prevailing wind may be read in Gittings, *Survey of the Sino-Soviet Dispute*, pp. 82–83.

22. For the text of the 1957 Moscow Declaration, see Hudson (*et al.*), *The Sino-Soviet Dispute*, pp. 46–56.

23. Grosser, *The Western Alliance*, pp. 183–92.

24. The 'Long Live Leninism' articles are reprinted in Hudson (*et al.*), *The Sino-Soviet Dispute*, pp. 82–112.

25. For the text of the 1960 Moscow Declaration, see ibid., pp. 177–205.

26. On Kennedy, see Arthur M. Schlesinger, *A Thousand Days: John F. Kennedy in The White House* (London: André Deutsch, 1975).

27. Ralph B. Smith, *An International History of the Vietnam War*, vol. 1, pp. 206–208, 226–28

28. Quoted in William Manchester, *Remembering Kennedy: One Brief Shining Moment* (London: Michael Joseph, 1983), p. 187.

29. The account which follows draws heavily on the discussion of the Berlin crisis of 1961 in Hannes Adomeit, *Soviet Risk-Taking and Crisis Behavior*.

30. The first round of defence cuts, implemented between 1955 and 1957, had reduced the size of the Soviet armed forces by about 1.8 million men from a 1955 peak of 5.7 million. The second reduction, implemented between 1958 and 1959, was much smaller, involving about 300,000 men. A third measure, announced in January 1960, was intended to effect a further reduction of 1.2 million, bringing the size of the Soviet armed forces down to 2.4 million by the autumn of 1961. Responding to Kennedy's defence outlays, which increased the size of the American armed forces by about 225,000 men, and also to the continued build-up of the West German armed forces, Khrushchev suspended the third round of Soviet defence cuts in July 1961. The Soviet armed forces stood at about 3 million men during the Berlin crisis of 1961. Ibid., pp. 238–41, 253–55, 261–64.

31. Ibid., pp. 220–25.

32. Ibid., p. 224.

33. Deutscher, *Russia, China and the West*, p, 233.

34. Adomeit, *Soviet Risk-Taking and Crisis Behavior*, p. 283, n. 238.

35. Ibid., pp 294–95.

36. Ibid., pp. 230–38.

37. Ibid., p. 308.

38. William Manchester, *Remembering Kennedy*, pp, 207–209.

39. Adomeit, *Soviet Risk-Taking and Crisis Behavior*, pp. 300–301.

40. Ibid., p. 302.

41. Ibid., p. 310, n.23.

42. For Khrushchev's motives during the Cuban Missile crisis, see Ulam, *Expansion and Coexistence*, pp. 667–77, and Robin Edmonds, *Soviet Foreign Policy 1962–1973* (London: Oxford University Press, 1975).

43. Gittings, *Survey of the Sino-Soviet Dispute*, pp. 181–83.

44. The controversies over Skybolt and MLF are discussed in Grosser, *The Western Alliance* and Morgan, *The United States and West Germany*.

45. Gittings, *Survey of the Sino-Soviet Dispute*, pp. 184–92.

46. Ibid., pp. 200–201.

4.   A DECADE OF DETENTE 1966–1976

1. On Gaullism, see Philip Cerney and Jolyon Howarth, 'National Independence and Atlanticism: the dialectic of French policies', in Kenneth Dyson (ed.), *European Détente: Case Studies in the Politics of East-West Relations* (London: Francis Pinter, 1986), pp. 195–220. Also, Josef Korbel, *Détente in Europe: Real or Imaginary?* (Princeton: Princeton University Press, 1972), pp. 40–60.

2. On the Gaullist-Atlanticist debate within West Germany, see Morgan, *The United States and West Germany*, and Korbel, *Détente in Europe*, pp. 141–86.

3. Korbel, *Détente in Europe*, pp. 154 and 187–89.

4. The text of the Harmel Report is printed in *Keesing's Contemporary Archives 1967–68*, pp. 224–25.

5. Cited in Robin Edmonds, *Soviet Foreign Policy: The Brezhnev Years* (Oxford: Oxford University Press, 1983), p. 72.

6. For Brandt's *Ostpolitik*, see Willy Brandt, *People and Politics* (London: Collins, 1978), esp. ch. 8.

7. Korbel, *Détente in Europe*, Table X.

8. Ibid., Tables XVa and XVb.

9. East Germany's policy towards West Germany is discussed by Martin McCauley, 'Soviet-GDR relations and European détente', in Dyson (ed.), *European Détente*, pp. 155–71.

10. Edmonds, *Soviet Foreign Policy: The Brezhnev Years*, pp. 63–64.

11. Korbel, *Détente in Europe*, pp. 190–92.

12. During his visit to Poland, Brandt paid homage to the victims of Hitler's Germany by kneeling before the memorial at the site of the Warsaw ghetto. His gesture was much appreciated by his Polish hosts. He was awarded the Nobel Peace Prize in October 1971.

13. On Berlin, see Eberhard Shultz, 'Berlin, the German question and the future of Europe: long-term perspectives', in Dyson (ed.), *European Détente*, pp. 113–33.

14. The text of the Treaty and Bonn's letter to East Berlin are reprinted in Roger Morgan, *The Unsettled Peace: A Study of the Cold War in Europe* (London: British Broadcasting Corporation, 1974), pp. 87–88.

15. On Vietnam, see Porter (ed.), *Vietnam*, vol. 2, and Ralph B. Smith, *An International History of the Vietnam War*, vol. 2, *The Struggle for South East Asia 1961–1965* (London: Macmillan, 1985).

16. Henry Kissinger, *The White House Years* (London: Weidenfeld and Nicolson, 1979), p. 227.

17. For a discussion of the financial crisis, see ibid., pp. 949–62, and Grosser, *The Western Alliance*, esp. ch. 8.

18. Figures cited in Colin Bown and Peter Mooney, *Cold War to Détente* (London: Heinemann, 1978), p. 161.

19. On the Nixon Doctrine and Vietnamisation, see Kissinger, *The White House Years*, pp. 222–25 and 271–77.

20. On the decision to bomb Cambodia, see ibid., pp. 483–504. For a savage indictment of the decision, see William Shawcross, *Sideshow: Kissinger, Nixon and the Destruction of Cambodia* (London: André Deutsch, 1979).

21. For American thinking on these issues, see Kissinger, *The White House Years*, pp. 163–94.

22. Ibid., p. 55.

23. Ibid., pp. 57–58.

24. Henry Kissinger, *Years of Upheaval* (London: Weidenfeld and Nicolson, 1982), p. 989.

25. For the development of this argument, see John Lewis Gaddis, 'The Rise, Fall and Future of Détente', *Foreign Affairs* (Winter 1983–84), pp. 354–77.

26. Kissinger, *Years of Upheaval*, p. 982.

27. Kissinger, *The White House Years*, p. 118.

28. Ibid., pp, 128–30.

29. Military Balance, 1969–70, cited in Edmonds, *Soviet Foreign Policy: The Brezhnev Years*, p. 41.

30. Arkady N. Schevchenko, *Breaking with Moscow* (London: Jonathan Cape, 1985), p 171.

31. For Sino-Soviet differences over Vietnam, see Gittings, *Survey of the Sino-Soviet Dispute*, pp. 254–70, and Keesing's Research Report, *The Sino-Soviet Dispute*, pp. 78–79.

32. Keesing's Research Report, *The Sino-Soviet Dispute*, pp. 105–107.

33. From an article, 'The Sino-Soviet Conflict: A Search for New Security Strategies' (1982), quoted in Bialer, *The Soviet Paradox*, p. 234.

34. Aaron L. Friedberg, 'The Collapsing Triangle: US and Soviet Policies towards China, 1969–1980', *Comparative Strategy* (vol. 4, no. 2, 1983), pp. 113–46.

35. Kissinger, *The White House Years*, p. 766.

36. Cited in Edmonds, *Soviet Foreign Policy: The Brezhnev Years*, p. 10.

37. Mikhail Suslov, cited in Fred Halliday, *Threat from the East?: Soviet Policy from Afghanistan and Iran to the Horn of Africa* (Harmondsworth: Penguin, 1982), p. 149 n. See also, Schevchenko, *Breaking with Moscow*, pp. 282–89.

38. Schevchenko, *Breaking with Moscow*, pp. 164–65.

39. Kissinger, *The White House Years*, p. 183.

40. Keesing's Research Report, *The Sino-Soviet Dispute*, p. 82.

41. The reorientation of China's foreign policy is discussed in Bill Brugger, *China: From Radicalism to Revisionism 1962–1979* (London: Croom Helm, 1981), pp. 134–35, 162–64, and John Gittings, 'China: Half a Superpower' in Noam Chomsky, Jonathan Steele and John Gittings, *Superpowers in Collision: The New Cold War of the 1980s* (Harmondsworth: Penguin, 2nd ed., 1984), pp. 87–120.

42. Kissinger, *The White House Years*, p. 1470.

43. On the Soviet-American summits, see Kissinger, *The White House Years* and *Years of Upheaval*. For the view from Moscow, see Edmonds, *Soviet Foreign Policy: The Brezhnev Years*; Schevchenko, *Breaking with Moscow*; and Joseph L. Nogge and Robert H. Donaldson, *Soviet Foreign Policy since World War II* (New York: Pergamon, 2nd ed., 1986).

44. On Helsinki, see Kenneth Dyson, 'The Conference on Security and Cooperation in Europe: Europe before and after the Helsinki Final Act', in Dyson (ed.), *European Détente*, pp. 83–112.

45. Franz Joseph Strauss compared the Helsinki Final Act to the Munich Agreement of 1938. Ibid., p. 92.

46. For the Soviet view of Helsinki, see Schevchenko, *Breaking with Moscow*, pp. 264–67 and John Erikson, 'The Soviet Union and European Détente' in Dyson (ed.), *European Détente*, pp. 172–97.

47. Kissinger, *Years of Upheaval*, p. 124.

48. On the Jackson-Vanik Amendment, see ibid., pp. 979–98.

49. Ibid., pp. 998–1020.

50. On Chile and Iran, see Fred Halliday, *The Making of the Second Cold War* (London: Verso, 1984), p. 207.

51. On the 1973 Arab-Israeli War, see Kissinger, *Years of Upheaval*, esp. chs 11 and 12; Edmonds, *Soviet Foreign Policy: The Brezhnev Years*, pp. 131–36; and Schevchenko, *Breaking with Moscow*, pp. 254–61.

52. Halliday, *The Making of the Second Cold War*, pp. 81–104.

53. On the crises in Europe, see 'The Atlantic Alliance: A Testing Time' *World Survey* (Atlantic Education Trust, no. 83, November 1975).

54. Schevchenko, *Breaking with Moscow*, pp. 212–13.

55. Kissinger, *Years of Upheaval*, p. 295.

56. Schevchenko. *Breaking with Moscow*, pp. 199–200.

57. Ibid., pp. 262–63.

58. The shifting fortunes of Soviet policies in Black Africa are discussed in the collection of essays edited by Robert H. Donaldson, *The Soviet Union in the Third World: Successes and Failures* (Boulder, Colo.: Westview, 1980).

59. 'The Fate of Portugese Africa', *World Survey* (Atlantic Education Trust, no. 83, November 1975).

60. Bialer, *The Soviet Paradox*, p. 314.

61. Halliday, *The Making of the Second Cold War*, pp. 114–16.

5. RETREAT FROM DETENTE: THE CARTER PRESIDENCY 1977–80

1. Zbigniew Brzezinski, *Power and Principle: Memoirs of the National Security Adviser 1977–1981* (London: Weidenfeld and Nicolson, 1983), p. 18.

2. Jimmy Carter, *Keeping Faith* (London: Collins, 1982), pp. 65–66.

3. Interview on *Newsnight*, BBC Television, March 1980.

4. Brzezinski, *Power and Principle*, pp. 3 and 53–56.

5. Ibid., p. 149.

6. Ibid., p. 147.

7. Ibid., p. 155.

8. On the Madrid and subsequent Security Conferences, see Dyson, 'The Conference on Security and Cooperation in Europe', in Dyson (ed.), *European Détente*, pp. 100–12.

9. Carter, *Keeping Faith*, p. 149.

10. For an assessment of Carter's military programmes, see Halliday, *The Making of The Second Cold War*, pp. 224–27.

11. For the Soviet response to the Vance proposals, see Edmonds, *Soviet Foreign Policy: The Brezhnev Years*, pp. 160–62.

12. For a discussion of SALT 2, see Lawrence Freedman, 'Nuclear Arms Control', in Phil Williams (ed.), *The Nuclear Debate: Issues and Politics*, Chatham House Special Paper published on behalf of the Royal Institute of International Affairs (London: Routledge and Kegan Paul, 1984), pp. 30–46.

13. It was decided that 464 cruise missiles were to be distributed among five European members of NATO, with 160 to be deployed in Britain, 112 in Italy (at Comiso in Sicily), 96 in West Germany, 48 in Holland and 48 in Belgium. In addition, the Bonn government agreed to deploy 108 Pershing II missiles in West Germany. The issues which led to the dual-track decision are discussed by Phil Williams, 'The Nuclear Debate', in ibid., pp. 1–29. The same publication includes articles by Christopher Coker and Gina Cowen on the peace movements in Britain and Europe.

14. For an interpretation of the crises in the Arc of South West Asia, and of Soviet involvement in particular, see Halliday, *Threat From the East?*

15. On Camp David, see Carter, *Keeping Faith*, pp. 273–429.

16. Brzezinski, *Power and Principle*, p. 186.

17. Ibid., p. 189.

18. On the power struggle in China between Deng Xiaoping and the Gang of Four, see Brugger, *China: Radicalism to Revisionism*, esp. ch. 7.

19. Bialer, *The Soviet Paradox*, p. 253.

20. Friedberg, 'The Collapsing Triangle', p. 137.

21. On the conflict between China and Vietnam, see C. G. Jacobsen, *Sino-Soviet Relations since Mao: The Chairman's Legacy* (New York: Praegar, 1981), pp. 92–107.

22. Carter, *Keeping Faith*, p. 206.

23. Bialer, *The Soviet Paradox*, pp. 187–88.

24. For the Soviet response to the Sino-Japanese peace treaty, see Jacobsen, *Sino-Soviet Relations*, pp. 123–45.

25. Carter, *Keeping Faith*, pp. 243–61.

26. Edmonds, *Soviet Foreign Policy: The Brezhnev Years*, p. 173.

27. On the Iranian crisis and the tensions which it engendered in the Carter administration, see Brzezinski, *Power and Principle*; Carter, *Keeping Faith*; and Halliday, *Threat From the East?*

28. On Afghanistan, see Edmonds, *Soviet Foreign Policy: The Brezhnev Years*, pp. 189–94, and Halliday, *Threat From the East?*, pp. 89–94.

29. Halliday, *Threat From the East?*, p. 93, and *The Making of the Second Cold War*, pp. 155–56.

30. South Yemen was the one country in Brzezinski's 'Arc of Crisis' in which the Soviet Union gained from a revolutionary upheaval. It was also a country in which the Russians did not intervene directly. A factional dispute between rival leaders of the ruling National Liberation Front culminated in 1978 in an unsuccessful coup which eliminated the faction most opposed to the Russian connection. South Yemen had been aligned to Moscow since 1969 but there is no evidence to suggest that the Russians were behind the events of 1978. However, the Soviet Union had an important stake in South Yemen. Soviet naval equipment (including a dry dock) had been installed in South

Yemen following the expulsion of the Russians from Somalia in 1977. Halliday, *Threat From the East?*, pp. 94-97.

31. When the UN General Assembly debated Afghanistan in November 1980, 111 countries voted in favour of an immediate withdrawal of foreign troops and 22 against. The 22 comprised: the Soviet Union, Byelorussia, Ukraine, Czechoslovakia, Poland, Mongolia, Bulgaria, East Germany, Hungary, Cuba, Afghanistan, Angola, Ethiopia, Grenada, Laos, Madagascar, Mozambique, Sâo Tomé, Seychelles, Syria, Vietnam and South Yemen. Halliday, *The Making of the Second Cold War*, pp. 101–102.

32. Carter, *Keeping Faith*, p. 483.

33. *The Times*, 5 and 6 February 1980.

6. FROM COLD WAR TO CONSTRUCTIVE CONFRONTATION 1981–87

1. See above, p. 60.

2. Halliday, *The Making of the Second Cold War*, pp. 108–109.

3. George Shultz, 'New Realities and New Ways of Thinking', *Foreign Affairs* (Spring 1985), p. 711.

4. *Newsweek*, 16 November 1987.

5. Cited in Edmonds, *Soviet Foreign Policy: The Brezhnev Years*, p. 205.

6. *The Economist*, 15 August 1987.

7. *The Times*, 28 May 1985.

8. Shultz, 'New Realities and New Ways of Thinking', pp. 706–708.

9. *The Sunday Times*, 22 November 1987.

10. *The Economist*, 5 September 1987.

11. *The Guardian Weekly*, 15 November 1987.

12. For an analysis of the problems posed by the budget deficit, see Robert Gilpin, 'American Policy in the Post-Reagan Era', *Daedalus* (vol. 116 no. 3, 1987). pp. 33–67

13. Ibid, p.61.

14. *The Guardian*, 20 October 1986.

15. On the Soviet leadership from Brezhnev to Gorbachev, see Bialer, *The Soviet Paradox*, chs 5, 6 and 7.

16. *The Guardian Weekly*, 1 March 1987.

17. *The Guardian*, 3 November 1987.

18. Bialer, *The Soviet Paradox*, p. 2.

19. For an early assessment of the Soviet Union under Gorbachev, see Philip D. Stewart, 'Gorbachev and Obstacles Toward Détente', *Political Science Quarterly* (vol. 101, no. 1, 1986), pp. 1–22.

20. *The Guardian Weekly*, 30 November 1986, 5 July 1987.

21. Ibid., 22 February 1987.

22. *The Sunday Times*, 4 October 1987.

23. Ibid.

24. *The Guardian*, 3 November 1987.

25. Stewart, 'Gorbachev and Obstacles Toward Détente', pp. 1–22.

26. *The Guardian Weekly*, 22 February 1987.

27. Stewart, 'Gorbachev and Obstacles Toward Détente', p.10

28. Ibid.

29. *The Guardian Weekly*, 1 March 1987

30. Bialer, *The Soviet Paradox*, p. 237.

31. *The Sunday Times*, 17 August 1986.

32. Syria's support for Iran against Arab Iraq angered most of the other Arab states. The Amman summit issued a strong declaration in favour of Iraq. President Assad of Syria was obliged to endorse the declaration in order to obtain much needed financial assistance from the Arab League and from Saudi Arabia in particular. The Amman summit also sanctioned the restoration of diplomatic relations between individual Arab countries and Egypt. For many Arab leaders, Iran had replaced Israel as the main danger and threat.

33. For Soviet policies in the Middle East, see Galia Golan, 'Gorbachev's Middle East Strategy', *Foreign Affairs* (Autumn 1987), pp. 41–57.

34. *The Guardian Weekly*, 5 July 1987.

35. *The Times*, 21 and 22 February 1984 and 7 and 16 March 1985.

36. *The Guardian Weekly*, 28 September 1986.

37. Ibid., 19 October 1986.

38. *The Guardian*, 20 October 1986.

39. *The Guardian Weekly*, 8 March 1987.

40. *The Guardian Weekly*, 3 and 10 May 1987.

41. Tables from *The Guardian Weekly*, 16 November 1986 and *Newsweek*, 28 September 1987.

42. Detail on the INF Treaty and the Washington summit from *Newsweek*, 7 December 1987; *The Guardian*, 12 December 1987 and *The Sunday Times*, 13 December 1987.

43. Dyson (ed.), *European Détente*, p. 258.

44. Bialer, *The Soviet Paradox*, pp. 192–93.

45. On the Polish crisis, see ibid., pp. 213–31 and Neal Ascherson, *The Polish August: The Self-Limiting Revolution* (Harmondsworth: Penguin, 1981).

46. *The Economist*, 21 February 1981.

47. Interview in *The Times*, 9 September 1982.

48. For details on intra-German relations at the time of the crises over Poland and the new NATO missiles, see Martin McCauley, 'Soviet-GDR relations and European Détente', in Dyson (ed.), *European Détente*, pp. 155–71.

49. Ibid, p. 167

50. Bialer, *The Soviet Paradox*, p. 209

51. *The Economist*, 5 September 1987.

52. Bialer, *The Soviet Paradox*, pp. 200–201

53. Ibid., p. 210

54. *The Guardian Weekly*, 22 March 1987.

55. *The Sunday Times*, 6 December 1987.

56. Bialer, *The Soviet Paradox*, p. 205.

57. *The Guardian Weekly*, 22 March 1987.

58. *Newsweek*, 7 December 1987.

59. *The Guardian Weekly*, 5 July 1987.

60. *The Times*, 28 October 1987.

Index

To avoid unnecessary duplication, this index does not include separate entries for the United States and the Soviet Union, References will be found under US presidents and Soviet leaders (eg. Reagan and Gorbachev), relations with other countries (eg, China, Federal Republic of Germany) and key issues (eg, détente, SALT).